The Newspaper Industry in the 1980s
An Assessment of Economics and Technology

Benjamin M. Compaine

Knowledge Industry Publications, Inc.,
White Plains, New York

Communications Library

The Newspaper Industry in the 1980s:
An Assessment of Economics and Technology

by Benjamin M. Compaine

Library of Congress Cataloging in Publication Data

Compaine, Benjamin M
 The newspaper industry in the 1980s.

 (Communications library)
 Bibliography: p.
 Includes index.
 1. Newspaper publishing—United States.
 I. Title. II. Series.
 PN4867.C6   071'.3   80-10121
 ISBN 0-914236-37-7

Printed in the United States of America

CONTENTS

LIST OF TABLES

LIST OF FIGURES

Preface

For most of its 300 years of existence, the newspaper has had the mass media arena to itself. Books and to a lesser extent magazines co-existed, but with so little overlap in function as to provide insignificant competition for readers and even less for advertising.

It has only been the 20th century—and most particularly the second half of the century—that has seen the widespread adoption of other media formats that threatened the position of the daily newspaper as a pre-eminent information vehicle for the populace. To be sure, daily newspapers are still selling 62 million copies every day, with newspapers of less frequency selling millions more. But that number has been stagnant for years, despite growth in the population and the number of households.

In 1980—a year for looking ahead to a new decade and the approaching end of a century—the mass media industry was active with further developments which may affect the future of the daily newspaper. The increasing penetration of cable, initially used to bring conventional broadcast television fare to homes with poor reception, has encouraged new programming and is attracting the interest of advertisers. This is closely related to the expanded use of earth satellites for the distribution of programming to local cable operators, making special interest programming—including a possible 24-hour news channel—available to millions of households. Video disc and video cassette machines were just starting to penetrate the consumer market, providing yet another means of bringing programming to the home. There were even steps taken to explore the use of roof-top antennae for residences to receive television programs directly from satellites, bypassing the cable (or over-the-air broadcaster) altogether.

Added to this grab-bag of devices, there has been the continued and rapid decrease in the cost of computer storage—a factor which has helped newspapers themselves profitably automate many production, control, and marketing functions. But while storage costs have decreased 25% annually, the basic raw material for newspapers—newsprint—has been increasing in price at a compound rate of more than 11%. These events have set the stage for the entry of yet another piece of technology, viewdata, sometimes misleadingly called the electronic newspaper. Using a video screen—perhaps adapting existing television sets—and telephone lines or cables to connect them with a computer somewhere, this technology could conceivably assume many of the functions of the print newspaper, as well as provide banking, shopping, library, entertainment, and other services. It may also have application as a vehicle for some advertisers.

In this context, therefore, it is a practical and timely exercise to take stock of the daily newspaper industry. This is not meant to be an historical analysis of the industry—although it often relies on historical data to trace trends. It is not intended to be an examination of the editorial mission of the newspaper, albeit the long-term marketability of the newspaper to consumers and advertisers depends on its ability to perform a useful editorial function.

Nor should this study be viewed as an *a priori* attempt to either promote or deflate the prospects of the newspaper industry. This study was not financed by any trade association or any special interest. As the author, I had no special axes to grind. Although much of my experience in the media has been as a newspaper journalist and manager, I had no stake in the industry at the time of writing this study.

This study, then, is no more nor less than an attempt to gather together and identify the significant trends in the major areas that affect newspapers as a business; i.e., circulation, advertising, production, labor, and competition, seasoned with what I hope readers will find to be some enlightened analysis and direction. Since newspapers are a relatively unregulated business, I have been spared having to include much on government policy and politics. Such an analysis should enable strategic planners within the industry, as well as students of the media, to better understand the structure and workings of newspapers as enterprises.

One of my greatest difficulties has been restricting the analysis to the newspaper industry alone, since it is becoming increasingly clear, as suggested just above and in the concluding chapters, that the traditionally discrete media industries—television, radio, book and magazine publishing, etc.—are becoming difficult to separate. They are relying on similar technology for gathering, processing and storing much of their information. With the ability of newspapers to transmit the content of their computers via telephone lines to a video screen just as easily (or more so) than making plates and rolling the press, the boundary between what is "newspaper" and what is "television" or some other medium is more tenuous. Nonetheless, I have drawn the line, using traditional criteria, to keep this book to manageable dimensions.

A word on the history of this volume. My first study of the newspaper industry began life with a commission from Efrem Sigel, editor in chief of Knowledge Industry Publications, Inc., to do a market study, which that firm published in 1973 as *Papers and Profits, A Special Report on the Newspaper Business.* In 1977, I completed a Ph.D. dissertation at Temple University's School of Communications and Theater under the weighty title of "The Daily Newspaper Industry in the United States (1977): An Analysis of Trends in Production Technology, Competition and Ownership, Economic Structure, Circulation, Advertising, Newsprint and Labor." That tome was edited and modified for publication by Knowledge Industry Publications as a marketing study. This current volume is a revision and updating of that project.

As always, a work of this magnitude required the cooperation of many individuals. These include the dozens of executives of newspaper companies as well as those who have compiled much of the statistical data for the industry. In particular, I must mention those who served on my dissertation committee. James H. Ottaway Jr., now Chairman of the Ottaway Newspaper subsidiary of Dow Jones Co., Inc., provided assistance at several stages. Jules Tewlow, Director of Special Projects for Lee Enterprises, Inc., is a valued source of ideas and insights. He is one of those rare individuals who can synthesize a great mass of conflicting information and make sense of it for practical applications. John Roberts and Jerry Knudson of Temple provided suggestions as part of the committee.

Finally, a public note of gratitude to Dr. Edward Trayes, professor of communications at Temple University. He encouraged me to assume the project, served as the committee chairman, and guided me along the way. This book would not have been written without his support.

To all those not mentioned, from sources to typist, I do thank you. With it all, however, I assume all responsibility for what is written—in the last analysis, the reasoning and assessments are mine alone.

Ben Compaine

Cambridge, Massachusetts
January 1980

This can be for no one but Martha, who has been patient, encouraging and much more through so many of my hours on the road and at the typewriter.

1

Introduction

This is a study of newspapers, not as an editorial product, but primarily as a business institution. It is an attempt at understanding some of the apparent paradoxes in the newspaper industry today, such as why, despite declining market penetration and circulation, newspaper firms are making more money than ever and seeking to buy papers for their groups at premium prices. More importantly, perhaps, this is also an evaluation of the future of the newspaper—not into the Buck Rogers future, but within the lifetime of most of us. Technological change in the mass media has come rapidly and its impact has been far reaching: first movies, then radio, television, and now cable, video disk, and tape. To some, including Marshall McLuhan, the newspaper as ink-on-newsprint is passé and destined to go the way of the horse-drawn carriage in the jet age. Others, however, including many who own or control the media companies, are not so ready to write off the newspaper in its current form.

The study at hand, therefore, explores the future by looking at some of the past of the newspaper and its rival media, then making a reasoned evaluation of what lies ahead. To be sure, speculating about the future is fraught with uncertainties. In 1955, Raymond Nixon, a respected student of the newspaper industry, boldly predicted a circulation for newspapers of 100 million copies daily by 1975. His supporting arguments at the time read logically, yet in 1975 audited circulation was, at just under 61 million, barely eight percent greater than in 1955. On the other hand, he concluded that the number of daily newspapers "should not fall much below the present figure of 1765." In fact, the number has stayed fairly consistent and stood at 1756 in 1978.

The uncertainties of forecasting notwithstanding, the primary use of this study is intended to be as a planning document. Planning is necessary to escape from the crises of the minute and to focus instead on goals, expectations, and changes. It allows decision-makers to make more efficient use of their resources, promotes coordination, and in general works toward reducing uncertainty.

SOME QUESTIONS AND HYPOTHESES

Specifically, this study set out to help find answers to questions such as:

- In this age of "electronic media," is the ink-on-print newspaper becoming obsolete?
- What will be the likely role of the daily newspaper by the year 2000?
- What will be the form of the daily newspaper in 2000?
- How, if at all, is the economic health of the newspaper industry affected by the new technology of production?

These questions give rise to hypotheses such as the following:

1. The rapid introduction of new technology into many phases of newspaper operations qualifies this print medium for inclusion as an "electronic" medium.

2. Although newspaper production may change, the final product, as received by the subscriber, will remain physically quite similar to the present form.

3. New technology will provide newspaper publishers with opportunities for new roles and formats for information distribution in the coming decades.

4. The daily newspaper has no replacement in the foreseeable future as a major vehicle for local advertisers to reach a mass audience.

5. Current trends notwithstanding, aggregate newspaper circulation has stabilized and will enjoy modest increases through the remainder of the century.

6. Direct newspaper competition within cities continues to diminish but the impact of this on readers and advertisers is not yet clear.

DEFINITIONS, ASSUMPTIONS, AND LIMITATIONS

The term "newspaper" is used to refer to a wide range of publications. It encompasses the local daily, but also weekly "shoppers" distributed free and in some cases completely devoid of any content but advertising. *The Wall Street Journal* is a national daily newspaper. *Grit* may be a newspaper; and in format and frequency, *Women's Wear Daily* can be included under this rubric as well.

But for the purpose of this book, a daily newspaper is published at least five days a week, with content of broad interest, and is eligible for listing in the daily newspaper section of *Editor & Publisher International Year Book*. Thus, *The Wall Street Journal* is included, but "special service" daily papers, such as legal papers, the *Daily Racing Form*, or *Women's Wear Daily* are generally excluded, as are foreign language dailies. Throughout this book, reference to "newspapers" means daily newspapers, except where indicated.

Circulation, unless otherwise indicated, is the weekday circulation reported to the Audit Bureau of Circulation (ABC) for September 30, 1978. For newspapers not reporting to ABC, sworn statements from post office filing statements are reported by the *Editor & Publisher International Year Book* and are for 1978.

Advertising linage is the total number of agate lines of paid advertising as reported either to Media Records, Inc., or to *Editor & Publisher*, as indicated.

Publicly owned newspapers refer to those newspapers owned by firms whose common stock is available to the general public and whose annual report and 10-K report must be filed with the federal Securities and Exchange Commission. (The 10-K is an annual form which must include specified information disclosing financial and management information in greater detail than is often included in the annual report sent to stockholders.)

The underlying assumption throughout this book is that the First Amendment will be interpreted for the various mass media as it has been in the past. Should the print media come under a type of governmental control equivalent to the FCC regulations affecting the broadcast media, the expectations for the future may have to be recast.

PREVIOUS STUDIES

As noted by Leo Bogart of the Newspaper Advertising Bureau, the substance and effect of newspapers has been the primary focus of researchers in this area. To be sure, there are studies and articles which deal with the declining circulation trends, chain ownership, advertising, and organization of newspapers. There are few studies, however, which present an overview of the newspaper industry with supporting data that can be meaningful and utilized by those for whom this study would be useful. And most of those which have summarized the conventional data, such as Udell's (1970) "Economic Trends in the Daily Newspaper Business 1946-1970," are short on analysis of the position of the newspaper during the decade of the 1980s. Another, Udell, et al (1928), *The Economics of the American Newspaper,* focuses on nuts and bolts rather than strategic issues.

A study in 1973 by Knowledge Industry Publications, Inc., *Paper and Profits: A Special Report on the Newspaper Business,* analyzed the circulation, advertising, technology, labor and management, newsprint, and government regulation aspects of the industry, concluding that, "The newspaper business today presents a paradox of an industry that is mature and stable . . . but which nevertheless exhibits a high potential for growth in profits over the next three to five years."

Some of the most insightful studies have come not from academia, but from the business community. Some stock brokerage firms which follow the publishing industry have research departments which turn out an occasional industry analysis for clients.

In a mid-1976 evaluation on "Economic Prospects for Newspapers . . . 1976 and Beyond," Lee Dirks, formerly of C.S. McKee & Co. and now working for the *Detroit Free Press,* told a meeting of newspaper advertising executives that he foresaw a "continuation of current earnings trends" for newspaper companies—earnings which have been above those of corporate profits generally. Looking ahead for five to 15 years, Dirks based his evaluation on three factors: (1) a "large reservoir of reasonable rate increases" which newspapers can still impose, particularly in the circulation area; (2) further savings through improving technology and production methods; and (3) a "clear" trend toward "more professional" management.

Another long-time financial analyst of the newspaper industry, R. Joseph Fuchs, made note of similar characteristics in a 1972 review of the industry from Kidder, Peabody

& Co., written for potential investors in newspaper securities. Fuchs found that newspapers represented "an opportunity for high quality, above-average investment growth and should not be considered simply as a short-term cyclical recovery vehicle." Among the reasons for this evaluation is the "almost total community monopoly conditions in relation to other newspaper publishers." This held true in 1980, as well.

FOCUSED STUDIES

Much of the more structured study of the newspaper industry has focused on either a single aspect, such as advertising or labor, or has come from an economist's viewpoint and looks at the economic structure as it affects competition or content.

One study tentatively concludes that, "Concentration of daily newspaper circulation in the hands of a single newspaper does appear to raise general and classified advertising rates to some significant extent."[1]

Another looked at newspapers which went from competitive to monopoly situations and from independent to chain-owned status and measured advertising cost, subscription price, and editorial quality. The documented findings were that consumers pay higher prices under monopoly and chain ownership with no compensating increase in quality.[2]

Nevertheless these studies have a narrow, technical orientation and lack the overview of the industry which would be useful to newspaper managers and owners.

Some of the histories of the newspaper in the United States by Emery (1978), Mott (1962), and Tebbel (1963) address themselves to such trends as declining circulation, the competitiveness of television for advertising dollars, the continued growth of the chains, and the demise of the independent newspaper, but are hesitant to draw conclusions about the future. A collection of readings edited by Udell (1978) provided superficial treatment of some aspects of the newspaper business, but little analysis or depth.

One of the few studies to treat the newspaper as a corporate enterprise, with an eye toward the future as well as its current status, is by Ben Bagdikian, formerly of the *Washington Post*. In a quick survey of profitability, circulation, advertising, labor, and chain ownership, Bagdikian found that, despite the stability and profits of the 1960s, most daily papers "have failed to use their freedom to use profits for maximum reinvestment to strengthen the paper in quality of content or even in preparation for a new technology."[3]

He does, however, see newspapers entering the uncertain world of "modern corporate finance and empire building" in part due to

> . . . a new competitor, broadcasting. From the start, newspapers and broadcasters have had a love-hate relationship, brutal infighting alternating between profitable marriages of convenience. New technology hints that in the not-too-distant future, newspapers and broadcasters, like some old married couples, may end up looking remarkably alike![4]

When it comes to technology, there have been questions about the viability of newspapers in an age of electronic information media, particularly television. Marshall

McLuhan (1964) hypothesizes that print, being linear and "hot," is detached from the participant, whereas television, as a representative of the new media, is instantaneous, "cool," and involving. The electronic media, he believes, are changing man's perceptual senses and thus print will become more and more passé. But McLuhan the philosopher may have been premature in his prediction of the demise of print. Bagdikian, working from a more empirical data base, concludes that "print is neither dead nor dying." Although it is being forced to co-exist with the "disrupting and even revolutionary" electronic media, the "alphabet and document are still indispensable to the efficient use of eye and brain and to the demands of the human rationality."[5]

What is more likely is that through the use of new technology and after a redefinition of the function of a newspaper publisher, the daily newspaper will take new forms. Toffler (1970) projects that the newspaper will become a home facsimile-produced medium (either hard copy or on a TV screen), with content being determined by the unique needs of each individual. In fact, the newspaper already has this characteristic: the ability to satisfy the diverse needs of many people in a single package.

In getting from the present to wherever it is we are going, however, newspaper publishers, readers, advertisers, investors, and researchers must consider the more mundane: What is being done to respond to stagnant circulation sales? How will personnel and unions respond to changes in technology? What is the gap between technological capability and economic feasibility? These are among the questions this study addresses.

SUMMARY

With few exceptions, previous studies deal with highly selective aspects of the newspaper business, such as its economic structure, effects of competition, or labor relations. The introduction of electronic technology to newspaper editorial and production functions brings this print form into the realm of other electronic media, and some newspaper executives and observers see this as a challenge to management to re-evaluate the nature of their product. At the same time, research on satisfaction and gratification provided by the newspaper indicates that the product apparently is still an important part in the daily lives of people in the United States.

The present report examines the economic condition of newspapers, the prospects for continuation of newspapers in their present form, competition from other media, and the impact on industry health of new production technology.

FOOTNOTES

1. James Rosse, "Daily Newspapers, Monopolistic Competition and Economies of Scale" (unpublished Doctor's Dissertation, University of Minnesota, 1966), p. 81.

2. Gerald L. Grotta, "Changes in the Ownership of Daily Newspapers and Selected Performance Characteristics, 1950-1968: An Investigation of Some Economic Implications of Concentration of Ownership" (Unpublished Doctor's Dissertation, Southern Illinois University, 1970), p. 21.

3. Ben H. Bagdikian, *The Information Machines* (New York: Harper & Row, Harper Torchbooks, 1971), p. 115.

4. Ibid, p. 136.

5. Ibid, p. 205.

2

An Overview
of the Newspaper Industry in the U.S.

This section will look at some of the general trends of the newspaper industry. It will cover some aggregate trends in circulation, advertising, profitability, and value of newspaper shipments relative to other measures of growth and selected industries.

The newspaper industry in the United States was born on September 25, 1690, with the publication of Benjamin Harris' *Publick Occurrences Both Foreign and Domestick.* This venture was suspended after a single three-page issue. But by 1765, Boston had three regular weekly newspapers, as did New York. Philadelphia had two English-language weeklies and a German-language newspaper.

In all, there were 23 newspapers in the colonies—all weeklies—as the colonies entered the Revolutionary War era. The first daily newspaper is attributed to *The Pennsylvania Evening Packet,* started by Benjamin Towne in Philadelphia in 1783.

By 1979, the newspaper industry included more than 11,000 publications, the vast majority published fewer than five days a week. There were about 40 foreign language daily papers and 90 professional, business, and special service daily newspapers. Most germane to this study, there were 1756 daily newspapers of general interest.

In 1978, the value of industry receipts was an estimated $14.8 billion, an increase of 10 percent from the previous year. By way of comparison, value of receipts for periodical publishers was $6.6 billion and for book publishers, only $4.8 billion.

The newspaper industry is also one of the country's largest manufacturing employers, third in numbers behind only the automobile and steel industries. Production workers now account for less than half of this work force and their proportion has been declining.

SOME GENERAL CHARACTERISTICS

Growth

With its origins dating back to the beginning of the nation, it should not be surprising that the newspaper industry is economically mature. Table 2.1 shows a growth which has lagged slightly behind the overall growth of the economy since 1960—newspapers growing at a rate of 7.4 percent annually compared to a growth rate of 8.2 percent yearly for the

Table 2.1 Value of All Newspaper Shipments Compared To Gross National Product, 1960 to 1978

(Index: 1970 = 100)

Year	GNP (current billions)	Growth Index	Year to Year % Increase	Value of Receipts (billions)	Growth Index	Year to Year % Increase
1960	$ 506.0	52	—	$ 4.1	59	—
1965	688.1	70	36.0%	5.2	74	26.8%
1970	982.4	100	42.7	7.0	100	34.6
1971	1,063.4	108	8.2	7.4	106	5.7
1972	1,171.1	119	10.1	8.3	119	12.2
1973	1,306.6	133	11.6	8.9	127	7.2
1974	1,412.9	144	8.2	9.6	137	7.9
1975	1,528.8	156	7.3	10.5	150	4.2
1976	1,706.5	174	11.6	11.7	167	12.0
1977	1,889.6	192	10.7	13.3*	190	13.7
1978	2,107.0	214	11.5	14.8*	211	10.4
Compound Annual % Increase	8.2%			7.4%		

*Estimates of U.S. Bureau of Domestic Commerce.

Source: GNP—U.S. Bureau of Economic Analysis. Newspaper Shipments—U.S. Dept. of Commerce, U.S. *Industrial Outlook*, annual.

Gross National Product. However, Table. 2.2 indicates that since 1970 advertising revenue, which provides the bulk of the proceeds for newspapers, exceeded general economic growth, and kept pace with the rate of increases in total advertising expenditures. As will be seen in Chapter 3, circulation, at 62.0 million in 1978, has been a particularly sluggish area for a variety of reasons. The record daily circulation was 63.1 million in 1973.

Table 2.2   Newspaper Advertising Revenues Compared to Total Advertising Expenditures and Gross National Product, 1945 to 1978 (Index: 1970 = 100)

Year	Total Advertising (million $)	Total Advertising Index	Total Newspaper Advertising Receipts (million $)	Newspaper Advertising Index	GNP Growth Index
1945	$ 2,875	15	$ 921	16	22
1950	5,710	29	2,076	36	29
1955	9,194	47	3,088	54	41
1960	11,932	61	3,703	64	52
1965	15,255	78	4,457	78	70
1970	19,600	100	5,745	100	100
1975	28,230	146	8,442	147	156
1976	33,720	175	10,022	174	174
1977	38,120	197	11,132	194	192
1978	43,740	223	12,690	221	214

Source: GNP—U.S. Bureau of Economic Analysis. Advertising — McCann Erickson Advertising Agency, Inc., N.Y., published by *Advertising Age.*

Consolidation

Notwithstanding the considerable attention which has been paid to the apparent consolidation in the ownership of daily newspapers, the industry as a whole was only slightly more concentrated in 1972 than in 1947, with the four largest entities actually accounting for a smaller portion of revenue in the most recent figures available. Table 2.3 also shows that both the periodical and book publishing industries are more concentrated than are newspapers.

In a sampling of industries outside of the publishing field, the four largest firms in each industry tend to be more dominant. The industries are:

aircraft manufacturers — 59%
bread and cake bakers — 29
cigarettes — 84

radio and TV sets   —   49
paper mills   —   24

There are, in fact, few industries which are more diversely held than newspapers.

Table 2.3   Share of Total Dollar Shipments by Largest Firms in Publishing Industries, Selected Years, 1947 to 1972

Year	Newspapers	Periodicals	Book Publishing
1947			
4 largest companies	21%	34%	18%
8 largest	26	43	29
50 largest	N.A.	N.A.	N.A.
1958			
4 largest companies	17	31	16
8 largest	24	41	29
50 largest	51	69	69
1963			
4 largest companies	15	28	20
8 largest	22	42	33
50 largest	52	73	76
1967			
4 largest companies	16	24	20
8 largest	25	37	32
50 largest	56	72	77
1972			
4 largest companies	17	26	19
8 largest	28	38	31
50 largest	60	69	77

N.A. Not Available.

Source: U.S. Bureau of Census, *Census of Manufacturers.*

Numbers

The number of daily newspapers, tallied in Table 2.4 and counted by *Editor & Publisher,* declined steadily from 1920 until 1944. But since that time, the number has been quite stable, rising to as many as 1786 in 1952 and falling to a low of 1748 in 1970.

Table 2.4   Number of Daily Newspapers, 1920 to 1978

Year	Daily Papers	Sunday Papers
1920	2,042	522
1925	2,008	548
1930	1,942	521
1935	1,950	518
1940	1,878	525
1944	1,744	481
1945	1,749	485
1950	1,772	549
1955	1,760	541
1960	1,763	563
1965	1,751	562
1970	1,748	586
1971	1,749	590
1972	1,761	605
1973	1,774	634
1974	1,768	641
1975	1,756	639
1976	1,762	650
1977	1,753	688
1978	1,756	696
Net Change	− 286	+ 174

Source: *Editor & Publisher International Year Book*, annual.

Sunday papers have been rising in numbers almost steadily since 1944. The impression that newspapers are dying may be largely the product of the well-publicized deaths of many of the New York City papers, including *The Herald Tribune*, and more recently permanent suspensions in Washington, D.C., Boston, and Hartford. But less attention has been given to start-ups, either as completely new newspapers such as *Newsday* on Long Island in 1940 or the *Philadelphia Journal* in 1977, or by converting a weekly or twice weekly to a daily basis, as was true with many small town papers which grew with their communities. For example, the three-times weekly *North Las Vegas Valley Times* became a daily in 1975. Table 2.5 summarizes the suspensions, mergers, and conversions of daily papers and the addition of new ones. Thus, there is some flux in the daily newspaper community, with new members replacing those who for one reason or another disappear.

Employment
Employment in the newspaper industry hit an estimated 386,000 in 1973, then fell in the next two years as part of the weakened economic climate before rebounding only

Table 2.5   Numbers of New, Suspended, Merged, and Changed Frequency U.S. Daily Newspapers, 1962 to 1978

Year	Outright Suspensions	Mergers	Conversions to Less Than Daily	Total Terminations	New Dailies	Net Gain (Loss)
1962	9	2	7	18	17	(1)
1963	11	1	8	20	21	1
1964	7	1	6	14	15	1
1965	8	4	3	15	13	(2)
1966	6	3	5	14	21	7
1967	7	4	4	15	10	(5)
1968	3	4	2	9	12	3
1969	13	5	4	22	26	4
1970	12	3	7	22	17	(5)
1971	8	4	5	17	16	(1)
1972	11	5	7	23	27	4
1973	6	4	4	14	35	21
1974	6	7	4	17	18	1
1975	7	6	2	15	13	(2)
1976	1	0	2	3	14	11
1978	8	3	3	14	27	13
Total	115	53	70	238	276	37

N.B.   These figures do not reconcile with the actual change in the number of daily newspapers reported by ANPA over the years. For example, in 1962, U.S. government figures report 1760 daily papers. A net change of 37 would presume 1797 in 1976, instead of the taillied 1762. Discrepancies may be explained in the greater publicity that attends the promotion of a new daily than the sometimes quiet suspension or conversion of a small town paper, which therefore may not show up in the figures.

Source: 1962-1970: Ben H. Bagdikian, "Report of An Exaggerated Death," Newspaper Survival Study, No. 1, p. 2. 1971-1978: Editor & Publisher International Year Book.

slightly since 1976. Although employment at newspapers grew faster than total U.S. employment generally between 1946 and 1960, the index in Table 2.6 shows that in more recent times newspaper industry employment has grown at a considerably lesser rate. This may be the result of production efficiencies (see Chapter 6) as well as a symptom of stagnation.

Profitability

If interest in buying and owning newspapers is any positive indicator of the financial health of this business, then the rapid rate at which they are being bought and sold at in-

Table 2.6 Newspaper Employment Compared to Total U.S. Civilian Employment, 1946-1978
(Index: 1960 = 100)

Year	Newspaper Employment (000)	Growth Index	Total U.S. Civilian Employment (000)	Growth Index
1946	248	76	57,039	86
1960	325	100	65,778	100
1965	345	106	71,088	108
1970	373	115	78,627	120
1971	370	114	79,120	120
1972	380	117	81,702	124
1973	386	119	84,409	128
1974	385	118	85,936	131
1975	379	117	84,786	129
1976	383	118	87,485	133
1977	393	121	90,546	138
1978	399[a]	123	93,200[b]	142
Compounded annual growth				
1946-1960	1.95%		1.02%	
1960-1978	1.15%		1.95%	

[a]Estimate.   [b]April average.

Sources: U.S. Bureau of Labor Statistics, *Employment and Earnings*, monthly; *U.S. Industrial Outlook, 1979.*

creasingly higher multiples of dollars per reader or earnings is a sign of a prosperous industry. Table 2.7 lists the revenues and profits of 15 firms whose revenues are derived totally or largely from daily newspaper holdings. These range from the conglomerate Times Mirror Co.—which owns the *Los Angeles Times, Newsday,* and the *Dallas Times Herald* in addition to major newsprint and wood products holdings, a group of special interest magazines, book publishers, and sundry other properties—to the small mid-western dailies in the Lee group. For these firms, most of which are publicly owned, the median net profit as a percentage of sales in 1978 was 8.8 percent, up from 8.6 percent in 1976. This compares to a median profit margin of 4.8 percent for the 500 largest manufacturing concerns in the United States and 8.4 percent for the largest firms in the printing and publishing category.

Table 2.8 compares this group of newspaper firms with median net profit margins for selected groups from the *Fortune 500* listing. The newspaper companies outperformed all except the broadcasting and motion picture firms, including office machinery, apparel,

Table 2.7 Revenues and Profits of 15 Selected Newspaper Publishing Firms, 1978
($ in millions)

	Revenues	Net Profits	Return on Sales
Affiliated	$ 159.8	$ 9.0	5.6%
Capital Cities	367.5	54.0	14.8
Dow Jones	363.6	44.2	12.1
Gannett	690.1	83.1	12.0
Harte-Hanks	184.6	15.7	8.5
Journal Co.	244.3	18.9	7.7
Knight-Ridder	878.9	76.8	8.7
Lee	104.7	15.9	15.2
Media General	243.7	18.0	7.4
Multimedia	110.6	15.6	14.1
New York Times	491.6	15.5	3.2
Thomson[a]	306.5	56.6	18.5
Times Mirror	1,427.9	125.1[b]	8.8
Tribune Co.	966.5	57.5	5.9
Washington Post	520.4	49.7	9.6

N.B. 1. All of these are publicly-held firms except the Journal Co. (publishes the *Milwaukee Journal* and *Sentinel*) and the Tribune Co. (publishes the *New York News* and *Chicago Tribune*).
2. Includes revenue from non-daily papers and other lines of business.

[a]Canadian dollars.

[b]Includes profit from sale of forest products assets.

Source: Company annual reports and other public reports.

and other categories. If the Journal Co. and Tribune Co. were not counted, the remaining all-publicly held firms would have a median margin of 9.6%, tied with broadcasting for the top of the list.

FINANCIAL STRUCTURE OF DAILY NEWSPAPERS

There were, at the end of 1978, 1756 daily, general circulation newspapers in the U.S., publishing 355 morning, 1419 evening editions. There were 696 Sunday editions. Table 2.9 lists the 25 largest circulation papers. These papers account for over 22 percent of the average daily circulation (see Table 3.1). Moreover, despite the general ratio of four evening papers for each morning paper, six of the top ten papers are published in the morning only and over half of the largest 25 dailies are morning papers. (The three so called "all-day" papers also have the bulk of their sales from their morning editions.)

Table 2.8 Median Return on Sales, Selected *Fortune* 500 Manufacturing Industries, Plus Newspapers, 1978

Industry	Median Profit Margin
Newspapers*	9.6%
Broadcasting and Motion Picture production and distribution	9.6
Pharmaceuticals	8.7
Printing and Publishing	8.4
Mining	8.1
Office Equipment (incl. computers)	7.9
Tobacco	6.4
Paper and Wood Products	5.3
Motor Vehicles and Parts	4.2
Apparel	3.3
Food	2.8
All Industries	4.8

* Publicly owned newspapers from Table 2.7.

Source: *Fortune*, May 7, 1979.

Newspaper revenues are derived from two constituents: advertisers, who provide 70 percent to 80 percent of revenue, and subscribers, who add the remaining 20 percent to 30 percent. Smaller newspapers tend more to the 70/30 advertising to circulation ratio, while the big city papers are more dependent on advertising revenue at about 80/20. This is found in an analysis of the composite operating statements for a big city daily of about 260,000 (Table 2.10) and for a small to medium size daily with 34,000 daily circulation (Table 2.11).

For the larger paper, local display advertising accounted for 43 percent of all revenue, national display about 5 percent, and classified advertising more than one-fifth of revenue. Proportions have been changing since 1967. Most significant has been the growth of preprinted inserts (see Chapter 4), which apparently has been replacing run of press local display advertising in many cases. Circulation revenue, which accounted for as little as 15 percent of total revenue (in 1972), has also become a more important contributor to revenue, in part as the result of more aggressive subscription and newsstand pricing newspapers have instituted during these years to help compensate for rising newsprint cost.[1]

Examination of advertising/circulation ratios of specific large newspapers, however, shows there is considerable latitude around the model newspaper. For the Times Mirror's newspapers, mostly large city papers, the composite ratio appears quite close to their 80/20 ad/circulation ratio. For *The New York Times*, the ratio in 1978 was also 80/20, compared to 75/24 in 1975. Lee Enterprises, which inlcudes newspapers in Davenport, Iowa, Billings, Montana and Madison, Wisconsin, had a 1978 ratio of 76/24, while the

Table 2.9   Twenty-Five Largest Newspapers in the United States by Circulation, 1978[a]

Newspaper (m — morning) (e — evening)	Daily (000)	Sunday (000)
1. New York News (m)	1,825	2,657
2. Los Angeles Times (m)	1,018	1,302
3. New York Times (m)	822	1,412
4. Chicago Tribune (all day)	724	1,139
5. Chicago Sun Times (m)	684	720
6. Detroit News (e)	632	820
7. Detroit Free Press (m)	618	716
8. New York Post (e)	613	—
9. Washington Post (m)	559	784
10. Newsday (Long Island) (e)	495	519
11. Philadelphia Bulletin (e)	486	585
12. San Francisco Chronicle (m)	494	663[b]
13. Boston Globe (all day)	481	670
14. Miami Herald (m)	420	529
15. Philadelphia Inquirer (m)	419	832
16. Newark Star-Ledger (m)	414	567
17. Cleveland Plain Dealer (m)	382	453
18. Baltimore Sun (all day)	345	359
19. Milwaukee Journal (e)	329	534
20. Washington Star (e)	329	309
21. Houston Chronicle (e)	324	418
22. Los Angeles Herald-Examiner (e)	316	321
23. Kansas City Times (m)	316	—
24. Cleveland Press (e)	309	—
25. Houston Post (m)	300	359
Total	13,724	16,668

morning: 13 papers = 8,271 daily
evening: 9 papers = 3,833 daily
all day: 3 papers = 1,620 daily

[a]Does not include *The Wall Street Journal,* national circulation 1.5 million in 1978. In 1979 the *New York News* fell 218,000, reflecting the long 1978 strike. *The Wall Street Journal* rose to 1.7 million.

[b]Joint edition with the *Examiner.*

Source: Audit Bureau of Circulation, Average Circulation for six months ending September 30, 1978, except *New York News,* March 31, 1978.

Gannett group, which has both large and small among the 78 dailies included in their 1978 total, reflects that mix with a 75/25 proportion.

Costs

The costs involved in publishing a newspaper include:

1. The cost of gathering and assembling the editorial material.
2. The expense of selling local, national, and classified advertising.
3. "First copy" production costs, including typesetting, plates, and plate production, and other makeready for running the press.
4. Printing, the actual expense of running the press, and consuming newsprint and ink.
5. Distribution expense, that is, getting the printed paper from the plant to subscribers and newsstands and collecting money from these sources.
6. Other necessary administrative, overhead, and general expenses, such as billing advertisers, soliciting for subscriptions, promotion, and similar tasks.

Each of the costs of publishing a newspaper varies with numerous qualitative or quantitative aspects of the newspaper and its audience. These include such factors as circulation, number of pages, population density, geographical extent of the market, editorial quality, and frequency of publication, among others.

Number four above, for example, is a completely variable one. That is, the amount of the expense varies directly with the number of copies printed. To a lesser extent, step five is a variable cost, since fewer papers may mean fewer trucks and stops. But much of the rest of a newspaper's expense has little or no variability within a given circulation range. Thus, a reporter who writes up the proceedings at City Hall is not paid based on the number of papers in which the story is printed. The cost of having the story written and edited is substantially the same whether it goes into a 10,000 circulation or 50,000 circulation paper. Likewise, a page which is typeset and pasted-up for a 100,000 circulation requires the same time and expense as a page on a 6000 circulation paper. A printing plate may have a useful printing life of 100,000 copies, even though it is used to print only 25,000 copies at a small paper.

Newsprint is by far the most costly item for a large newspaper, accounting for almost 30 percent of all revenue and 36 percent of total expenses. Although this is not much different than the 1967 percentage, before the rapid escalation in newsprint prices, it comes only as a result of stringent waste reduction methods incorporated into procedures by the industry in the past several years (see Chapter 9) and has been responsible to much of the increases in subscription and advertising rates.

Some observers have voiced concern about the diminishing proportion of expenditures going into editorial services. These declined from 9.6 percent to 9.0 percent of total revenue for large newspapers, but were proportionately higher for medium size papers in 1978 compared to 1971. On the other hand, in 1975, for the first time, "administrative" expenses actually exceeded editorial expenses for large papers, the former having climbed

**Table 2.10 Operating Revenues and Expenses of a Composite
Large City Newspaper, 1967, 1971, 1975 and 1978
($ in thousands)**

	1967	Percentage of Total Revenue	1971	Percentage of Total Revenue
Revenue				
Advertising				
Display local	$ 7,446	47.8%	$10,691	49.3%
Display national	1,636	10.5	1,974	9.1
Classified	3,239	20.8	4,993	23.0
Inserts & other	147	1.0	549	2.5
Total	12,468	80.1	18,207	84.0
Circulation	3,043	19.5	3,378	15.6
Other	53	0.4	100	0.5
Total	15,564	100.0%	21,685	100.0%
Expenses				
Direct				
Editorial	$ 1,502	9.6%	$ 1,923	8.9%
Advertising	742	4.8	978	4.5
Production	2,115	13.6	3,180	14.6
Newsprint & ink	4,538	29.2	6,012	27.8
Total	8,896	57.2	12,093	55.8
Indirect				
Building	$ 263	1.7%	$ 378	1.8%
Circulation	1,200	7.7	1,612	7.4
Administration	1,199	7.7	1,717	7.9
Total	2,662	17.1	3,707	17.1
Supplements	$ 101	0.6%	$ 94	0.4%
Depreciation	302	2.9	455	2.0
Bad debt & other	74	0.5	296	1.4
Total	477	3.1	845	3.9
Total Expenses	$12,035	77.4%	$16,645	76.8%
Operating Profit	$ 3,529	22.6%	$ 5,040	23.2%
Average Circulation		254,130		257,320

Table 2.10 continued

	1975	Percentage of Total Revenue	1978	Percentage of Total Revenue
Revenue				
Advertising				
Display local	$15,861	50.2%	$13,929	43.3%
Display national	2,048	6.5	1,630	5.1
Classified	6,450	20.4	7,435	23.1
Inserts & other	603	1.9	1,684	5.2
Total	24,678	76.8		
Circulation	6,561	20.8	7,323	22.8
Other	43	0.1	152	0.5
Total	31,567	100.0%	32,153	100.0%
Expenses				
Direct				
Editorial	$ 2,466	7.8%	$ 2,894	9.0%
Advertising	1,370	4.3	1,656	5.2
Production	4,384	13.9	3,128	9.7
Newsprint & ink	9,306	29.5	9,296	28.9
Total	17,526	55.5	16,974	52.8
Indirect				
Building	$ 635	2.0%	$ 709	2.2%
Circulation	2,280	7.2	3,307	10.3
Administration	3,348	10.6	3,248	10.1
Total	6,263	19.8	7,264	22.6
Supplements	$ 33	0.1%	$ 81	0.3%
Depreciation	544	1.7	627	2.0
Bad debt & other	325	1.0	553	1.7
Total	903	2.9	1,261	3.9
Total Expenses	$24,691	78.2%	$25,500	79.3%
Operating Profit	$ 6,876	21.8%	$ 6,653	20.7%
Average Circulation		262,035		260,402

Source: Compiled by Newspaper Analysis Service, Cincinnati, Ohio, for *Editor & Publisher*. Percentage calculated by author.

Table 2.11   Operating Ratios for An Average Medium Size Daily
Newspaper, 1971 and 1978, Expressed in Percentage of Revenue[a]

	1971 Percent of Revenue		1978 Percent of Revenue	
Revenue				
Display local	49.8%		37.3%	
Display national	5.5		4.3	
Classified	11.1		17.2	
Inserts & other	4.7		8.4	
Total advertising		71.1		67.2
Circulation		28.3		29.2
Other		0.6		3.6
Total Income		100.0%		100.0%
Expenses				
Direct				
Editorial	11.3%		12.6%	
Advertising	7.5		8.4	
Production	21.4		7.7	
Newsprint & ink	9.5		14.1	
Total direct		49.7%		42.8%
Indirect				
Building	3.1%		1.8%	
Circulation	9.1		6.8	
Administrative	7.0		8.4	
Total indirect		19.2%		17.0%
Other				
Bad debt	0.8%		0.2%	
Depreciation	2.2		2.9	
Employee Benefits	6.5		5.7	
Total Other		9.5		8.8
Total Expenses		78.4%		68.6%
Operating Profit (before tax)		21.6		31.4
Provision for Income Tax		11.4		15.1
Net Income		10.2%		16.3%

[a]Based on an estimated total revenue of $5,890,713, from daily circulation newspaper of
34,470 in 1978 and $3,525,000 revenue and 33,700 circulation in 1971.

Source: Editor & Publisher, May 7, 1973 and May 12, 1979.

171 percent since 1967, to the point where this expense accounted for over ten percent of all revenue, up from 7.7 percent 11 years earlier.

Small newspapers appear to be even more profitable than their big city counterparts, but their revenue and expense structure is somewhat different. Advertising accounts for proportionately less revenue, with circulation therefore carrying the larger share. This is not necessarily because small newspapers charge the reader more; rather, they have a smaller advertising constituency, especially among national accounts. The most striking expense difference between the large and small papers is the expenditure for newsprint. Carrying less advertising, lower circulation papers tend to have fewer pages, thus using proportionately less newsprint than metropolitan dailies. Smaller papers do tend to spend relatively more on editorial, however.

A 34,000-circulation paper averaged 30 pages daily in 1978. The larger papers published an average of 83 pages. Thus, newsprint and ink account for less than half the amount than that of a large paper. Figures gathered by the Inland Daily Press Association, cited in Table 9.3, show a direct relationship between increasing circulation and higher proportionate newsprint expense.

On the small paper, production costs have fallen below the percentage level of the larger paper. As recently as 1972, production expenses were 22.6 percent of total revenue for the composite small paper. By 1975 they had dropped to the point where, for the first time, editorial expenses exceeded production costs. In 1978 editorial expenses were almost 64 percent greater than production costs. Big city newspapers, frequently more hampered by union contracts, and up to 1976 slower to switch to cold type technology, did not as a group experience much of a change in relative production costs until 1977.

The small newspaper has not seen as dramatic an increase in administrative expenses, although this area did account for only 7.0 percent of expense in 1971, compared to 8.4 percent in 1978. Total wages and salaries as a percentage of revenue ends up being quite similar for the two types of papers, accounting for 28.3 percent for the smaller paper and 25.7 percent for the larger paper (down from 31.2 percent and 35.0 percent, respectively, in 1976).

ADVERTISING/COPY RATIOS

The proportion of the newspaper devoted to advertising has increased rather steadily since 1945, when it was about half advertising, half editorial copy. Table 2.12 shows that by 1973, advertising accounted for 65.3 percent of all space. The number of pages of these newspapers had increased more than 170 percent between 1945 and 1978, but the number of pages and the advertising proportion has stabilized in the 1970s.

According to Media Records, Inc., the percentage of the newspaper which is not advertising is primarily, but not completely, editorial matter. A separate category of "house ads," i.e., notices about patronizing our advertisers or promotions for classified advertising, accounts for one to two percent of remaining space. Nonetheless, despite the considerably higher advertising percentage, the "news hole," that portion of the paper devoted to editorial matter, has grown with the size of the paper. In 1945, the 22 average pages would be divided approximately 11/11 advertising/editorial (and house). In 1978, the larger newspaper had more than twice the space devoted to non-advertising copy, or about 23 pages.

Table 2.12   Daily and Sunday Newspaper Pages Per Issue and Proportion of Advertising Content, Selected Years, 1945-1978[a]

Year	Daily Total Pages	Advertising Percentage[b]	Sunday Total Pages	Advertising Percentage
1945	22	51.5%	70	49.6%
1950	36	59.0	112	54.6
1955	40	61.4	132	58.2
1960	43	60.3	142	56.4
1965	50	61.0	167	59.1
1970	47	61.5	145	61.5
1971	51	62.6	162	63.1
1972	56	64.4	176	64.4
1973	59	65.3	182	66.2
1974	60	65.2	188	66.8
1975	57	63.1	180	65.7
1978	60	62.1	196	69.0

[a]Compiled for subscriber newspapers. This is not a random sample or a projection for all newspapers. Included 145 daily and 93 Sunday papers in 1978.

[b]Includes all non-editorial content.

Sources: 1945-1975 Media Records, Inc., New York. 1978: *Editor & Publisher*, March 17, 1979, p. 64.

© Media Records, Inc. Reprinted with permission.

At least one top newspaper chain executive warns that one must be careful when you quote ANPA and other industry ratios of editorial to advertising content of daily newspapers because large city newspapers run as little as 30 percent news, while small and medium-sized papers run 45 to 55 percent news. In fact, Leo Bogart of Newspaper Advertising Bureau presented figures for 37 big city papers for 1973 which indicate that "news pages as percent of total" pages are as low as 28 percent, although the number of total pages may average as high as 76 pages, so that even these papers may be devoting more actual space to editorial copy than the low copy percentage may at first indicate.[2]

THE ROLE AND RESPONSIBILITY OF THE DAILY NEWSPAPER

The quick and easy answer to the question "What is the role of the daily newspaper in the United States?" would likely be answered by a newspaper subscriber as "to provide the news" or to "distribute information." Students of mass communication see further roles. In addition to informing, newspapers may be said to educate, entertain, and sell. For the reader/client, the information function may be the most important, but many features such as comics and crossword puzzles are entertainment which for some may be their primary reason for buying the paper.

For the advertiser, the newspaper is a means to reach a market for a product or service. A general interest newspaper must, by its very nature, deliver a generalized market, held together mostly by a geographical boundary.

In this general sense, the role of the newspaper would seem to differ little from that of the other commercial mass media. However, if priorities were assigned to these four functions, both publishers and readers would probably consider the informing function first and, depending on one's point of view, selling or entertaining last. Commercial television and most radio typically have entertaining as the top priority, while all-news radio would parallel more closely the newspaper's role.

As a business, the newspaper publishing company has the unique position of being part of the only industry singled out in the Constitution for special protection. Although the freedom of the press is not absolute, the product itself is largely immune from prior control of the government. As will be seen in Chapter 5, this does not free the newspaper firm from government controls which affect it solely as a business, such as minimum wage, normal taxes, or antitrust rules, but it does place the owner of the newspaper in a special position. However, it also brings with it certain responsibilities, especially in communities lacking competing newspapers. Thus, Rivers and Schramm argue:

> The energy and imagination which in a multiple situation the newspaperman might devote to beating the competition must be given to creating a marketplace of ideas. He must seek out opinions and present them in an equitable balance.[3]

This introduces the entire question of access to the columns of the newspaper by voices which differ from those expressed by the editors or the advertisers. It is beyond the scope of this study to engage this issue, other than to point out that it is at the heart of the responsibility of the newspaper—as well as the other mass media.

Besides informing, educating, and entertaining readers and selling for advertisers, newspapers have an added role and constituency: that of returning a profit on the invested capital of their owners. A newspaper which is family-owned may choose to maximize or minimize this role at its whim. But as more newspapers are bought by publicly owned chains or turn to the public money market for capital to expand, they acquire a broader ownership and then they are obligated to provide reasonable returns, returns which some may argue are at odds with their information and education role. Thus, the publisher must grow and earn a profit, yet satisfy his responsibility of providing acceptable, if not quality, journalism.

At least one voice speaks often to this dichotomy. Katharine Graham told stockholders of The Washington Post Company in 1973:

> These two commitments are in no way contradictory. Indeed, they complement each other—and there is not better proof of that than the company's record during the past year . . . 1972 was a year of real journalistic achievement for all divisions of the company. It was also—and this was no coincidence—the greatest financial year in the company's history, with record sales and earnings that enable us to double the dividend.

There is evidence at the *Post* and at Knight-Ridder's *Philadelphia Inquirer* and elsewhere that quality journalism can produce long-run economic benefits. Even in one-newspaper cities, readers may buy a newspaper only if they consider it has information they want and cannot get through other media.

It may be reasonably argued, therefore, that to optimize profits and satisfy stockholders, a newspaper must sell advertising, which in turn depends on attracting subscribers with good editorial coverage. Strengthened circulation thus helps the advertiser, while providing a service to the reader. This may not describe the operations of all publishers, but it is a connection of the common interests of the newspaper's multiple clientele.

SUMMARY

The recent history of the daily newspaper industry has been one of slow growth, but substantial profits. It is more concentrated in ownership than it was in 1947, but the largest firms still control a considerably smaller portion of its revenues than the largest firms in other communications industries.

The number of newspapers has been consistent, ranging between 1749 and 1774 since 1945. Newspaper employment has grown at a much slower pace than has total civilian employment since 1946.

The 25 largest circulation daily newspapers account for about 22 percent of total daily newspaper circulation in the country. A large circulation newspaper could expect 18 to 22 percent pre-tax profit on operations, with newsprint and ink the largest single expense category. A medium-sized newspaper had a somewhat larger pre-tax profit in 1978, but newsprint expense was a much smaller proportion of expense.

The advertising to copy ratio has grown to the point where advertising accounts for over 60 percent of all space, but the absolute newshole has expanded because the number of pages in an average large paper more than doubled between 1945 and 1978.

The role of the newspaper is to inform, educate, entertain, and sell. It is also expected to produce a profit for its owners. However, it has been argued that in performing the newspaper's functions properly for the readers, it will enhance its service to the advertisers and stockholders.

In examining the profitability of newspaper companies which release information on their earnings, it appears that such firms do tend to be more profitable than firms in other manufacturing industries. This would also hold true by comparing the average large and medium-sized newspaper's profit to other industries' averages.

FOOTNOTES

1. These factors will be discussed more fully in Chapters 3 and 9.

2. Leo Bogart, "How the Challenge of Television News Affects the Prosperity of Daily Newspapers," *Journalism Quarterly* 52:409, Autumn, 1975.

3. William L. Rivers and Wilbur Schramm, *Responsibility in Mass Communication* (rev. ed.; New York: Harper & Row, 1969), p. 160.

3

Circulation

Circulation refers to the number of copies of the newspaper sold each day. Although circulation may not be the major source of revenue for newspapers, the viability of newspapers depends on people buying them. If circulation drops, advertisers find the newspaper vehicle of less use in reaching a desired audience. Circulation, therefore, might be judged to be a daily reminder to the publisher of the worth of the product. Circulation levels provide constant feedback on how good a job a newspaper is doing in satisfying some want or need within the population.

This chapter examines some of the factors which appear to affect circulation rates in general. It investigates the research which has been done into readership patterns. Finally, it looks at distribution and some of the problems being encountered and several of the solutions being investigated.

In the end, the chapter should help address the hypothesis: Current trends notwithstanding, aggregate newspaper circulation has stabilized and will enjoy modest increases through the remainder of this century.

Table 3.1 shows that after decades of continued gains, daily newspaper circulation stalled in the mid-1960s, edged to a peak in 1973, then retreated to levels of the previous decade before beginning to inch upward. Sunday circulation has continued rising, albeit very slowly as more newspapers add Sunday editions. (See also Table 3.7.)

Table 3.2 shows that circulation has been lagging behind the growth in both the adult population and households. The latter—the primary buying unit for newspapers—have increased even faster than the adult population, as the size of the average household has gotten smaller. Between 1960 and 1978, net newspaper circulation increased only 5.3 percent, while households rose by over 40 percent and adult population by nearly 30 percent. The result is seen in the declining penetration of newspapers per household.

The reasons given for this phenomenon are numerous. Within the industry, concern is expressed about the editorial product itself and whether it meets the needs of today's readers. One executive editor does not put the blame on circulation or marketing personnel "but on the editors," many of whom "are simply delivering a weak product." Other concerns include rising newsprint costs and the pressure to raise prices accordingly, changing lifestyles that place more emphasis on the electronic media, and circulation and delivery practices which are inefficient and outmoded.

Table 3.1   Morning, Evening, and Sunday Daily Newspapers in the U.S., 1920-1978

	A.M. Papers		P.M. Papers		Total Daily		Sunday	
	Number	Circ.	Number	Circ.	Number	Circ.	Number	Circ.
1920	437	N.A.	1,605	N.A.	2,042	27,791	522	17,084
1930	388	N.A.	1,554	N.A.	1,942	39,589	521	26,413
1940	380	16,114	1,498	25,018	1,878	41,132	525	32,371
1950	322	21,266	1,450	32,563	1,772	53,829	549	46,582
1960	312	24,029	1,459	34,853	1,763	58,882	563	47,699
1965	320	24,107	1,444	36,251	1,751	60,358	562	48,600
1970	334	25,934	1,429	36,174	1,748	62,108	586	49,217
1971	339	26,116	1,425	36,115	1,749	62,231	540	49,665
1972	337	26,078	1,441	36,432	1,761	62,510	603	49,339
1973	343	26,524	1,451	36,623	1,774	63,147	634	51,717
1974	340	26,145	1,449	35,732	1,768	61,877	641	51,679
1975	339	25,490	1,436	35,165	1,756	60,655	639	51,096
1976	346	25,858	1,435	35,119	1,762	60,977	650	51,565
1977	339	26,747	1,403	34,750	1,753	61,498	668	52,468
1978	355	27,657	1,419	34,333	1,756	61,990	696	53,990

N.B.   In 1960 through 1976 circulation of "all-day" papers is apportioned between both morning and evening figures. These papers are counted in both the a.m. and p.m. paper number, but only once in total daily count.

Source: *Editor & Publisher International Year Book.* Figures for number of papers on December 31 of each year, based on September circulation audit or statement.

Table 3.2 Daily Newspaper Circulation Growth Compared to Adult Population* and Households,
Selected Years 1930-1977
(Index: 1930 = 100)

Year	Households (000)	Adult Population (000)	Circulation Index	Household Index	Population Index	Circulation Per Household	Circulation Per 100 Adults
1930	29,905	75,166	100	100	100	1.32	52.7
1940	34,949	86,363	104	117	115	1.18	47.6
1950	43,559	98,341	136	146	131	1.24	54.7
1960	52,799	108,124	149	177	144	1.12	54.5
1970	63,401	122,722	157	212	163	0.99	50.7
1975	71,120	134,421	153	238	179	0.85	45.1
1977	74,142	139,320	157	248	185	0.84	44.5
% Change							
1930-1977	147.9%	85.3%				−36.4%	−15.6%
1960-1977	40.4%	28.9%				−25.0%	−18.3%

* 21 years old and over.

Source: U.S. Bureau of the Census, *Current Population Reports*.

BASIC TRENDS

Both sociological and economic factors may affect the newspaper buying patterns of Americans. Few studies have found any definite evidence to explain what specifically makes people buy or not buy a newspaper on a regular basis, although numerous factors have been suggested.

Economic Factors—The Price of Newspapers

As seen in Chapter 2, newspapers derive 20 to 30 percent of their operating revenue from circulation sales. But to maintain this proportion as advertising revenues increase, they have had to raise subscription prices. As recently as 1972, 1407 dailies still charged 10 cents for the daily paper, and only 350 charged 15 cents. By the end of 1978, most papers —1031—were up to the higher figure, with only 140 at 10 cents. More papers—56 in all—charged 25 cents, while the predominant trend was toward the 20 cent daily, the rate for 56 newspapers in 1978.

The price increase also helped the industry reverse a trend which saw circulation income covering a decreasing proportion of the physical cost of the newspaper's basic raw materials—ink and newsprint. As seen in Table 3.3, the large city newspaper recovered the erosion in circulation income as a percentage of newsprint and ink cost which had continued from 1967 until 1974, when the widespread boost of circulation price to 15 cents began to more than offset added materials costs in those years.

Table 3.3   Percentage of Newsprint and Ink Expense Covered by Circulation Revenue for a 250,000 Circulation Daily Newspaper, 1967 to 1978

	Newsprint & Ink Expense (million $)	Circulation Income (million $)	Circulation Revenue As % of Newsprint & Ink Expense
1967	$4.5	$3.0	66.7%
1968	4.7	3.1	66.0
1969	5.5	3.2	58.2
1970	5.6	3.3	56.7
1971	6.0	3.4	56.7
1973	6.7	3.7	55.2
1974	8.0	5.0	62.5
1975	9.3	6.6	71.0
1976	9.4	7.3	77.7
1977	9.5	7.2	75.8
1978	9.3	7.3	78.5

Source: Calculated from data compiled by Newspaper Analysis Service, as published in *Editor & Publisher.*

Although the rise in price to 20 or 25 cents represents a large percentage increase at one time, newspaper prices have, in fact, changed little in relative terms. Table 3.4 indicates that the average price of the newspaper in 1978, expressed in 1967 dollars, is 8.4 cents. The newspaper of 1889, also translated into 1967 terms, would have been 8.5 cents. Thus, relative to income levels, the average price of a newspaper in 1976 is comparable to that of 87 years earlier.

Thus, the increased price of newspapers can only be a contributing factor to the sluggish circulation gains and, at the least, may have helped to discourage multiple newspaper households. The small and medium-sized papers owned by one group have noted the biggest fall off in subscribers among the older, fixed-income readers as prices at most of their papers moved up to 20 cents. A drop of five percent in Sunday circulation followed after a boost in price from 35 cents to 50 cents. This confirms the observation made in an interview by Edward A. Koehler, circulation director of the *Providence* (RI) *Journal* and *Bulletin*, that older people and families in three-family apartment houses have taken to sharing the paper to spread the increased cost. And that cost is considerable: At 20 cents daily plus 70 cents on Sunday, subscribers were paying almost $100 annually for a daily newspaper.

Table 3.4 Newspaper Prices in Constant Dollars, Selected Years, 1880 to 1978

Year	Newspaper Price (cents/copy)	Consumer Price Index (1967 = 100)	Real Newspaper Price (1967 cents)
1880	3.1	29	10.7
1885	2.7	27	10.0
1889	2.3	27	8.5
1899	1.3	25	5.2
1909	1.4	27	5.2
1919/20	1.9	56	3.4
1929/30	3.0	51	5.9
1970	9.2	116	7.9
1976	14.7	170	8.7
1978	16.4	195	8.4

Sources: Newspaper Prices 1880-1970: Bruce Owen, *Economics & Freedom of Expression*, Table 2A-12, which summarizes data he assembled from several sources. He warns that newspaper prices prior to 1899 are based on a handful of sample cities, while from 1899 onward, price includes weekly and periodical data.

1976: Weighted average taken from *Editor & Publisher*, Feb. 12, 1977, p. 29.

1978: Weighted average calculated from "ANPA General Bulletin," No. 6, Feb. 14, 1979, p. 42.

Consumer Prices: U.S. Bureau of Labor Statistics, *Monthly Labor Review*.

One study of the effects of price increases on circulation found that in 239 cases of price increases from 202 daily newspapers picked in a random sample, circulation continued to climb in 142 instances (59.4 percent).[1] These took place over a ten-year period, 1965 to 1974. However, the results were not the same in all circulation categories. The data presented in Table 3.5 indicate that the larger the circulation, the greater the likelihood that circulation will decrease if the price is raised. The correlation between circulation size and decreased circulation is a strong −.94, suggesting that smaller newspapers, perhaps more often in one-newspaper communities and more affluent suburbs, face fewer difficulties in passing on circulation increases than bigger city papers. However, the alternative is that the smaller papers are younger or are in expanding towns which have brought natural growth. In the absence of a control group of newspapers, it cannot be known how much more the smaller papers may have grown without the price hikes.

The effects of inflation have caused families to make adjustments in their lifestyles as well. According to one study by Yankelovich, Skelly and White, 21 percent of families considered cutting back on magazine and newspaper subscriptions as one aspect of coping.[2] This is, however, a far lower priority than not buying as many clothes (44 percent), not eating out in restaurants (37 percent), and fewer trips to the barber shop or hairdresser (25 percent). But it is more frequent than buying less beer or liquor (19 percent).

Some circulation also has been eliminated or held down, especially by regional dailies, by consciously reducing the delivery area. As the cost of delivery escalates through labor and fuel costs, along with substantially increased newsprint costs, publishers may find that fringe circulation costs more than the revenue it brings in. This is because the newspaper cannot really charge the local advertiser for circulation in areas beyond their regular trading area. When the marginal revenue doesn't even cover the incremental cost, that circulation is economically expendable.

Several newspapers are charging higher rates for subscribers in outlying areas, such as the *Chicago Tribune*'s extra five cents a day or the *Louisville Courier*'s premium of a nickel weekly on home-delivered copies. Other papers have just eliminated circulation which was not paying its way. *The Salt Lake City Tribune* and *Deseret News* lopped off over 12,000 daily and Sunday subscribers in 1973 when they discontinued circulation to Idaho, Nevada, and other neighboring states. The *Portland Oregonian* and *Oregon Journal* had about 40,000 subscribers beyond a 100-mile limit of the city and stopped taking out-of-state orders. Others are making similar concessions to the escalating price of newsprint (see Chapter 9) and transportation.

Sociological Factors

The 1960s and 1970s have seen numerous changes in the ways people live and their relationships with one another:

• The intrusion of television into the home has taken time away from the newspaper and contributed to fewer multiple newspaper households. To an extent, TV also fulfills the need for news for many who once depended on newspapers.

Table 3.5   Changes in Circulation Size When Subscription Rates Change, 1965-1974

Daily Circulation Category	No. of Newspapers	Total No. Of Changes in Prices	No. of Price Changes Followed by Circulation Increases	% of Total Category	No. of Price Changes Followed by Circulation Decrease	% of Total Category	No. of Price Changes Followed by No Change in Circulation
100,000 or more	18	19	5	26%	14	74%	0
50,000 to 99,999	15	18	8	44	10	56	0
25,000 to 49,999	30	32	17	53	14	44	1
10,000 to 24,999	61	79	53	66	25	32	1
Under 10,000	78	91	59	65	31	34	1
Total	202	239	142		94		3

Correlation coefficient (r) between category size and percentage of decreased circulation papers = −0.94.

Source: Jeff Clark, "Circulation Increase Despite Higher Subscription Rates," *Editor & Publisher*, February 14, 1976, p. 32.

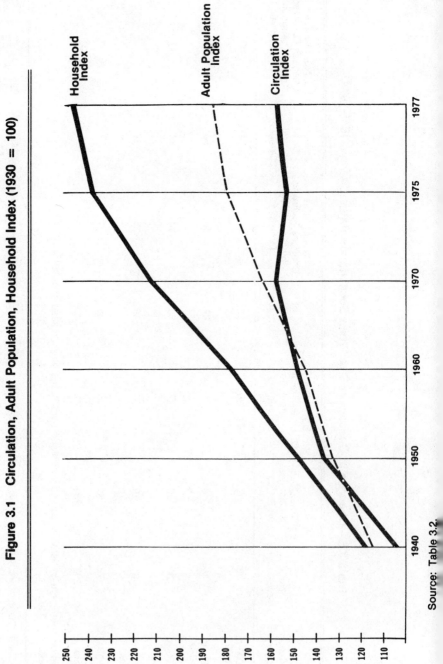

Figure 3.1   Circulation, Adult Population, Household Index (1930 = 100)

Source: Table 3.2

- The larger size newspapers (Table 2.11) also mean more time is needed to read the paper and thus less time to read a second or third paper.

- A rising standard of living has been accompanied by an increase in leisure time. Ironically, this may result in decreased readership as people spend more time in camping, sports, fishing, and related activities outside the home.

- The trend toward suburban living and working has decreased the reliance of many on the big city dailies, while making it more difficult for the city dailies to reach their prospective customers. Fear of being in the city at night has reduced newsstand sales, while urban traffic problems have made delivery more difficult.

- High-rise dwellers, whether in the city or suburbs, are generally more difficult to reach than families in single-family homes or garden apartments. Since 1960 the number of housing units in multi-family dwellings increased from 23.6 percent to 32.4 percent in 1976. In apartment buildings, managers may refuse to allow carriers to place newspapers at hall doors and sales teams have trouble gaining entry.

- Black and other non-white ethnic groups are becoming a larger proportion of the population in many cities. A study from Temple University found evidence that circulation suffers the most in those cities where the white population has fallen.

- The seemingly irreversible love affair of Americans with their automobiles for commuting and the resulting impact on mass transportation means that fewer workers have time to read the paper on their way to or from work. The eventual impact of the energy shortage may ultimately force a change in this equation.

- More women than ever before are in the labor force—48 percent in 1977—thus reducing their time to read the paper.

- Finally, as seen in Table 3.6, readership tends to be highest among older people. Young adults, 18 to 24, have been shown to be the least intensive group of newspaper readers. In 1960, this group accounted for 13.6 percent of the 18 year-old and over population. In 1975, that age bracket hit its highest expected penetration for this century at 18.6 percent. Not surprisingly, a higher level of readership is associated with greater education and income, although in both cases the peak is attained at relatively low levels, then remains constant even as education or income increases. Although men and women read the paper at the same level, there is a difference between blacks and whites.

Table 3.6   Newspaper Readership by Age, Income, Education, and Sex, 1975-76

	Percent using "Yesterday"
Education:	
Grade school	51%
Some high school	64
Completed high school	73
Some college	73
College graduate	74
Income:	
Under $5,000	53%
$ 5,000 – $ 9,999	65
$10,000 – $14,999	72
$15,000 – $24,999	74
$25,000 and up	75
Age:	
18 – 24	51%
25 – 29	51
30 – 39	66
40 – 49	67
50 – 59	79
60 – 65	87
66 and older	90
Race:	
White	68%
Black	58
Sex:	
Male	70%
Female	67

Source: John P. Robinson, "Daily News Habits of the American Public," *ANPA News Research Report,* No. 15, September 22, 1978, p. 3.

DIFFERENCES IN A.M. AND P.M. DAILIES

Big city newspapers are suffering the most in circulation efforts, with papers published for afternoon delivery feeling the most pronounced declines, due to traffic problems and competition from television's evening news. Although a 1976 study by Bagdikian generally minimizes the difficulties of afternoon papers compared to their morning brethren, he does note that of the 12 newspapers with 100,000 or more circulation that suspended operations between 1961 and 1970, eight were evening papers that represented 67 percent of the circulation of the 12 papers.[3] In 1965, evening papers overall represented 60 percent of total daily circulation (compared to 55 percent by 1978).

Morning papers, although accounting for the same percentage of total papers in 1978 as in 1940, accounted for a somewhat greater proportion of total daily circulation. As seen in Table. 3.7 morning papers amount to 20.2 percent of daily newspapers but account for 44.6 percent of total circulation.

Table 3.7   Circulation of Morning Daily Papers and Sunday Papers as a Percentage of Total Daily Circulation, Selected Years, 1920-1978

	A.M.		Sunday	
	% of Papers	% of Circulation	% of Papers w/ Sunday Edition	% of Daily Circulation
1920	21.4%	N.A.	25.6%	61.5%
1930	20.0	N.A.	26.8	66.7
1940	20.2	39.2%	28.0	78.7
1950	18.2	39.5	31.0	86.5
1960	17.7	40.8	31.9	81.0
1970	19.1	41.8	33.5	79.2
1975	19.3	42.0	36.4	84.2
1978	20.2	44.6	39.6	87.1

Source: Calculated from data in the *Editor & Publisher International Year Book,* annual.

Although New York lost some well-known morning papers in the 1960s, most notably the *Herald Tribune* in 1967, the list of suspended big city afternoon papers since 1960 is formidable: *The World Journal Tribune, Chicago Today, New York Journal-American, Detroit Times, Cleveland News, Hartford Times.* Under stiff competition from the morning *Los Angeles Times,* and intensified by internal turmoil, the evening *Herald-Examiner,* a Hearst paper, plunged in circulation from about 718,000 in 1965 to 316,206 in 1978, a drop of almost 56 percent. In Philadelphia, the leading *Bulletin,* an evening paper, fell more than 20 percent in a steady decline from 1972 to 1978 with its Sunday edition down 13 percent. The morning *Inquirer,* on the other hand, slowed its mostly downward trend by 1976 and in 1978 was only 7 percent behind the 1972 level.

Of course, these and other trends are not just related to the morning or evening position of the papers. Big city newspapers in general have been losing circulation steadily. In 1948, daily circulation in cities over one million population accounted for 27.2 percent of all circulation. By 1978, this category sold only 19.4 percent of all newspapers (although this was an improvement from even lower percentages in past years).

THE MARKET FOR NEWSPAPERS

There was a time when practically all literate people seemed to read a newspaper—back when circulation per household was well over one. Generally, people take their newspaper for granted—except when for some reason, such as a strike, it is suddenly not there. Sociologist Bernard Berelson used one such opportunity—the New York newspaper strike of 1945—to gauge public reaction toward newspapers. Among the uses of the newspaper articulated by those interviewed in the Berelson study were: (1) for information about and interpretation of public affairs; (2) as a tool for daily living (radio listings, retail advertisements); (3) for respite ("escape" from the reader's immediate world); (4) for prestige ("You have to read in order to keep up in a conversation with other people"); and (5) for social contact (human interest stories and advice/gossip columns, etc.). However, the interviews also turned up "the ritualistic and near compulsive character for newspaper reading." At least half the respondents referred to this habit and this helps explain the strength of the drive which sent thousands of people to the central offices of the various newspapers to buy copies of the paper during the strike.[4]

Are people as in need of the newspaper in this age of television? On Sunday, February 13, 1977, the *Philadelphia Bulletin,* faced with truck drivers who refused to cross a picket line set up by striking employees of the shut-down *Philadelphia Inquirer* and *Daily News,* sold 150,000 copies of the paper over the counter of the main office. This had followed an over-the-counter sale of 50,000 copies the previous Friday (compared to circulation 540,000 on a normal day). Circulation Director Jack Betson noted: "I have never seen anything like this in my life. The readers simply flooded the area. Something like this ought to dispel the negative thinking about the lessening attraction of newspapers."

Readers and Nonreaders
Newspaper managers would like to know what factors separate regular readers from those who do not read their product. A better understanding of who their customers are might help newspapers serve this group better while at the same time be better able to pinpoint and direct sales to those who have heretofore been nonreaders.

One study in 1964 by Westley and Severin[5] found that, in Wisconsin at least, nonreaders were, as a group, relatively old or young, residents of a rural area, and low in income, education, and occupational achievement. However, although the correlation between nonreaders and any of these factors was statistically significant, the magnitude of the correlations was moderate. For example, 93 percent of the respondents were daily readers in households headed by persons earning at least $10,000 annually compared to 81 percent in households headed by individuals with annual earnings under $5000.

Similar results are found in a 1971 study sponsored by the Newspaper Advertising Bureau.[6] Newspaper reading was positively related to increased education, income, and age, and showed little difference by sex. But even at the low end of each category, there were substantial majorities of the population who read the newspaper.

Another approach decided that an index combining two or more indicators might be more productive.[7] Of the several indices constructed, the Household Index was found to be the most reliable predictor of subscribers vs. nonsubscribers. The items in the Index which favored newspaper subscribers were annual income of over $5000, home ownership, and residence in the county (where the study was done) by at least one member of the household for at least three years. In households where all three criteria were met, 89 percent subscribed to the newspaper. Where only two criteria were met, 77 percent subscribed. And where none of the criteria was found, only 20 percent of the households studied bought the paper.

A survey by Penrose in 1974 substantiated a "real decline" in the use of the daily newspaper.[8] In this study, many more persons fell into the nonreader categories across the spectrum of socioeconomic characteristics than in the 1964 project. Of considerable interest, moreover, should be the finding that those who watch television news were more likely to see the daily newspaper, with only 20 percent of those who watched TV news being nonreaders, compared to 41 percent who were not regular viewers.

Although most studies indicate that newspaper readership increases with age, a series of newspaper readership surveys between 1962 and 1973 by Market Opinion Research (MOR) yielded evidence that penetration dropped 12 percent in the 35-44 year old age group—supposedly the solid, prime newspaper reading years. During this same period, MOR surveys indicate newspaper penetration among all adults fell eight percent, the same rate as in the 25-34 year old group. But among young adults 18-24, readership penetration dropped only four percent. Thus, it may not be enough to merely "mount a campaign among our young people between the ages of 20 and 35," as has been typically suggested as a remedy to circulation problems, concluded the researchers.[9]

Finally, a study conducted between 1972 and 1976 suggests that no single set of audience characteristics can predict newspaper circulation.[10] For example, while higher income and more education have been associated with reading a newspaper every day, they are also correlated with choosing a larger metropolitan newspaper over the local newspaper. Higher television viewing time was related to lower circulation only in that these people would tend to read one newspaper rather than two, but it was also strongly tied to reading that one paper every day. The study uncovered other characteristics related to readership that had previously received little attention, including marital status, political participation and the gratifications sought from newspaper use.

Where the Readers Are

The shift of the population to the suburbs has brought with it a shift in circulation patterns. The smaller city and suburban newspapers are growing at the expense of the large regional papers. Table 3.8 shows how newspapers in all city-size categories increased between 1948 and 1978, except the large, mostly older cities of over one million population. Newspapers based in cities of over one million persons have frequently tried to follow their fleeing readers into the suburbs with various zoned editions, but this effort has not prevented the substantial decline in their proportion of total circulation.

Table 3.8   Growth in Circulation by Size of City, 1948, 1959, 1978

City Size	Daily Circulation (000)			% Change
(1970 Census)	1948	1959	1978	1948-1978
Over 1,000,000	13,947	12,045	12,006	– 13.9%
500,001 – 1,000,000	8,533	9,012	10,586	24.1
100,001 – 500,000	13,908	16,907	15,902	14.3
100,000 and under	14,956	19,273	23,496	57.1
All U.S. Papers	51,345	57,237	61,890	20.5

Sources: 1978: *Editor & Publisher International Year Book, 1979.*

1959 and 1948: Benjamin M. Compaine, *Future Directions of the Newspaper Industry: The 1980s and Beyond* (White Plains, NY: Knowledge Industry Publications, 1977), p. 57.

Table 3.9 shows what is probably another trend, and that is the movement of newspaper growth away from the Northeastern cities to the Sunbelt of the South and West. The table highlights the decline in the Northeast and the marginal dip in the North Central states, in contrast to substantial increases, albeit on a much smaller base, in the rest of the country.

Overall, in 1978, the 31 newspapers in the largest cities represented only 1.8 percent of all newspapers, but over 19 percent of total circulation. Table 3.10 shows the number of dailies as well as the percentage of circulation they accounted for in cities of various sizes. Cities of between 100,000 and 500,000 accounted for the largest block of newspaper circulation of any category, 25.7 percent, although they comprise only 12 percent of the number of papers. On the other hand, the smallest 52.7 percent of the papers together sell only 14.6 percent of daily papers.

What People Read and How They Read The Paper

An Audits & Surveys, Inc. study for the Newspaper Advertising Bureau conducted in 1971 reported that 84 percent of the pages (other than classified) are opened by the typical reader, with general news pages the highest (88 percent) and business and sports tied for the lowest at 75 percent each (but that would likely include a very high proportion of male

Table 3.9 Changes in Daily and Sunday Circulation by Region Between 1959 and 1975

	Daily Circulation (000)			Sunday Circulation (000)		
	1959	1975	% Change	1959	1975	% Change
Northeast	17,466	15,546	– 11.0%	14,725	13,633	– 7.4%
North Central	17,142	16,562	– 3.4	13,428	12,820	– 4.5
South	14,223	16,594	16.7	11,561	15,460	33.7
West	8,406	9,785	16.4	7,351	8,675	18.0
Total U.S.	57,237	58,487	2.2	47,065	50,589	7.5

N.B. Excludes *Wall Street Journal, Christian Science Monitor, Journal of Commerce.*

Source: American Newspaper Publishers Association, "U.S. Economic Growth and Newsprint Consumption," Newsprint & Traffic Bulletin, No. 1, January 5, 1977.

readers). The study estimated that 81 percent of all advertisements of 100 lines or more, with the exception of classifieds, were exposed to readers.

More than nine out of ten of the adult respondents reported turning through the entire newspaper, the majority starting with the front page. Moreover, the average respondent picked up the daily edition a median of 2.3 times before being finished with it. Total time spent with the newspaper averaged 34 minutes each weekday. Consistent with the results of others, this study also found that those who watched television news spent slightly longer with the paper than did nonviewers.

The amount of advertising content has been found to be as important as editorial material. Leo Bogart of the Newspaper Advertising Bureau reported that a survey in 1974 found that 75 percent of women respondents agreed with the statement: "When I read the newspaper, I am about equally interested in the advertising and news stories." Advertising information is an integral part of the newspaper package in that it is "specific, practical, and informative."[11]

DISTRIBUTION

Newspaper readers may subscribe to a newspaper for enjoyment or because of the prominence of a particular paper, but delivery problems ranked as the number one reason why people cancel their subscriptions. A survey for ANPA in 1973 reported that 21.7 percent of those who canceled their subscriptions did so because of unreliable, improper, or late delivery of their newspaper. This ranked far above the cost (8.8 percent), disinterest (6.7 percent), or objections to the editorial stance (1.7 percent).

Table 3.10   Percentage of Newspapers and Circulation Accounted for by Size of City, 1978

Number of Dailies	1970 Population						
	Over 1 million	500,000-1 million	100,000-500,000	50,000-100,000	25,000-50,000	Under 25,000	Total
% of Total Newspapers	1.8	3.1	11.9	13.3	17.2	52.7	100.0
% of Total Circulation	19.4	17.1	25.7	12.8	10.5	14.6	100.0
% of Morning Papers	5.4	8.2	25.9	20.0	17.7	22.8	100.0
% of Evening Papers	0.9	1.8	8.5	11.9	17.2	59.6	99.9
% with Sunday Editions	54.8	58.2	56.0	57.7	51.7	25.8	—

N.B. May not total 100.0 due to rounding.

Source: Calculated from data in *Editor & Publisher International Year Book, 1979.*

Yet with minor exceptions, there have been few substantial advances or changes in the distribution of the newspaper, a process which still frequently culminates with a 12-year-old kid tossing the paper on the subscriber's lawn each day. Vending machines have made newspapers more available to commuters, but filling them still depends on trucks and drivers and district managers and the newsboy. And far too often circulation directors perceive themselves as managers of a delivery system rather than as head of a sales organization.

At one time, it seemed that facsimile transmission of the newspaper directly to the home would be a technological solution to distribution problems. But technology and cost have never come together in a method that would be practical and economical. As discussed in Chapter 6, it appears that the facsimile approach has been written off as a substitute for present methods in the foreseeable future. Although facsimile may be used eventually as a supplemental means of bringing some types of information into the home, both hard copy and television tube receipt continue to present significant drawbacks.

The Little Merchant

The "little merchant," an independent news carrier, has been cited as a major reason for circulation problems, but has also been rigorously defended. For many newspapers, the newspaper deliverer is a young 12- or 13-year old boy who is treated as an independent businessman. He receives newspapers at a discount from their selling price and generally is responsible for delivery and collection on a given route. The newsboy is frequently the only contact between the newspaper publishing firm and the customer. The newsboy is also expected to solicit for new customers and make weekly or monthly collections from his subscribers. Newspapers thus count as circulation revenue only the net revenue received from carriers, not the full price of the newspaper. Nor are carrier expenses thus included in the income statement.

Carrier turnover is generally high, with reports of up to 175 percent a year. At one midwestern newspaper, district managers who supervise carriers were terminating "almost as fast as new subscriptions."[12]

A vocal critic of the "little merchant" system, Francis Dale, when publisher of the *Cincinnati Enquirer,* asked a conference of circulation managers:

> Can you seriously contend that your carriers are qualified to persuade a family to subscribe to your daily paper, the reputation of your columnists [sic], the dedication of reporters, the public service of the newspaper, or the number of different news items reported on each day?
> Are we going to leave the job of selling the product to the least trained, least controlled, least challenged, least knowledgeable and least qualified people there are who are in any way related to us?[13]

Those who defend the newsboy arrangement refer to the large numbers of readers who subscribe to papers because of this little merchant. "One cannot 'buy' a friendly smile of earnest youthful appeal of our boys and girls . . . ," wrote one circulation manager in response to Dale's evaluation. Or they promote the "opportunity to receive some quality training and motivation" or be " 'turned on' by the extra profits he or she can personally generate."[14]

Innovations in Distribution

Most innovation in physical delivery systems has been in trying to streamline the basic existing process. To avoid downtown traffic problems, large city papers such as the *St. Louis Post-Dispatch, New York Times, Los Angeles Times,* and the *Detroit News* have built suburban printing plants to supplement their in-town plants. This is obviously an expensive proposition and is justified only for the largest of newspapers, particularly evening papers.

Another gimmick that was tried involved having delivery men operate out of vans, getting instructions through earphones from a central dispatcher or computer.

In a more direct attack on basic problems in the existing system, the *Fort Wayne* (Ind) *News-Sentinel* decided to revamp its network. Previously, contract haulers delivered the paper each day to 650 individual carriers, who then made local deliveries and biweekly collections. The carriers were responsible to eight full-time district managers. In 1973, the district managers were replaced by carrier "counselors," primarily housewives working part time. The newspaper bundles are now dropped off with the counselors, who in turn deliver them to the news carriers. The counselors also work with carriers at sales meetings and make missed paper deliveries. The *News-Sentinel* reports the costs are about the same as before, but deliveries are made about 25 minutes earlier and counselor turnover is low.

Faced with the problems of making deliveries and collecting money in the inner city, many papers have given their routes to adults, who are less likely to be hassled or robbed than the youngsters who traditionally have fulfilled that role.

Replacing the Independent Merchant

Given that the newspaper must be individually delivered to each subscriber in its current form, the realm of innovation is relatively limited. There is considerable interest, therefore, in the steps which have been taken by *The Los Angeles Times,* among others, in completely eliminating the independent carrier system and replacing it with a network of 200 full-time and 1000 new part-time employees to act as full-time collectors, managers, and part-time distributors to stores, racks, and vendors. The independent home-delivery dealers became independent delivery agents only.

Under the *Times'* system, implemented in 1976, all sales, billing, and customer contact is the responsibility of the *Times.* The new procedure gives the *Times* a computerized list with the names and addresses of nearly 750,000 home subscribers—information which previously had been solely in the hands of the independent agent. The start-up cost for the switch was $5 million. The system resulted in an additional $23 million in circulation revenue in its first year of operation, although Times Mirror management reported associated costs of about $27 million in the same period. But for the longer run, the company now controls its own distribution network and for the first time actually knows who its subscribers are.

The *Nashville Tennessean* and *Banner* have similarly changed to a system of deliveries paid on an hourly wage basis, with billings from the central office. The Nashville papers expected to increase net income from the new set-up within three years.

Several industry leaders see this trend intensifying in coming years. Even the general manager of the International Circulation Managers Association predicts that by 1985, "what carrier boys there are will be newspaper employees whose sole function will be to deliver the newspaper." But in most instances, the youngsters will be replaced by adults. Not everyone agrees, however, including circulation directors at large papers such as the *Washington Star, Baltimore Sun, Boston Globe,* and *Philadelphia Bulletin.*

Factors Promoting Change

Several factors appear to strongly support the movement for newspaper-owned distribution systems.

Anti-trust Legislation.   A Supreme Court ruling several years ago held that newspaper firms could not arbitrarily fix prices or restrain sales territories. That means that independent dealers could not be restricted in what they wanted to charge once they bought their papers, nor could they be stopped from infringing on the territory allocated to another distributor by the newspaper. Distributors could also file antitrust suits should the newspaper try to enforce other than voluntary compliance with "recommended" prices and territory. If the papers take over their own distribution, they do not have to fear such litigation and they also can make sure a distributor is not selling the paper at other than the suggested price.

Paid-In-Advance Subscriptions.   Newspapers are showing increasing interest in billing subscribers in much the same way as magazines have done—in advance of receiving the publication. This can be handled either through monthly, or less frequent renewal billings from the paper, or automatically charging through a bank credit card. The attraction to the subscriber is in not having to be constantly bothered by the news carrier collecting at inconvenient times. It also provides a ready receipt of payments made. The advantage for the newspaper is that it frees the carrier from what is typically the most difficult part of the job—making weekly or biweekly collections—and thus helps reduce carrier turnover. It also accelerates the cash flow of the firm—bringing in the money in advance of delivery of the paper rather than collecting in arrears.

There is, on the other hand, the cost of billing or the discount which the credit card operations deduct from the gross. Nonetheless, in Richmond, Va., the *Times-Dispatch* and *News Leader* has found it could actually make money by emphasizing credit card payment in advance (PIA) rather than newspaper billing. And the idea was quite popular with subscribers, with 50,000 out of 220,000 carrier-served readers converting to PIA during a single two-month promotion in fall 1974. In Atlanta, the *Journal* and *Constitution* have 30 percent of their subscribers on a PIA basis. In Miami this practice has seen tremendous growth.

As more papers and subscribers promote PIA, the role of the newspaper carrier becomes more that of a deliverer who may never see the subscribers. Readers will deal directly with the newspaper. Thus, there may be an added inducement to merely pay delivery agents a wage similar to the Nashville approach.

It is unlikely, however, that newspapers can ever hope to become totally paid for in advance. Small papers may not have the volume to make it economical for credit card companies to grant a small discount rate or for the computer to do their own billing economically. People on fixed incomes or of limited means may resist having to pay large amounts at once. As one newspaper executive warned, he had a fear of making people realize how much they were paying for their newspaper. In his case, at the *Providence* (R.I.) *Journal* and *Bulletin,* this would be about $25 every three months.

Legal Restrictions on Little Merchants.   Since 1948, a series of rulings by the National Labor Relations Board has exempted independent carriers from minimum wage and worker compensation laws, agreeing with newspaper owners that the little merchants and other carriers are independent contractors. Some states, New York, New Jersey, Maryland, and California among them, do require that newspaper carriers be covered by workmen's compensation insurance.

However, the conditions under which the independent contractor is exempted from employee rules strictly limits the authority newspapers have over them. For example, in NLRB v. Lindsay Newspapers, Inc., the status of the carrier may be ruled that of an employee if several of the following factors are found:

• The company selects and controls the scope of the distributor's territory.

• The company alone establishes the price at which papers are to be bought and sold.

• The company assists in obtaining new subscribers.

• The firm requires that certain subscribers be serviced whether or not the distributor wishes to do so.

• The newspaper firm insists that delivery be made in paper tubes even if the distributor objects.

• The firm retains payments made by subscribers for more than three months in advance.

• The firm requires papers to be waxed under certain weather conditions.

There are ten other such factors, but they all involve the extent to which the publisher can dictate what the "independent" carrier must or cannot do. For example, one method newspaper firms use during a subscription drive is a "blitz" during which teams of agents go into a neighborhood to knock on doors or call homes to solicit subscriptions. The U.S. Labor Department has ruled that such work of carriers is not exempt from the Fair Labor Standards Act if they obtain subscriptions for carriers on routes other than their own. In that case, they are subject to minimum wage, overtime, and child labor provisions of the law. Even employee carriers are exempt from these laws so long as they deliver only newspapers.

Thus, newspapers which use paid-in-advance plans, solicitation teams, or who otherwise engage in actions which might be regarded as close supervision and control, may find themselves having to convert to systems similar to those in Los Angeles or Nashville.

Ancillary Uses of the Distribution Network

Distribution systems can be used for delivering more than just the daily newspaper to homes. In an attempt to gain additional advertising, some newspapers are offering a service to deliver pre-printed advertisements, usually inserted into the newspaper, to homes of nonsubscribers as well, giving the advertiser "total market coverage." The *Detroit Free Press, Newsday, Washington Star,* and *Minneapolis Star-Tribune* are among the large papers which have experimented with such service. (See Chapter 4 for more on total market coverage.)

U.S. Suburban Press, Inc. has used carriers to deliver samples of a General Mills product tied to an advertisement inserted in the paper. Arthur Diaz, former sales director of the *St. Louis Post-Dispatch*, felt that the economic potential for such ventures is great. "Newspapers have a distribution organization that can deliver a service or small product anywhere in the metropolitan area in a matter of hours," he observed.

Perhaps the most extensive experiments in the use of newspaper delivery networks have been for the delivery of magazines. The *Louisville Courier-Journal* and *Times,* the *Passaic* (N.J.) *Herald-News,* and the *Boston Globe* are among those who have delivered *Time* magazine on a trial basis.

Newspaper publishers are interested in these programs because of the considerable fixed costs of their circulation system, which is set up to deliver a newspaper during a relatively short period of time once or twice a day. Using the same network to spread the cost over more products can thus improve, stabilize, or reduce the costs in the future overall circulation system. Louisville tested the delivery of magazines by carrier as well as by address, catalogues by address, and promotion material to all housing units along a carrier's route.

In one test, with *Time,* 63 Louisville carriers were delivering 1800 copies of *Time* each Tuesday along with 7600 copies of the afternoon *Times.* Each of the walking carriers had 12 to 40 magazines; motor delivery route drivers accounted for 60 to 250 each. The system depended on computer-generated manifests for each route. Copies of *Time* were bulk shipped to Louisville and dropped in bulk to the carriers with their Tuesday papers. The manifest told the carrier which of four editions of *Time* (students, business, doctor, or regular) any given subscriber should be given. Thus, there were no mailing addresses on each copy.

Time paid the Louisville papers ten cents for each copy delivered, four cents of which went to the carrier. Although this is more expensive to *Time* than the 4.5 cents it then paid through the mail, complaints with the U.S. Postal Service and rates of about 14 cents to deliver each copy in 1980 have initiated the search on the part of the magazine publishers for alternative delivery modes.

Cyrus L. MacKinnon, president of the parent company in Louisville, reports that the newspaper and *Time* have been satisfied with the results—a modest $1000 profit during the first six months. Walking carriers have reported feeling undercompensated for their extra effort, but are willing to go along.

One consideration, however, is the legal grounds when dealing with employee carriers. In the case of independent contractors, all that is required is a rewriting of contracts to include a provision for supplemental delivery items. With employee carriers, however, once they start delivering anything besides newspapers, the exemptions from minimum wage, child labor laws, social security payments, etc., are lost. This might be a serious consideration in a publisher's deliberation on the best type of distribution system, given the revenue potential of delivering products besides newspapers.

Dow Jones, which relies heavily on the Postal Service to deliver its daily *Wall Street Journal* and weekly *Barron's*, has been expanding its own direct delivery service, with company-employed deliverers as well as the independent contractors it used during an experimental phase. With a postal bill which soared from $6 million in 1971 to an estimated $66 million in 1983, the company expects to have about 600,000 *Journals* delivered each day (out of over 1.7 million) through its own network by the end of 1983 at an additional cost of $23 million.

IMPROVING CIRCULATION AND DISTRIBUTION

The stagnation in newspaper circulation in the decade of the 1970s has been a situation of great concern to publishers, editors, circulation managers, and advertisers. Many of the proposed remedies may be lumped under the topic of increased emphasis on the marketing of the newspaper.

Marketing Efforts

Improved Editorial Presentation. Both editorial product and layout have been accused recently of being "damn dull" by one editor who also considers them to be out of touch with a new constituency of readers or potential readers.[15] In buying fewer papers relative to the number of households and population, readers are saying that the newspaper is not as essential as it once was, whether due to greater interest in television or simply because of changing lifestyles. Thus, as the price of the newspaper increases, subscribers become less frequent purchasers. *The Wall Street Journal,* on the other hand, is one of a few large newspapers which has been increasing steadily in circulation, despite a strict magazine-like paid-in-advance policy and a cost of 30 cents a day or $63 a year. To continue to do this, says Dow Jones president Warren Phillips, "We must see that the reader gets a feeling of additional value." And value, to Leo Bogart "means that there is something in it [the newspaper] that the reader doesn't get from TV news."

There is some evidence that superior editorial copy is translated into circulation. Bogart reports that there is an apparent positive correlation between circulation increases and the number of major journalism awards a newspaper claims. Between 1963 and 1972,

17 major newspapers winning three or more Pulitzer, Sigma Delta Chi, or Overseas Press Club awards had an aggregate circulation increase of 18 percent. On the other hand, 81 large papers which won no such awards dropped 16 percent in circulation. The tally is seen in Table 3.11.

What all this requires is further research into the newspaper market to better answer the question: What can the newspaper editor realistically do to make the content more appealing to the audience?

Table 3.11 Relationship Between Papers Winning Major Journalism Awards and Circulation, 1963-1972

Number of Awards Won	Number of Papers	Percent Circulation Change, 1963-1972
3 or more	17	+ 18
1 or 2	28	no change
none	81	− 16

Source: *Journalism Quarterly*, Autumn 1975, p. 409.

One advertising agency executive thinks that newspapers have been taken for granted so long that they should be introduced as a new product, with bright new designs to promote a feeling of being lively and aware and a promotion campaign which emphasizes the unique features of the newspaper: You can't read a box score or do the crossword puzzle on TV, he notes.

Among the other marketing steps being suggested for newspapers are:

Attracting Younger Readers. This means more than adding a rock music column. Newsapers have the greatest chance of success with this group if they perform very well their traditional functions of reporting and explaining the world, Bogart says. A number of papers are making changes in this direction. The *Chicago Tribune* reported that their study of newspaper readers found rejection of "unnecessary complexity" in the news and expression of growing interest in personal improvement. To promote a younger image, the *Tribune* has added a new Wednesday section, "Venture," which gives news and advice about partcipatory sports such as tennis, cycling, and backpacking. Other changes include general news and business news capsule stories and a new design for the "Tempo" entertainment and arts section, all specifically done with the younger reader in mind.

The New York Times also has reported increased circulation since the addition of its Friday "Weekend" entertainment and culture section.

Paid Spot Television Promotion. The top ten daily papers using spot TV to promote themselves in 1975 spent over $3 million. Designed to reach the viewer of the competition, TV sports can be used to demonstrate the different treatment a story can get in the newspaper and answer questions that television cannot.

Zoning. The geographically zoned editorial editions allow newspapers to run advertisements for suburban merchants, while printing news which is presumably of local interest to readers, thus wooing them away from smaller suburban dailies or providing information which the TV news does not have time to pay attention to. The pioneer in zoning was the *Chicago Tribune*, whose efforts go back to 1927.

But the real need for this process was not apparent until the expansion of suburbia after World War II. Between 1950 and 1977, the population in central cities increased 14.5 percent, from 53.7 million to 61.5 million. During the same period, suburban areas grew 104.2 percent, from 40.9 million to 83.5 million. This proved to be a source of great growth for smaller papers, but hurt the big city dailies.

Although news staffers may think covering a suburban beat is a dull job, it is a way of life in many newsrooms. The *Philadelphia Bulletin* produces three separate zoned editions each day, as well as an almost completely different paper, the *Jersey Bulletin,* which has been added to compete with Gannett's highly successful *Camden Courier-Post* in the rapidly growing South New Jersey suburb. *The New York Times,* a late-comer into zoned editorial editions, watched Times Mirror's *Newsday* erode its Long Island subscribers, Gannett's Westchester-Rockland chain of papers gain strength in the north suburbs, and several Connecticut dailies move in on the Fairfield County suburbs, as well as long established New Jersey competition expand, before beginning to strike back with weekly special Sunday editions in each of those areas.

Meanwhile, in something of a reverse pattern, *Newsday* began a Sunday edition aimed at the Queens borough of New York City, perhaps in anticipation of the demise of the Queens-oriented *Long Island Press.* Subsequently, *Newsday* began distributing its daily edition in that portion of Queens nearest to Nassau County, thus confronting the *Daily News,* the *Post* and, to a lesser extent, the *Times* with added competition.

The emphasis on gaining suburban readers for the large city may mean putting a particular slant on what is printed, as exemplified in an internal memo from the news editor of the *Detroit News* to his assistant,[16] quoted in *Advertising Age* of June 28, 1976. Said the memo in part: "We are aiming our product at the people who make more than $18,000 a year and are in the 28-40 year age group." As a "fine example" of this policy, the memo cited a column that described a rape and robbery following a minor traffic accident between a suburban car and a Detroit car: "It dealt with Detroit and its horrors that are discussed at suburban cocktail parties. . . ."

In introducing its weekly Westchester and Fairfield County editions in 1977, *The New York Times* has not sought out broad mass market, but, in the pattern of many special interest magazines, it aspires to appeal to a defined target audience identified by a market research study. Not only are the editions aimed at an upscale market, e.g., $25,000 annual family income, four years of college, or a managerial position, but at psychographic types identified as prototypes and seekers. The former, which makes up the highest percentage of *Times* readers in the suburbs, are print-oriented and use these media to find out about the world outside their immediate community. They value education highly for its own sake, and tend to be socially liberal. The seeker is younger and more self-involved than the prototype, but holds similar liberal views. He or she is more broadcast-media oriented.

Thus, the editorial content of the paper, while not dictated by the marketing department, will be that which is of interest to these suburban readers: home-owning, families, transportation, college life, and Long Island Sound-oriented sports and leisure-time activities. Unlike many zoned editions, however, these sections do not replace any section of the regular paper, but are supplements to them. Thus, no reader is denied something available to other readers of the *Times.*

Market Research. Some newspaper chains have been moving heavily into the use of this long neglected tool which can help management better understand the perceptions and needs of their dual reader (and nonreader)/advertiser constituency. As just described, the *Times* has used such information in designing its new supplements. The Harte-Hanks chain commissioned a study on the causes of disinterest in newspapers on the part of the under-30 year group. Significantly, management found that newspaper people had a different explanation than the under-30 people. The former ranked TV competition, the "visual generation" and declining reading skills as the main reasons for circulation drop-off. The young stressed the "irrelevant" content of the dailies, their "formal language," as well as too many jumps, dull formats, and a perceived dislike for the young audience on the part of the newspaper. What they did seek were more features and capsules, a more fast-paced graphics approach, and more extensive coverage of inflation and unemployment.

Richard Hare, a marketing management consultant, sees the need for greater investigation into nonreaders: who they are, where they are. He suggests research into section-by-section ratings of each part of the newspaper, as well as the overall image of the newspaper. Delivery people would want to know where people purchase their newspaper, what time they get it, how much time they spend reading it. Which stores do readers patronize? Unlike many academic studies which aspire to generalize to the population of newspaper readers and nonreaders, these studies should be performed by newspapers in their own circulation areas. The Harte-Hanks group has done this and the Ottaway chain undertook such research in several of its markets in 1977. The industry took a general approach as well by instituting the Newspaper Readership Project, a three-year study budgeted for about $1.2 million and intended to investigate readership habits, promotion, and circulation.

A Repackaged Product. The outcome of much of the readership market research has already been put to use at some newspapers. The changes at the *Chicago Tribune* and *The New York Times* have already been noted. Numerous other examples exist around the country, often lead by the smaller, no-competition papers of the group owners.

Because the electronic media can beat even the fastest deadlines on any story, newspapers must offer their product on different terms than screaming headlines. Westchester-Rockland newspapers' executive editor Joseph Ungaro suggests that newspapers should meet the changing needs of the reader by:

- being consistently organized, with a regular place for each feature every day;

- having type and headline faces that are easy to read and that attract the reader;

- using news digests for the busy reader who may have missed the TV news;

- having key stories in-depth for those who want more detail;

- placing more emphasis on relating government news to the reader;

- giving more emphasis to "soft news" such as food, fashion, travel, home furnishing, and participatory sports.

Technology in Circulation Systems

Most of the new technology has been in the production process, where labor savings were obvious and returned a quick payback (see Chapter 6). Some large papers are just beginning to use the computer and storage devices to help the paper increase profits by improving business. One way was demonstrated in the example of delivery of *Time* or other products to selected households using computer-generated lists of addresses. Continued cost reduction and improvements in microcomputer technology have made it possible for even a small paper to use off-the-shelf Radio Shack computers and packaged programs for many circulation functions.

Another avenue of use is computer-based circulation systems, such as the Atlanta Newspapers On-Line Circulation System (ANOCS) now in operation. The system has all subscribers available in random access storage by name, address, and route. Whenever a subscriber has a question or complaint, the receiving operator can get an immediate video display of all the customer's account information.

The system can improve numerous types of transactions. For example, if a customer wants to stop paper delivery for two weeks while on vacation, the operator enters the stop and start dates on the terminal and the carrier will receive a printout—as well as a reduced or expanded number of newspapers to accommodate the change. Or, a carrier who knows he or she will be late in making deliveries can call in, so that should a subscriber call to complain of a missed delivery, the terminal will display information about the carrier's lateness and the expected delivery time. Paid-in-advance accounts or a new subscriber file can be entered and the carrier's paper allotment can be updated by a single key-stroke entry.

Some of the benefits to the newspaper of this type of system are self-evident, e.g., customer and carrier problems can be more quickly handled and resolved. Customers thus receive quick satisfaction. Others are less obvious:

(1) Management control. Before, the circulation department knew virtually nothing about 90 percent of its 500,000 customers. All was in the hands of the carrier. If he disappeared, his list might go with him.

The new system will eventually put all subscribers on computer file. Moreover, service errors by route and district are available as requested from the computer, for greater control of problem areas. Reports will also show how problems were resolved.

(2) Customer relations. Before, the Atlanta newspapers found it took up to 38 days to handle a problem. One-fourth of those who wanted to start a subscription had to call four times before they received their first issue. Stops and starts, other problems are easily handled on-line.

(3) Lower employee turnover. The job of handling customer complaints by circulation department personnel has been upgraded. Instead of just receiving it, the operators can actually deal with the problem, because all the information is immediately on the screen. There is more positive feedback. Pay has been increased because of this upgrading and employees find the job more satisfying.

(4) Fewer errors. Because the data processing system is so visible, entry errors were reduced by 20 percent. They expect to cut the service error rate down to almost nothing, with human keystroke errors being the only source of mistakes.

(5) Improved profits. The system in Atlanta may result in a direct net savings over the old system of $30,000 a year, based on labor savings of $120,000 and offset by an estimated equipment, running, and support cost of an incremental $90,000. For example, certain clerical functions which had taken almost 900 man-hours were reduced to under 500 hours. Moreover, there may be considerable indirect savings from improved adjustments, billing, cut-off of paper draws to carriers during a vacation, and in fewer lists which must be generated for each carrier, since the new system provides a printout only when there is some change affecting that particular route—and the printout includes just changes, so they are given immediate notice by the carrier.

The savings come only after the cost of the system's development and equipment has been paid back, a period which was initially estimated at only 20 months, but was re-evaluated to be 50 months because of added costs. This is not the best investment for a newspaper, "but it does make customers happy," an executive of the newspapers said in an interview. Thus, the system has some long-run benefit which may not show up explicitly but could be translated into fewer cancellations due to delivery problems or otherwise increased circulation.

Furthermore, the system provides the basis for a total marketing operation, since once all subscribers are stored in the computer, the next step, already accomplished by the Minneapolis newspapers, is an expanded file which adds the names and addresses of non-subscribers. With this, newspapers have the potential of becoming the most complete and reliable source of information about their own markets. They can sell this information to shopping center developers, use it to show advertisers the various market segments they can specially address, or use it for total marketing advertising campaigns. Thus, the information gathered for circulation can itself become a revenue-producing center for many newspapers.

There is no convincing evidence that circulation patterns have reversed the slump of the 1960s and mid-1970s. Thus, the hypothesis regarding resumption of circulation growth cannot be given unqualified support. Yet 1976 did see a small upturn in sales, which continued through 1979. Newspaper managers also seem to be coming to grips more seriously with the problem. As a result, they appear to be taking steps to make both their editorial product more appealing and their distribution systems more responsive. In specific instances, such as with *The New York Times,* the result of one or a combination of these improvements do have or seem to be having a positive effect. There are, therefore, grounds for optimism that newspaper sales will continue making steady gains.

SUMMARY

Newspaper owners and managers are concerned about the stagnant circulation penetration of the daily paper. The level in 1978 was only 5.3 percent greater than circulation in 1960 and was down from the peak of 1973. This, despite increased education and higher incomes. Circulation per household has declined steadily since 1945. Several trends have been advanced as causes of this erosion, including competition from television news, changing living patterns, higher circulation prices, and even planned reduction in fringe circulation due to higher newsprint costs.

Circulation has been strongest in smaller cities and towns, as well as in the Southern and Western states.

Distribution continues to be a problem, since technology has not been able to do much to replace newsboys as a primary delivery vehicle. There is some debate in the industry whether to stick with this "little merchant" system or convert to a newspaper-owned delivery organization. There are legal as well as economic considerations which complicate the solution.

More newspapers are promoting paid-in-advance subscriptions, some with noteworthy success. But there is still the fear expressed by some circulation managers that subscribers will balk at seeing how much their daily and Sunday paper is really costing them when they are asked to pay three months or more in advance.

Newspapers are experimenting with using their distribution systems to handle other goods, such as magazines.

A number of approaches are being attempted to try to rejuvenate lagging circulation: zoned edition of large city papers, stepped-up marketing efforts, including "new look" formats aimed at attracting younger readers, paid promotion spots on television and radio, and market research. Computer technology is also being adapted to circulation and distribution, to keep closer track of subscribers and service problems.

FOOTNOTES

1. Jeff Clark, "Circulation Increase Despite Higher Subscription Rates," *Editor & Publisher*, February 14, 1976, p. 32.

2. *The General Mills American Family Report 1974-75* (Minneapolis: General Mills, Inc., 1975), p. 83.

3. Ben H. Bagdikian, "Report of an Exaggerated Death: Daily Newspapers that Failed, 1961-70" (Oakland, Calif: The Newspaper Survival Study, N.D. [1976]), p. 8.

4. "What the Missing Newspaper Means," *The Process and Effects of Mass Communication,* Wilbur Schramm, ed. (Urbana, Ill: University of Illinois Press, 1965), pp. 36-47.

5. Bruce H. Westley and Werner J. Severin, "A Profile of the Daily Newspaper Non-Reader," *Journalism Quarterly* 41: 45-50, 156, winter 1964.

6. Conducted by Audits & Surveys, Inc., New York.

7. Galen Rarick, "Differences Between Daily Newspaper Subscribers and Non-Subscribers," *Journalism Quarterly* 50: 265-270, summer 1973.

8. Jeanne Penrose, et al., The Newspaper Nonreader 10 Years Later: A Partial Replication of Westley-Severin," *Journalism Quarterly* 51: 631-638, winter 1974.

9. Frederick R. Currier and John E. Pollack, "Evolving Measures of Newspaper Readership," (Detroit: Market Opinion Research, 1976), pp. 27-31.

10. Jack McLeod and Sun Yuel Choe, "An Analysis of Five Factors Affecting Newspaper Circulation, *ANPA News Research Report,* No. 10, March 14, 1978.

11. Unpublished study conducted among 6000 housewives by Response Analysis Corporation for the Newspaper Advertising Bureau, Inc. and the Newsprint Information Committee.

12. Gerald B. Healey, "Carrier Counseling Program," *Editor & Publisher,* April 7, 1973, p. 31.

13. Gerald B. Healey, "Sluggish Circulation Growth Linked to 'Little Merchant'," *Editor & Publisher,* June 23, 1973, p. 9.

14. Letters to the Editor, *Editor & Publisher,* July 21, 1973, p. 7.

15. Lenora Williamson, "Circulation Drop Linked to Dull Newspapers," *Editor & Publisher,* October 2, 1976, p. 11; "Publishers Listen to Ways to Attract New Readers," *Editor & Publisher,* May 8, 1976, p. 11.

16. Ralph Gray, " 'Detroit News' Memo on Coverage Angers Mayor," *Advertising Age,* June 28, 1976, p. 1.

4

Advertising in Newspapers

The daily newspaper has two constituencies. One, the subscriber or purchaser, was discussed in Chapter 3. The other is the advertiser, who wishes to reach a particular audience with a message. To have this message included in the pages of the newspaper, the advertiser pays the publisher a fee which varies depending on the size of the advertisement and the circulation of the newspaper. Typically, the greater the number of regular purchasers of the newspaper, the more a publisher is able to charge for any given size of advertisement.

The role of advertising in promoting a free and vigorous newspaper industry should not be underestimated. Although circulation and advertising revenues are interdependent, the latter nonetheless plays the more dominant role in the newspaper economics, since they provide (as seen in Tables 2.11 and 2.12) 70 percent to 80 percent of a publisher's revenues. There is some indication that advertising is an integral part of the reading material the newspaper can use to attract readership (Chapter 3). And newspapers ultimately fail not for the lack of editorial content, but for a dearth of advertiser support.

A newspaper must achieve substantial advertising revenue in order to most fully support its editorial function, a relationship that Washington Post Co. chairman Katharine Graham discusses frequently. "Financial independence," she insists, "is essential to support the talent and resources required for modern news-gathering."[1]

As a basis for examining the role of advertising in newspapers, this chapter will therefore investigate newspapers relative to other mass media. It will include the strengths and weakness of the newspaper medium and its cost compared to other media. The discussion includes an analysis of advertising rates and sources of newspaper advertising revenue. Finally, this chapter will look at the newer developments in the battle for the advertiser's dollar: preprints and Total Market Coverage.

ADVERTISING EXPENDITURES

Total expenditures on advertising in all forms surpassed $43.7 billion in 1978, an increase of more than 122 percent since 1970. However—as seen in Table 4.1—since 1940, advertising expense as a percentage of GNP has held near two percent, representing a substantial decrease from its 1920 level of 3.2 percent.

Table 4.1   Total U. S. Advertising Expenditures as a Percentage of Gross National Product, Selected Years, 1920 to 1978

Year	Gross National Product (GNP) (billions)	Advertising Expenditures (billions)	Advertising Expenditures as % of GNP
1920	$ 91.5	$ 2.9	3.2%
1930	90.7	2.6	2.9
1940	100.0	2.1	2.1
1950	286.2	5.7	2.0
1960	506.0	11.9	2.4
1970	982.4	19.6	2.0
1976	1,706.5	33.7	2.0
1977	1,889.6	38.1	2.0
1978	2,107.0	43.7	2.1

Sources: GNP: U.S. Bureau of Economic Analysis. Advertising: McCann-Erickson Advertising Agency, Inc., New York, as published by *Advertising Age*.

Increasing Competition for Newspapers

Newspapers, which at one time had little mass media competition for advertising dollars, have had their share cut over the years first by commercial radio and then by television. Table 4.2 and Figure 4.1 compare advertising dollars spent in each major medium since 1935 and their percentage share of the total. Although newspaper managers today consider television their major media rival, the data in Table 4.2 appear to emphasize the significant impact radio had on newspaper advertising and the relatively minor effect of television. In 1935, while commercial radio was still young, newspapers accounted for over 45 percent of the advertising dollar and radio under seven percent. By 1945, however, aided partially by wartime restrictions on newsprint, newspapers had fallen to only 32 percent of ad revenue, while radio more than doubled to 14.7 percent.

Magazines also made substantial gains. But as television gained penetration in the 1950s and 1960s, newspaper share first rebounded, then slid gradually to about 30 percent, where it has apparently stabilized. Television, the new medium, of course grew quickly at first, and now represents about one fifth of advertising expenditures. Radio seems to have been hurt more than newspapers by the rival broadcast medium. Since 1945, moreover, among the then existing media, newspaper revenue growth has been the fastest growing on a compounded annual basis. Thus, in 1978, newspapers remained by far the largest single mass medium for advertising.

Nonetheless, these revenue increases for newspapers are not always the product of fatter newspapers. In 1972, for example, 1295 daily papers were measured as running 16.8 billion agate lines of advertising. In 1975, revenue was higher, but 1319 measured

Table 4.2 Annual Advertising Expenditures by Medium
(in millions)

	Total Advertising (in billions)	Newspapers Total	Newspapers % of Total	Television Total	Television % of Total	Consumer Magazines Total	Consumer Magazines % of Total	Radio Total	Radio % of Total	Direct Mail Total	Direct Mail % of Total	Other Total	Other % of Total
1935	$ 1,690	$ 762	45.1%	—	—	$ 136	8.0%	$ 113	6.7%	$ 282	16.7%	$ 398	23.6%
1945	2,875	921	32.0	—	—	365	12.7	424	14.7	290	10.1	875	30.4
1950	5,710	2,076	36.4	$ 171	3.0%	515	9.0	605	10.6	803	14.1	1,540	27.0
1955	9,194	3,088	33.6	1,025	11.1	729	7.9	545	5.9	1,299	14.1	2,508	24.3
1960	11,932	3,703	30.8	1,590	13.5	941	7.9	692	5.8	1,830	15.3	3,176	26.6
1965	15,255	4,457	29.0	2,515	16.5	1,199	7.9	917	6.0	2,324	15.2	3,843	25.2
1970	19,600	5,745	29.2	3,596	18.4	1,323	6.8	1,308	6.7	2,766	14.1	4,862	24.8
1975	28,230	8,447	29.9	5,263	18.6	1,465	5.2	1,980	7.0	4,181	14.8	6,899	24.4
1976	33,420	10,022	30.0	6,575	19.7	1,775	5.3	2,228	6.7	4,725	14.1	8,095	24.2
1978	43,740	12,690	29.0	8,850	20.2	2,595	5.9	2,955	6.8	6,030	13.8	10,620	24.3

Compounded Average Annual Percentage Change

	Total Advertising	Newspapers	Television	Consumer Magazines	Radio	Direct Mail	Other
1945-1950	14.7%	17.7%	—	7.1%	7.4%	22.6%	12.0%
1950-1955	10.0	8.3	43.1%	7.2	-2.1	10.1	10.2
1955-1960	5.4	3.7	9.2	5.2	4.9	7.1	4.8
1960-1965	5.0	3.8	9.6	5.0	5.8	4.9	3.9
1965-1970	5.1	5.2	7.4	2.0	7.4	3.5	4.8
1970-1975	7.6	8.0	7.9	2.1	8.6	8.6	7.2
1975-1978	15.7	14.6	18.9	21.0	14.3	12.9	15.5
1945-1978	10.2	9.8	15.1[a]	6.1	6.1	9.6	7.9

[a] 1950-1978.

Source: McCann-Erickson Advertising Agency, Inc., New York. Compiled for *Advertising Age* ©. Percentage derived by author.

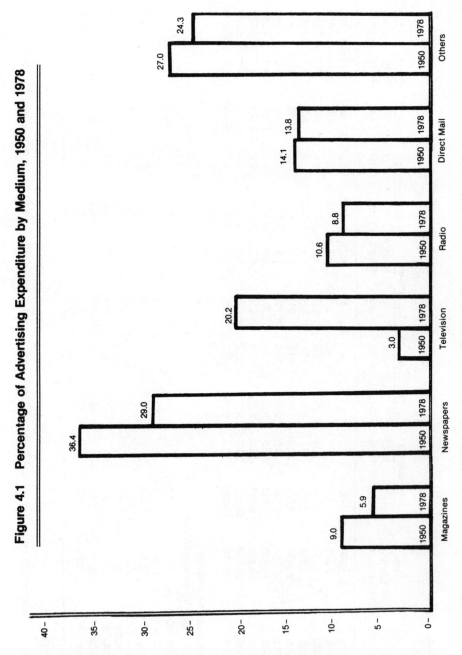

Figure 4.1   Percentage of Advertising Expenditure by Medium, 1950 and 1978

Source: Table 4.2.

newspapers carried only 13.8 billion lines. The higher revenue came from rate increases which more than made up for the linage drop. Table 4.3 lists the 15 leading newspapers in advertising linage in 1978.

NEWSPAPERS COMPARED TO OTHER MEDIA

Newspapers provide the advertiser with several features which are unique to the medium.

• Their frequency and close deadlines allow for precise placement of the ad message at a time when it will do the most good: an ad for snow tires immediately after a snow storm, for example.

• Their local identity in metropolitan, suburban, small town, and zoned editions

Table 4.3   Leading Newspapers in Advertising Linage, 1978[a]

Newspaper	Full Run Linage (000)	Part-Run Linage (000)	Total Linage (000)
1. Los Angeles Times (m)	104,975	48,630	153,605
2. Chicago Tribune (m/e)	71,956	47,130	119,086
3. Houston Chronicle (e)	101,515	10,092	111,607
4. Fort Lauderdale News (e)	85,102	·6,183	91,285
5. Washington Post (m)	79,806	11,163	90,969
6. Miami Herald (m)	69,363	18,883	88,246
7. Houston Post (m)	75,103	8,008	83,111
8. Milwaukee Journal (e)	62,805	15,596	78,401
9. Dallas Times-Herald (e)	66,086	3,565	69,651
10. Detroit News (e)	58,039	11,604	69,643
11. St. Petersburg Times (m)	51,876	16,471	68,347
12. Atlanta Journal (e)	66,191	1,576	67,767
13. Cleveland Plain Dealer (m)	61,421	5,059	66,480
14. Chicago Sun-Times[b] (m)	48,207	13,268	61,475
15. Tampa Tribune (m)	48,289	10,111	58,400

[a]Converted to 8 column format. Includes daily and Sunday.

[b]Tabloid, 6 columns.

Note: *The New York Times* ran 57,846,000 lines, but did not publish for 3 months (August-November) due to a strike.

Source: Compiled from *Editor & Publisher*, "Report of Newspaper Advertising Linage for 1978," May 26, 1979. Based on measurement by Media Records, Inc. of 203 newspapers published in 69 cities.

provides considerable territorial segmentation. Thus, newspapers offer advertisers both time and place utility.

• Newspapers, as a print medium, are hard copy, so the advertiser can furnish as little or as much information in the space as is deemed appropriate, since the message is delivered at the speed determined by the reader, based on his or her own interest and comprehension. The reader can come back to an ad or clip it to save for later reference.

• Since newspaper readership is a daily habit among a large segment of the adult population, advertisers can put their name and their message before a regular audience with almost unlimited repetition.

• The broad market coverage means that a sizeable majority of households in a given market can be reached in just one or several major papers.

• There are more creative possibilities than newspapers are usually given credit for. Ads can be all copy or employ large portions of white space. They can support a complex rational approach or make a strong emotional impact.

• Advertisements may benefit from the editorial product with which they are associated. A food ad in the living, style, or women's pages provides position with editorial copy of similar interest to the ad copy. Research has also shown that people who give high ratings to editorial content are also more apt than other readers to say that they look at and appreciate most of the ads.

On the other hand, the newspaper does present some drawbacks:

• The newspaper medium lacks the sight and sound impact which is available to television advertisers.

• It cannot provide the same entertainment value as a television or radio ad might.

• Its production quality, although enhanced by increased use of offset presses and color, is still poor by magazine standards.

• The structure of the newspaper also places the advertiser's message in immediate and juxtaposed competition with an often overwhelming number of other advertising messages.

• There is little opportunity for repeat impressions. Unlike many magazines, a newspaper is looked through just once (although not necessarily in one sitting).

Based on the strength of its timing, geographical flexibility, and regular readership, newspapers are highly suited as an advertising outlet for local advertisers selling goods and services with an established identity or brand, but not as effectively for introduction of an unfamiliar product or service. As seen in Table 4.9, local advertising, including classifieds, accounts for over 80 percent of newspaper ad revenue. For the national advertiser, it is often used to present a cents-off coupon for a product or to provide a short-term boost to a product in a localized market. Finally, newspapers can be effectively used instead of magazines for a test market campaign in a specific market.

Competition with Television

Sears, Roebuck, one of the largest newspaper advertisers, found in one survey that while television could offer a retailer in a local market high "gross rating points" in general store or image advertising, such reach falls drastically on a per-item basis. Thus, the actual rating points fall 40 percent when tire prices appear on the screen. Moreover, since television is an instantaneous medium, to build an acceptable net reach with an advertisement, a commercial may have to be run several times. For example, a newspaper ad may have a net reach of 61 percent at a cost of $2457. A television ad run three times would have a total net reach (unduplicated audience) of 74 percent, but at a cost of $7641.

The Newspaper Advertising Bureau (NAB) puts much of its promotional efforts into supporting the role of newspapers against the threat of increased encroachments by television for the local advertiser. Among the studies which the NAB has sponsored or promoted supporting newspaper effectiveness or television ineffectiveness, are the following:

• Newspaper advertising is used extensively by motion picture companies to promote their pictures and by movie houses to announce show times. Television would like to attract some of this advertising. In one test, a 20th Century-Fox film was introduced in the Dallas area with a 100 percent newspaper advertising schedule. In Atlanta, the same movie had 70 percent of the budget in television spots. The results: For 14 previous pictures from the studio, the average first week's gross receipts were 27 percent higher in Dallas than in Atlanta. For the picture in the study, however, Dallas receipts were 147 percent higher, while media costs were only 26 percent greater. Follow-up questionnaires to those attending the film in both cities found almost as high a pattern of newspaper usage for movie information in Atlanta as in Dallas.

• In a test of aided and unaided recall of advertisements aired during the television showing of "The Godfather," a survey sponsored by the *Rochester Democrat-Chronicle* (but independently conducted) found that only seven percent of those who saw some part of the show could the next day recall, unaided, any of the commercials shown once or twice. One sponsor, which had seven commercials shown, had a 24 percent recall. Aided recall scores were not much higher, with eight percent recalling commercials run just once, at a network cost of $225,000 per minute.

• A similar type of telephone survey was conducted by the *Miami Herald* and *Miami News* immediately following the 1974 Super Bowl. They reported that even after prodding, only three percent recalled seeing a Datsun advertisement. When told that one commercial was for beer, 20 percent recalled Schlitz as the product. The Miami papers also reported that, by pre-arrangement with the city water authority, they were able to measure a five-pound drop in the water pressure during the game's half-time activities—the so-called "flush factor."

Implications of These Studies

These and similar studies do not necessarily prove that one medium is better than another. Nor do they shed light on the question of which is more effective in changing or converting opinions. But they do serve newspapers in that they bring into question the usefulness of the "boxcar" numbers of viewers and low cost-per-thousand figures which television can use in promoting itself.

Newspapers, for example, are primarily an adult medium, and their circulation and readership are usually compared to adult population. Television ratings, however, are based on "millions of viewers" or households, where only children may be watching at a given time during the day. Thus, Uldis Grave of the NAB suggests converting household TV ratings into adult ratings by multiplying the former by 75 percent during prime time or by as little as 50 percent during the day.

Nonetheless, one ongoing series of surveys sponsored by the television industry and conducted by the Roper Organization has found that since November, 1963, more of the public has gotten its news from television than from newspapers and by late 1976, 64 percent considered television their primary news source, compared to only 49 percent for newspapers. The same study showed a significant drop from previous years in the percentage of viewers who agreed that having commercials "is a fair price to pay for being able to watch it [television]."

Another study, under the presumably more impartial sponsorship of the American Association of Advertising Agencies, concluded that those surveyed considered newspapers the best-liked advertising medium. Figure 4.2 shows that magazines rated second, radio third, while direct mail was the most disliked medium, with over 30 percent rating it "completely unfavorable."

Competition with Other Media

Magazines, becoming ever more specialized, cannot compete with newspapers for local retail advertising. City and regional magazines such as *Philadelphia* or *Washingtonian,* as monthlies, can make only minimal inroads into this area. Direct mail is being hit hard by rapidly escalating postal rates, which may actually benefit newspapers by making preprint inserts more attractive to some advertisers.

Radio, more than television, is probably the daily paper's major competitor for the local advertiser. The high degree of audience segmentation available due to radio specialization in different types of formats in larger cities and their equally local audience provides many advertisers with an effective way of reaching certain audiences. Nonetheless,

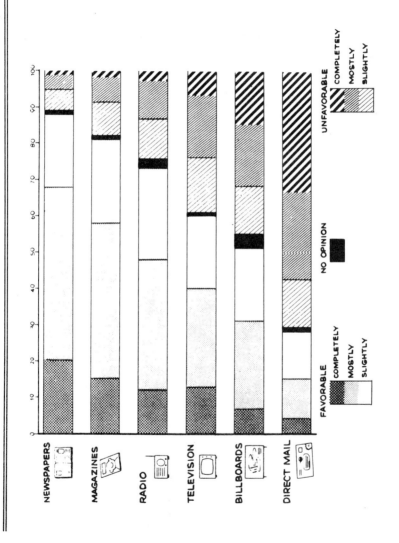

Figure 4.2 How People Feel About the Advertising They See in Each Medium

Source: American Association of Advertising Agencies, as published in *Editor & Publisher*, March 29, 1975, p. 12.

the instantaneous and sound-only qualities of radio make frequent repetition of messages necessary and therefore expensive for general advertisers, and inappropriate as a vehicle to replace the classified ad. Thus, it does not loom as a particular threat to newspaper domination of the local market.

Although locally originated, cable-produced programs are currently a minuscule factor in the local advertising competition, they do have the potential for catering to the needs of the local advertiser. Cable systems in Manhattan, Philadelphia, and elsewhere which televise home sporting events have made a start in this direction. As locally produced programming, such as neighborhood newscasts, for highly segmented audiences becomes more common, these cable systems will be more aggressive in seeking a share of the local ad dollar. "Superstations" and other new programmers for the cable market are offering their product to cablecasters with the presumption that the cable operators will be able to sell advertising, a prospect becoming increasingly likely as cable becomes more widespread.

Another natural use of the many channels available to cable is the ability to devote one to the display of nothing but classified advertisements. At first these may be displayed for a fixed time on a rotating basis, but later interactive systems may permit viewers to actually request specific categories for display on demand (see Chapter 6).

Under any circumstance, significant competition from local cable should not be an important factor until well into the 1980s. But it is the type of competition which newspapers should be planning to meet.

For all media, however, it is clear from the figures of Table 4.1 that advertising expenditures are unlikely to grow over the long run any faster than the general economy. Thus, major expansion in any one medium must come at the expense of a decrease in another. In that regard, newspapers, like magazines, may actually benefit from increased advertiser demand. Unlike television, which has a fixed number of minutes it can devote to commercials, newspapers can expand newspaper size to accommodate a larger advertising volume.

Cost of Advertising in Competitive Media

Between 1967 and 1978, average newspaper advertising costs rose slightly faster than the composite for all major media. Table 4.4a shows that network television rates were up 150 percent and outdoor 121 percent, while spot (local) television rates increased at about the same rate as did newspapers. But when the rates are adjusted for audience size, as in Table 4.4b, newspapers are seen to have edged out even network television in the rate of increase. This is because newspaper circulation has been relatively stagnant, while television audiences continued to grow during that period. Radio and magazines, media that encountered some rough times during these years, experienced the lowest rate increases for advertising.

Table 4.4a   Media Cost Index, Unit of Advertising, 1970-1978
(1967 = 100)

	1970	1972	1973	1974	1975	1976	1977	1978
Magazines	109	110	110	115	122	127	136	150
Network TV	113	125	140	151	160	189	223	250
Spot TV	105	117	127	135	145	181	195	207
Newspapers	115	123	128	140	160	176	192	209
Network Radio	101	105	105	106	112	128	147	165
Spot Radio	107	109	114	119	125	135	146	155
Outdoor	125	145	155	166	178	192	207	221
Composite	111	120	126	136	149	168	185	202

Table 4.4b   Media Cost Index, Cost per Thousand, 1970-1978
(1967 = 100)

	1970	1972	1973	1974	1975	1976	1977	1978
Magazines	106	112	109	113	120	125	132	143
Network TV	108	105	114	120	126	149	174	194
Spot TV	99	104	109	112	119	147	157	166
Newspapers	115	122	126	135	154	169	183	197
Network Radio	96	96	95	94	98	111	127	141
Spot Radio	102	102	106	108	114	122	130	136
Outdoor	117	130	136	142	151	161	173	183
Composite	109	111	118	124	136	152	166	178

Source: *Advertising Age,* September 25, 1978, p. 126.

NEWSPAPER ADVERTISING RATES AND LINAGE

Newspaper advertising revenue is the function of two components: total agate lines times the rate per line. Meaningful long-run comparison of linage trends is difficult because of changes in the number of newspapers included in the compilation provided by Media Records, Inc., the firm which is the industry's advertising statistician. In 1972, for example, it counted the 5.25 billion lines in 247 newspapers, but in 1978, the 4.87 billion lines came from only 203 papers. Per newspaper, the average linage was greater in 1978, but since the measured newspapers are not a true sample and reflect those which subscribe to and pay for the service, the comparison is of limited significance.

With this caveat, the general trend as seen in Table 4.5 shows modest growth, at under half the compounded rate of all newspaper advertising revenue found in Table 4.2. Table 4.6 traces the increase in daily and Sunday milline rates from 1945. Combining the 3.9 percent compound yearly growth in linage from the Media Records group with the 4.4 percent increase in milline rates yields a growth figure that approaches the 9.8 percent compound annual increase in newspaper ad revenues seen in Table 4.2.

Much of the increase in rates came in the years of rapid inflation between 1970 and 1978. In comparison to the overall rise in the consumer price index, milline rates actually trailed the cost of living until the most recent period, when rate boosts outstripped the increases in consumer prices in general.

Advertising sales are sensitive to changes in the general economy, and this can be quite cyclical. Table 4.7, for instance, lists the ten leading newspapers in combined daily and Sunday linage for 1975. Each of them added linage in 1973 from the previous year. The Gross National Product, as an indicator of economic activity, increased 5.5 percent in 1973. A recession began in 1974, however, and deepened in 1975 before an upturn took hold in 1976. As the recession came on, newspaper linage slackened, as only half the papers made linage gains in 1974, and even those were modest. In 1975, each of the papers lost linage, reflecting a relatively poor economic year for newspapers.

In years when linage drops, publishers often try to keep up their revenue by increasing linage rates faster. Thus, in 1973, a good year, morning papers boosted their rates an average of 5.1 percent, and evening papers only slightly more. But as linage fell in 1974, papers posted boosts of 18.3 and 16.6 percent for morning and evening, respectively.

Table 4.5   Daily Newspaper Advertising Linage as Reported by Media Records, Selected Years, 1945 to 1978

Year	Total Advertising Linage	Percentage Growth
1945	1,391.6	—
1950	2,440.1	75.3%
1955	2,843.4	16.5
1960	2,888.6	1.6
1965	3,164.6	9.6
1970	3,443.8	8.8
1975	3,973.6	15.4
1978	4,874.8	22.7
Compounded Yearly Increase 1945-1978		3.9%

Source: *Editor & Publisher,* "Report on Newspaper Linage," annual in May. Media Records, Inc. measures about 70 newspapers in about 70 cities, with some variation year to year.

Table 4.6 Milline Rates for Daily Newspapers, Selected Years, 1945 to 1978 (Index: 1967 = 100)

Year	Milline Rate	% Change From Previous Year	Index	Consumer Price Index
1945	$ 2.90	—	53	54
1950	3.50	20.7%	64	72
1955	4.09	16.9	74	80
1960	4.75	17.0	87	89
1965	5.17	8.8	94	95
1970	6.30	21.9	115	116
1975	9.26	47.0	169	161
1978	12.00	29.6	219	195
Compounded Growth Rate				
1945 to 1978	4.4%			4.0%

Sources: Milline rate calculated from figures in *Editor & Publisher International Year Book,* annual; CPI from U.S. Bureau of Labor Statistics, *Monthly Labor Report.*

Table 4.7 Advertising Linage Changes in the Ten Linage Leading Newspapers, 1972-1975

	Percent Change 1972-73	Percent Change 1973-74	Percent Change 1974-75
1. Los Angeles Times (M/S)	6.9%	1.8%	− 8.2%
2. Chicago Tribune (AD/S)	13.5	1.8	− 6.7
3. Houston Chronicle (E/S)	6.7	0.6	− 9.1
4. Miami Herald (M/S)	4.1	− 6.6	− 18.9
5. Washington Post (M/S)	7.6	− 1.1	− 12.5
6. Fort Lauderdale News (E/S)	10.1	0.9	− 9.3
7. New York Times (M/S)	0.5	− 6.0	− 8.0
8. San Jose Mercury & Mercury News (M/S)	2.7	− 2.0	− 3.2
9. Milwaukee Journal (E/S)	4.1	3.9	− 9.6
10. St. Petersburg Times (M/S)	17.0	− 0.1	− 15.4
Median	6.8	0.2	− 9.2
GNP (constant 1972 dollars)	5.5	− 1.7	− 1.8

Source: Calculated from linage figures reported by Media Records and compiled by *Editor & Publisher.*

Rates went up another 13.4 percent and 11.8 percent, respectively, in 1975. This was especially necessary given the flat circulation and rapidly escalating costs newspapers faced in this period.

These increases have left many local merchants upset and newspaper executives worried. In Providence, Rhode Island, local trade associations have met with newspaper management to protest the rate hikes. One large retail user complained that costs "are going up faster than our profits and faster than our customers can absorb if we raise our retail prices. We don't have a chance to catch up."[2]

Effect of Newspaper Competition on Rates

Advertising rates for newspapers, unlike magazines, are not tied to a strict cost per thousand level, although there is certainly a general relationship between increased household penetration and the ability of a publisher to charge higher prices.

Advertising rates appear to be largely a product of the competition among other media, the revenue a publisher requires, and what he thinks merchants are willing to pay. These combine to presumably produce an optimum rate. These latter two characteristics are largely what *Los Angeles Times* publisher Otis Chandler suggests when he claims a newspaper publisher without competition can "generate revenues almost arbitrarily."[3] (See Chapter 5.)

Yet there does not appear to be convincing evidence that newspapers which have no other newspaper competition have significantly different rates than those of similar size which do have competition. Table 4.8 presents the open linage rate (minimum when available) of 11 newspapers which face competition and ten newspapers in non-competitive cities. Although this does not pretend to be a carefully drawn random sample, it nonetheless serves to illustrate that the mere lack of newspaper competition does not permit a publisher to demand rates which deviate greatly from "going" rates. In fact, for this group, the average milline rate for the non-competitive newspapers was lower than that for papers which faced direct competitors. Interestingly, the rates of the *Camden* (NJ) *Courier Post,* one of the highest in the list, are competitive with those of the similarly high Philadelphia newspapers with which it faces some competition in the South New Jersey territory.

COMPONENTS OF THE ADVERTISING DOLLAR

Local Retail

Local retail advertising, as seen in Table 4.9, accounts for the major portion of advertising revenues in newspapers. Since 1950, this component has grown at about the same rate as total ad revenue.

Growth in retail advertising expenditures is closely keyed to general economic conditions in the locality. Department store and shopping mall openings in the suburbs, urban renewal in downtown areas, and supermarket competition all augur well for the local advertising picture. For example, in 1975 Houston was the fastest growing Standard

Table 4.8 Linage Rates Among Competing and Non-Competing Newspapers

Competitive Newspaper Markets		Non-Competitive Newspaper Markets	
City/Paper	Open Milline Rate	City/Paper	Open Milline Rate
NEW YORK		ATLANTA	
Times	$ 6.65	Constitution	$6.47
Post	7.34	Journal	5.96
News	4.27	Combination	4.49
LOS ANGELES		MILWAUKEE	
Times	4.10	Journal	5.03
Herald-Examiner	6.95	Sentinel	6.26
		Combination	4.65
CHICAGO			
Daily News	6.06	AUSTIN	
Sun-Times	5.68	American-Statesman	5.55
Combination	5.84		
Tribune	5.18	SCHENECTADY	
		Gazette	6.32
PHILADELPHIA			
Inquirer	10.17	CAMDEN	
Daily News	8.74	Courier-Post	7.20
Combination	7.58		
Bulletin	7.77	PROVIDENCE	
		Bulletin/Journal	
Mean Milline Rate	$ 6.63	Combination	7.37
(excluding combination)			
		KANSAS CITY	
Mean of Combination Rates		Star	6.13
Only	$ 6.71	Tribune	5.94
		Combination	5.14
		Mean	$6.09
		Mean (combination)	$5.41

Source: Computed from *Editor & Publisher International Year Book, 1976*. Based on open or minimum rate stated.

Metropolitan Statistical Area (SMSA) with over two million population. It also outdistanced all other major SMSA's between 1972 and 1975 with a 64.6 percent increase in retail sales.

During the same period, a recessionary period as seen in Table 4.7, the Houston newspapers gained 7.5 percent in linage (although it was down from its peak in 1973). In the New York SMSA, on the other hand, retail sales grew only 14.1 percent, and retail advertising linage fell 7.1 percent. Table 4.10 compares linage change between 1972 and 1975 for three fast-growing SMSA's among the top 50 in retail sales and three of the

Table 4.9   Composition of Newspaper Advertising, 1950-1978[a]
(millions)

Year	National	%	Retail	%	Classified	%	Total
1950	$ 518	25%	1,175	57%	377	18%	2,070
1955	712	23	1,755	57	610	20	3,077
1960	778	21	2,100	57	803	22	3,681
1965	783	18	2,429	55	1,214	27	4,426
1970	891	16	3,292	58	1,521	27	5,704
1975	1,221	14	4,958	59	2,263	27	8,442
1978	1,787	14	6,994	55	3,926	31	12,707
Compounded Growth Rate							
1950-1955	6.6%		8.4%		10.1%		8.3%
1955-1960	1.8		3.7		5.7		3.6
1960-1965	0.1		3.0		8.6		3.8
1965-1970	2.6		6.3		4.6		5.2
1970-1975	6.5		8.5		8.3		8.2
1975-1978	13.5		12.2		20.2		14.6

[a]Production cost estimates included.

Sources: McCann-Erickson, Inc., New York; H.C. McDonald for classified, 1949-1966;
Newspaper Advertising Bureau estimates for classified, 1967-1978.

slowest. Although retail linage for the three fast-growing areas managed to hold its own in this period, the others showed a more typical downturn.*

Local advertising often comes from national accounts whose outlets have discretionary budgeting authority. Sears, Roebuck, for example, although a national chain, put 73 percent of its total mass media budget (not counting catalogues and direct mail) into local newspapers in 1975. Penney's spent 86 percent and Montgomery Ward 85 percent of their budgets in newspapers, accounted for as local retail advertising. Another significant portion counted as local is actually cooperative advertising placed by the local retailer but paid for in part by the product's manufacturer.

To capture a greater amount of the suburban retail dollar, many papers have gone to extensively zoned editions, thereby making part-run rates more competitive and practical for non-chain neighborhood stores. Combined with local news, this part-run circulation serves a need for the diverse interests in a metropolitan area and provides an additional source of income for the newspapers.

---

*This is merely to illustrate the importance that a healthy local economy can have for newspapers. There may be other factors which influence local linage, and this example is not meant to prove a cause-and-effect relationship between retail sales and retail linage.

Table 4.10   Retail Linage in Daily Newspapers in Three Fast- and Three Slow-Growing Retail Markets in the Largest 50 Standard Metropolitan Statistical Areas, 1972 and 1975

	Retail Linage (million)			% Change in Retail Sales 1972-1975
	1972	1975	% Change	
Fast-Growing SMSA's				
Houston, Tex.	77.1	76.4	− 0.9%	+ 64.6%
Indianapolis, Ind.	46.8	47.0	+ 0.4	+ 56.7
Fort Lauderdale-Hollywood, Fla.	63.6	60.7	− 4.6	+ 50.5
Average	62.5	61.4	− 1.8	+ 57.3
Slow-Growing SMSA's				
New York, N.Y.	84.4	78.4	− 7.1	+ 14.1
Dayton, Ohio	46.0	43.3	− 5.9	+ 16.1
Albany-Schenectady, N.Y.	58.2	48.2	− 17.2	+ 16.9
Average	62.9	56.6	− 10.0	+ 15.7

Sources: Retail Sales: *Advertising Age,* December 13, 1976, p. 26, compiled by Marketing Economics Institute, Inc. Linage: *Editor & Publisher,* "Report on Newspaper Advertising Linage," May 26, 1973, May 29, 1976.

During the 1972 to 1975 period, when overall linage decreased, part-run advertising gained 41.8 percent, representing 7.4 percent of all linage run by the 184 newspapers surveyed by Media Records, Inc. At some papers, part-run linage is a greater portion. For *The Los Angeles Times,* which must cover a sprawling Southern California territory, part-run linage represented 32 percent of its 1978 total. For the *Chicago Tribune,* 40 percent is part-run. These figures include classified ads.

Television has been doing its best to make inroads on the newspapers' hold on the retail market. For the most part, TV has been too expensive and too shotgun for all but the largest retailers. In 1960, newspapers accounted for 62.4 percent of all local advertising expenditures, television only 6.0 percent. Overall, only 2.3 percent of TV advertising revenue was locally derived. By 1978, however, TV's share of the local ad dollar was up to 12 percent, as newspapers slipped to 55 percent. Local dollars now account for 26 percent of television's ad revenue. UHF stations in particular appear to attract retailers, with their low rates. However, the nature of the television medium would appear to restrict its appeal to retailers for concept or image advertising, in conjunction with newspapers. For example, a 30-second spot for a supermarket can hardly list all its specials. Instead, it may emphasize the quality or lower prices of the chain, then suggest that the viewer "see our ad in today's newspaper for details." Typical of such a media mix is that explained by an executive of a large retail carpet chain:

"Our theme, 'We Buy By the Mile—You Save by the Yard,' makes a solid impact on the electronic media [sic]. . . . It tells our audience that when they need
carpeting, Allen Carpets is the place to go. Newspaper ads have the hard sell. Having been exposed to the Allen concept on TV, the prospect, when he comes across
our newspaper ads, will act on them more readily. Our TV makes our print more effective."[4]

How much of the money which retailers are putting into television is additional
money and how much is coming out of newspaper budgets is hard to ascertain. At Sears,
Penney's, and Wards, the newspaper share of the 1975 budgets was down slightly from
1971 levels, but higher than some interim years. But spot TV expenditures have fared even
worse. One newspaper executive who informally monitors TV stations in his market ad-
mits to seeing more local commercials than ever, but also notes a fast turnover of advertisers. Gimbel's, the New York retail department store chain, started using local TV spots in
1974, with the $1 million budget coming out of funds formerly applied to newspaper and
radio expenditures. It is this prospect that should be of concern to the older media.

At least one analyst of the newspaper industry believes that other print media—such
as shoppers (all-advertising, give-away papers), paid suburban weeklies, and direct mail—
present an even greater threat to the daily newspaper's local advertising base than does
television.

Classified Advertising

Since 1950, classified advertising has grown at a rate greater than all newspaper advertising, to the point where it accounted for 31 percent of all newspaper advertising
revenue in 1978. The reasons for this growth may be traced to more aggressive selling of
this outlet by advertising departments and the success that small business people such as
manufacturing reps and distributors have had in reaching customers at a minimal cost.

The bulk of classified ads are not the notices placed by individuals; a majority of
newspapers get more than 60 percent of their classified advertising from accounts who
place linage contracts. Funds for much of this advertising are supplied from cooperative
advertising programs provided by manufacturers to retailers and dealers in such fields as
automobiles, boats, mobile homes, and camping equipment.

The classified ad illustrates one of the major strengths of the newspaper as an advertising vehicle and is least subject to encroachment by other media. It is one of the few
forms of advertising which readers actually seek out. A study by Audits & Surveys, Inc. in
1973 found that 40 million Americans over the age of 18 years read the classified ad columns of daily newspapers on an average weekday.[5] They include active prospects for
homes, apartments, new and used cars, and employment. Among the study's findings:

• About 1.15 million workers who said they would change jobs in the next year read
classified employment ads on an average weekday, as well as another 12.4 million persons
over 18 years old.

• Every weekday about 100,000 adults move their residences, but more than 5.5

million people planning to move in the next year read the real estate classified ads on the average weekday, as do 11.5 million other adults.

• About five million adults who planned to purchase an automobile in the following year read classified automobile want ads each day, as did an additional 5.5 million adults.

Table 4.11 indicates that classified advertising is particularly sensitive to economic conditions. Help wanted notices drop as unemployment rises. During the mild slump of 1970, for example, when average unemployment increased from 3.5 percent to 4.9 percent of the labor force, classified advertising revenue fell 5.2 percent. In the six years between 1960 and 1976 in which the average unemployment rate increased from a year earlier, classified revenue increased an average of only 1.3 percent, despite rate increases. In the nine years in which unemployment decreased, classified revenue increases averaged 14.4 percent. The recovery in 1976 from the worst recession in this period also brought the largest year-to-year jump in this area of advertising revenue. This correlation between rising unemployment and decreased classified revenue is − 0.63.

Table 4.11   Unemployment Rate and Classified Advertising Revenue Changes, 1960 to 1976

	Unemployment	Change From Previous Year	% Change in Classified Ad Revenue from Previous Year
1960	5.5%	—	—
1961	6.7	+ 1.2%	+ 0.1%
1962	5.5	− 1.2	+ 3.7
1963	5.7	+ 0.2	+ 4.0
1964	5.2	− 0.5	+ 15.7
1965	4.5	− 0.7	+ 21.0
1966	3.8	− 0.7	+ 9.9
1967	3.8	N.C.	− 2.2
1968	3.6	− 0.2	+ 9.2
1969	3.5	− 0.1	+ 12.7
1970	4.9	+ 1.4	− 5.2
1971	5.9	+ 1.0	+ 8.2
1972	5.6	− 0.3	+ 18.4
1973	4.9	− 0.7	+ 15.4
1974	5.6	+ 1.3	+ 0.3
1975	8.5	+ 3.1	+ 0.4
1976	7.7	− 0.8	+ 24.0

Correlation Coefficient (r) = − 0.63

Sources: Unemployment from U.S. Bureau of Labor Statistics. Classified revenue: See source note, Table 4.9.

Classified advertising is not equally important to all newspapers. Large metropolitan papers tend to depend on it the most, small town newspapers the least. At the *Philadelphia Inquirer*, 37 percent of all 1978 linage was in classifieds. It was 33 percent at the *Chicago Tribune*. But at the *Auburn* (N.Y.) *Citizen* and the *Jackson* (Tenn.) *Sun*, for example, classifieds accounted for only 12 and 16 percent, respectively. Thus it is the big paper which more often feels the impact of drops in this classification most acutely—and reaps the benefits in boom times.

Some large newspapers offer classified advertising options in zoned editions, at reduced rates. *The New York News*, for example, has applied computer capability to offer classified users of an ad in the full classified section, in its proper category and in alphabetical order, but only in copies of the paper distributed in a zoned area. Thus, the *News'* system allows zoned classifieds to appear among the full-run ads, instead of split off into a separate section which might not get full exposure. It thus enables private local users to afford a lower priced zoned ad (reaching as many as 338,000 readers in Brooklyn) instead of paying for the total million circulation.

National Advertising

National advertising has declined continuously since 1950 as a proportion of total aggregate newspaper advertising revenue. And most of the $1.8 billion that there was in 1978 went to the larger newspapers. Advertisers who wish to reach a national market on a mass basis can often turn to television and magazines as more efficient media than having to prepare advertisements for hundreds of separate newspapers. Moreover, the linage rate for national advertisers is considerably above that charged to local retailers. In 1976, the rate differential between the two averaged 50.4 percent, the greatest disparity since 1970.

Newspapers, along with magazines, have been the beneficiaries of the ban on cigarette advertising in the broadcast media. By far the largest single classification of national advertising in newspapers is cigarettes and tobacco as seen in Table 4.12. Other large spenders are airlines, food processors, liquor, beer and wine distributors, communications companies, and automobile manufacturers. Many of the ads for food companies are in the form of "cents-off" coupons.

It should not be surprising, given the top categories, that the two top national newspaper advertisers in 1978 were R.J. Reynolds, Inc. and Phillip Morris, Inc., cigarette manufacturers which have also diversified into food and related consumer items. The remainder of the top 25 national advertisers is heavily laced with automobile manufacturers, airlines, and food processors, including General Motors and Ford (third and fourth); Ligget Group, American Brands, British American Tobacco (seven through nine); Delta Airlines, UAL Inc., Eastern, TWA and American Airlines (10, 14, 16, 17, 18, respectively); Procter & Gamble (21) and General Foods (23). In election years, such as 1976, political advertising adds to the national advertising totals.

While the Newspaper Advertising Bureau is actively making the case for newspapers with large national advertisers and agencies, a survey of advertising agencies found that newspapers rated last among the major media—television, radio, magazines—in relationships with the agencies. Television had the highest rating. Agencies complained of poor

Table 4.12 Leading Categories of National Advertising in Newspapers Among Largest 100 Advertisers, 1978

Category	Expenditures (000)
1. Cigarettes and Tobacco	$167,038
2. Automobiles	104,790
3. Food	65,694
4. Airlines	62,308
5. Communications, Entertainment	35,233
6. Appliances, TV, Radio	29,892
7. Wine, Beer, Liquor	18,107
8. Soaps and Cleansers	16,398

Source: Calculated from *Advertising Age,* September 6, 1979, p. 12.

position for their clients' ads, lack of service, poor billing, poor reproduction quality and sales representatives, and varying page and column sizes.

This last point has been the result of an explosion in the number of layout formats newspapers have adopted in recent years, due to changes in technology and newsprint shortages and cost. For many years, wire service transmission widths, coded on the paper tape that drove linecasters, largely dictated column widths for news and advertising. To reset the copy in another width meant considerable added composing room expense.

With the widespread use of computers and photocomposition, adjusting column widths to a publisher's own desires became economically practical. As part of the drive to conserve newsprint, numerous page widths and column width variations were adopted— almost 300 altogether. This did not affect local advertisers greatly, since they prepared their ad copy to the specifications of only one or two newspapers. But national advertisers and others providing already made-up advertisements for co-op advertisements placed by local merchants were faced with this proliferation of dimension standards for six or eight or nine column formats on sheets of widths from 52 to 62.5 inches wide. To prepare ads for a national market of newspapers, they had to remake an ad many times, or often purchase unneeded space so an ad could be "floated" in an extra column.

From this confusion, the National Retailers Group, in the spring of 1975, asked the American Newspaper Publishers Association (ANPA) to do something, and the result was the "ADS System." This provided for a scheme whereby all possible formats for newspapers could be accommodated by prepared ads for only six different sizes, designated ADS A, B, C, D, E, and F. Newspapers could thus notify the NAB and Standard Rate & Data Service which of the six classifications best suited their own format. Two of the sizes, C and F, were the most strongly recommended by the ANPA as being compatible with the widest range of newspaper needs.

National advertisers are still complaining about the great rate differential they pay over the local retailer. The newspapers justify the need for higher rates because:

1. The day-after-day local advertiser is the newspaper's bread and butter.

2. Newspapers must deduct a 15 percent commission for the agency which places the ad, and sometimes a two percent cash discount as well.

Nonetheless, some, such as James Ottaway, Jr., believe that no premium above the 15 and two percent discounts is justified. And since small papers get such little national advertising in the first place, any that they did get would be "found money."

About 70 newspapers have eliminated the differential, including the *Louisville Courier* and *Journal,* the *Trenton Times*, the *Chicago Daily News/Sun-Times* combination, and the *New York Daily News.* In the case of the *News*, rates were reduced to the retail rate plus the 15 percent commission, but only for those advertisers who agree to run at least twice in a seven-day period. Some accounts, primarily financial, responded by boosting linage, but the experience of other cities indicates that the reduced rate does not significantly increase national linage. Thus, there appears to be no general movement on the part of other newspapers to do anything more than gradually move toward lower differentials.

The NAB feels that it is not individual papers that are put on an advertisers' media schedule, but rather "newspapers" in general. "First we need the big papers on the media list, then the small ones will be added," explains the NAB's Bogart. He further believes that newspapers will at the least hold on to their current volume of national advertising dollars. Among the factors he sees which may help national penetration for newspapers are:

• Declining cost efficiency of television and the increased "clutter" as 60-second commercials are replaced by 30-, 20-, and even ten-second spots.

• Cable and video disk adding to the fractionalization of the broadcast market.

• Localization of selling. The Universal Product Coding of goods sold in supermarkets helps in promoting the demand for greater accountability of the ad medium. The daily volume of sales of each product could be correlated to advertising in a newspaper. Selling strategies are likewise becoming more localized.

National advertisers find newspapers most applicable to ad campaigns coordinated with television spots or to bolster sales in a lagging market. As seen in the extensive use made of coupon promotions, newspapers are utilized for new product introductions or promotion. Trans World Airlines, for example, had a television campaign in 1977 with the theme "Being the Best Isn't Everything, It's The Only Thing." Besides announcing on TV how its planes are on-time most often, TWA ran newspaper ads in various markets comparing its times from that city to other cities with competing airlines' times.

PREPRINTS

Not all advertising in newspapers is that which is printed as part of the newspaper—or run-of-press (ROP). Increasingly, advertisers have been turning to preprinted inserts. These may be full-page color ads on rolls which are fed into the newspaper as it is run through the press or free-standing inserts—separate cards or brochures—inserted into the newspaper after it is printed. In either case, preprints are not printed by the newspaper, but instead use the newspaper merely as a delivery vehicle. Distribution through newspapers may replace direct mail or private door-to-door distribution.

Table 4.13 traces the 154 percent increase in the volume of preprint circulation between 1970 and 1977. Only the recession of 1975 halted temporarily their momentum upward. Growth resumed in the recovery of 1976, with volume hitting 18 billion pieces.

Inserts themselves are not new, but had been restricted largely to magazine supplements such as *Parade* and *Family Weekly* or comic sections stuffed by hand into the Sunday paper. The dramatic upsurge in the use of preprints by national advertisers is related to several developments.

First, there is the fairly recent development of high-speed stuffing machines, such as the Sheridan 72-P, which are connected to the press and can add inserts to papers at the speed with which they come off the press (as fast as 40,000 to 50,000 papers per hour). In-

Table 4.13   Volume of Preprinted Inserts Distributed by Daily Newspapers 1970 to 1977

Year	Circulation (Billions of Newspapers)	% Increase
1970	8.0	—
1971	10.0	25.0%
1972	11.8	18.0
1973	12.8	8.5
1974	16.0	25.0
1975	16.0	0.0
1976	18.0	12.5
1977	20.3	12.7
Compounded Annual Growth Rate, 1970-1977		14.2%

Source: Newspaper Advertising Bureau, New York, Insert Division.

stead of hand stuffing by mailers or by the carrier, on-line inserting makes preprints economical to add even to daily editions.

Second, increased postal rates make delivery of preprinted catalogues or other material more economical in many cases for reaching a mass, local market. Pricing of preprints varies widely among papers. Some may charge merely the cost of inserting plus a small mark-up. Others base it strictly on their regular ROP rate for the same size advertisement, less savings in newsprint, ink, and makeready. However, for a 9 inch by 12 inch card, the average charge by a newspaper for inserting is about $24 per thousand. The direct mail cost for sending the card is $84 per thousand for postage alone.*

Third, the Hi-Fi and SpectaColor roll-fed inserts give the advertisers the added advantage of higher quality color reproduction, since they are printed separately and then shipped to the newspapers for insertion. These had a particular advantage several years ago when other inserts had to be hand stuffed. With the stuffing machines, these two processes have become less popular.

Although many publishers consider preprint revenue found money, others are not so enthusiastic. In its favor is the fact that the newspaper saves all material and production costs, yet receives revenue which far exceeds its stuffing cost. Thus, the profit margin can be much above that of ROP advertising. But others are more restrained in their enthusiasm. Large advertisers, they contend, will switch from ROP to preprints with a net loss of revenue, since they will be selling advertising in effect for perhaps half the ROP rate. A sampling of New England newspaper ad directors showed concern that their papers would become primarily "distribution centers for retail circulars rather than carriers and distributors of news." The president of a chain of small papers found seven percent of his ad revenue coming from preprints.

A longer range concern is that if enough ROP advertisers switched to preprints, the size of the paper would shrink and editors would find less news hole unless the ad copy ratio was decreased. "Preprints are advertising and we need all we can get," notes an executive of the *Concord* (NH) *Monitor,* "but we also need enough newspaper to wrap around those preprints." The *Monitor* reported a five percent to eight percent loss of ROP space formerly run by K-Mart, Sears, and IGA (a supermarket co-op) when those chains moved to greater use of preprints.

The Times Mirror Co. was the first to begin a separate breakout of preprint linage in its newspapers from other linage categories. In its first such reporting period, for January 1977, the linage increase from the same period in 1976 was 8.1 percent but that came as the result of a 14.5 percent *decrease* in retail advertising, combined with a nearly 20 percent *increase* in classified and a *doubling* in preprint linage. All of Times Mirror's papers had their strongest gains in preprint linage.

There has been some study of the effectiveness of preprints. Detractors have claimed that since they fall out or are easily separated from the rest of the paper and are readily

---

*Printing costs are extra and would be about $30 to $40 per thousand for a single four-color piece in either case.

discarded, they are not as good as ROP. Moreover, as more inserts are used, they produce a certain clutter which further detracts from any single one getting noticed. On the other hand, by falling out of the paper onto the floor, they in fact gain special attention. They are usually printed on heavier paper stock as well.

One study of effectiveness, by the advertising agency Dancer-Fitzgerald-Sample in 1974, compared free-standing coupon inserts with delivery of coupons via a color page in a Sunday supplement, a magazine color page, a magazine insert card, ROP newspaper ads of 600 and 1200 lines, and co-op direct mail (with several coupons). The free-standing insert was found to be more effective than all but the direct mail, but the insert method was less expensive.[6] Another study, which was undertaken for a major appliance manufacturer, found that a four-color preprint was recalled by 83 percent of the recipients and almost half remembered the message, a superior showing to most television network commercials. A survey of the NAB found interest from women in preprints ran high even with several preprints in a single issue.

Mail order advertisers like to use direct mail because they are generally trying to reach a specific audience. Yet trying to reach a broad audience by mail is prohibitively expensive. A study found that newspaper preprints, backed up by TV ads worth about 15 percent of the preprint budget, can increase the effectiveness of inserts by 95 percent and reduce the cost of acquiring a response by 41 percent.[7]

TOTAL MARKET COVERAGE (TMC)

The combination of preprints plus a computer can allow a publisher to offer an advertiser complete saturation of the paper's entire distribution area or any part of it. Some computer programs are sophisticated enough to permit a newspaper to provide a pinpointed geographical or demographic audience for a direct-mail advertiser, thus providing the lower cost of newspaper delivery with the segmentation of direct mail.

By having the names and addresses of all households in the newspaper's marketing territory, it can sell the direct mailer 100 percent nonduplicated coverage. Subscribers to the newspaper get the insert in the newspaper. A computer then generates a list of remaining nonsubscriber addresses, which can then be sent the insert either via carriers along the routes or through the mail. An advertiser might want only certain economic categories, in which case specific zip codes or other designated areas which have certain known income levels can be singled out for coverage.

These, of course, are more possibilities than reality. But some papers are using TMC. One-third of Gannett newspapers are using a TMC program of some sort, with considerable success. *Newsday,* which initially sent nonsubscriber inserts by mail, now delivers them by hand. *Newsday* also offers regular ROP advertisers TMC. For a slightly higher charge, it runs the advertiser's copy in a special weekly edition that is distributed to every household in its market. A survey by the International Newspaper Advertising Association in 1976 found that 141 newspaper organizations were offering some form of TMC to advertisers, including many newspapers under 10,000 in circulation.

One of the first and most sophisticated of all the systems was attempted at the Minneapolis newspapers, which built a file of all names and addresses in their circulation area. Each household is identified by street, as well as by 23 demographic characteristics. Conceivably, the system could provide not only total market coverage, but it could add a new dimension to target marketing by being able to tell a manufacturer, for example, what stores are close to where the person lives and how many children he or she has. However, the advertising sales department found it difficult to generate much enthusiasm for its use from advertisers so it was turned into the basis for the paper's circulation system pending further development.

TECHNOLOGY AS AN ADVERTISING TOOL

Computers are already helping newspapers with TMC and in composing advertising copy. The use of computer data banks, such as that put together by Minneapolis, is another possible use, with long-run development as a profit center. A newspaper has the capability for being the single most authoritative source of information about its marketing territory: number and locations of households, education level and incomes, number of children, real estate values and trends, etc. Part of the information can be gathered as part of the newspaper's ongoing reporting activities (such as recording real estate transactions), and part can be gathered specifically to help an advertiser, especially a national advertiser, learn what a given market can offer. Currently information of this sort is compiled in some form by such marketing services as Standard Rate & Data Service and the Audit Bureau of Circulation.

Classified advertising has been improved with the on-line systems described in Chapter 6. All advertisers, contract and individual, can get better service by the on-line responses these systems can provide.

But these systems may just be providing the basis for the classified advertising function of the future. Although classified sections are well read, relatively few people may look at any given section. One of the first applications of home VDT display of information may be the ability of newspaper subscribers to access a computer's storage for specific items in its classified file. Someone interested in used foreign sportcars under $4000 could request a display of just those notices. A business might pay to access "situation wanted" for a particular job it has available. Or a subscriber could ask for only "help wanted" ads that apply to his or her own qualifications.

SUMMARY

Despite increased competition from newer media, newspapers have shown a stubborn tenacity in maintaining the largest share of the advertising dollar. In 1978, they accounted for over 50 percent more dollars than their closest rival, television. However, they have held this position despite consistent erosion of their share of national advertising.

The strength of newspapers is as a local medium, and thus classified advertising has taken up most of the slack from weak national advertising.

The continued strength of newspapers in attracting local retail and classified advertising tends to support the hypothesis of the medium's firm hold on the market for local advertising. Weekly shopper newspapers may be more of a threat than local television.

The cost of newspaper advertising has risen more steeply since 1970 than competing media.

Advertising revenue is a product of both linage and the rate per line. Newspapers are able to offset linage decreases with rate increases. But linage is quite sensitive to the economy, especially classified. Help wanted notices decline measurably during periods of rising unemployment. Newspapers in cities with rapidly expanding retail bases have fared much better than those with a more slowly growing retail environment.

The proliferation of page formats and the continuation of premium rates for national advertisers have been blamed for decreasing national advertiser interest. Progress is being made in both areas, however, with the ADS System for formats and some realignment of national rates at several papers.

Preprints are a rapidly growing phenomenon and account for much of the increased linage. Some fear that they diminish the role of the newspaper, but others are happy for the revenue they produce.

Total Market Coverage is the package many newspapers are now offering advertisers to make up for the lower market penetration of newspapers. It is aided by computerized lists in some cities.

FOOTNOTES

1. Statement to the Dirks Newspaper Seminar, New Orleans, La., June 12, 1973.

2. Dan Lionel, "Rising Advertising Rates Plague Carpet Merchant," *Editor & Publisher,* April 13, 1976, p. 12.

3. "The Big Money Hunts for Independent Newspapers," *Business Week,* February 21, 1977, p. 59.

4. Lionel, "Rising Advertising Rates Plague Carpet Merchant," p. 12.

5. Cited in a press release from the Newspaper Advertising Bureau (New York, June 23, 1973).

6. "Agency Surveys Free Standing Insert Field," *Editor & Publisher,* April 13, 1974. Survey was conducted by Dancer-Fitzgerald-Sample, Inc., New York.

7. Dan Lionel, "Researcher Finds TV Hypos Suffer Results," *Editor & Publisher,* December 13, 1975, p. 20. Research was conducted by Chairman L. Jain, associate professor at St. Johns University.

5

Competition and Group Ownership

This section will look at the effects of the lack of competition in one-newspaper cities and the roles of various group owners. A group is defined as the ownership of two or more daily newspapers by a single firm or individual. Newspaper competition refers to separate ownership of two or more general interest daily newspapers in the same city. It will be seen, however, that competition may also be given a broader definition.

BACKGROUND

In the heyday of multi-newspaper cities and many independent owners, newspapers were thin—in 1900 even big city papers often consisted of only eight pages. Type was still hand set until the Linotype came into widespread use about the same time. Many daily newspapers were designed to appeal to a select group, and there was a newspaper which expressed the political views of seemingly every faction which sprang up. Newspapers did not really compete for the same audiences. James Gordon Bennett wrote in his first issue of the *New York Herald* in 1835:

> There are in this city at least 150,000 persons who glance over one or more newspapers every day and only 42,000 daily sheets are issued to supply them. We have plenty of room, therefore, without jostling neighbors, rivals, or friends, to pick up at least 20,000 or 30,000 for the *Herald,* and leave something for those who come after us!

Today, a newspaper can grow primarily by taking a subscriber from another newspaper. Moreover, the cost of newer and faster presses, Linotypes and then other technology, and the demands of the new advertisers in the 1880s for circulation, brought about economies of scale which demanded that a newspaper be sold at a low price to a mass audience. The cost of entry increased as well. Increased specialization required by the technology of 1900 reduced the extent to which newspapers could depend on job printing during off hours as a means of subsidizing competing newspapers.

Improved transportation made it possible to distribute a single paper to a larger territory, and the telephone and telegraph aided the same papers in covering the more distant suburbs. Advertisers could also depend on customers from a wider area to patronize their stores, and could therefore make use of the broadened circulation. Other trends during the beginning of the 20th century, as identified by historian Frank Luther Mott, include:

• A decline in political partnership which had demanded that each group have a newspaper representing its view. Thus, fewer newspapers were needed.

• Advertisers found it cheaper to buy space in one general circulation newspaper than in several with overlapping circulation.

• The Associated Press rules for new memberships made acquisition of a paper with membership the easiest way to join.[1]

Radio, then television, made inroads into newspaper functions. Perhaps the most significant factor is that newspapers are still considered an important mass medium.

Confidence in the future of the daily newspaper can be demonstrated in no better way than in the rate at which firms are spending to acquire new newspaper properties. In 1978, 53 daily newspaper properties changed hands. Forty-six of these involved the purchase of one chain by another, such as the acquisition of Combined Communications, Inc., with its two large dailies, by Gannett Co., Inc. But the total also included many small, independently owned newspapers which group owners have been buying steadily. In 1923, for example, there were 31 newspaper groups publishing 153 papers. By 1954, that number of chains had tripled to 95 and by 1978, 167 groups published an aggregate of 1098 newspapers—accounting for 62% of all daily newspapers.

As newspaper groups have grown, competition among newspapers within cities has diminished. Table 5.1 reveals the steady decline in the number of cities with competing papers. In 1923, 502 cities had two or more competing newspapers. By 1978, only 35 cities, or 2.3 percent of all cities, had newspaper competition.

Thus, the newspaper industry is concerned with two related trends in ownership: (1) the apparently increased concentration of ownership, and (2) the decrease in newspaper competition. Table 5.1 shows that, ironically, more cities had at least one daily newspaper than at any time since 1923.

CONCENTRATION OF OWNERSHIP

Concentration of ownership is not a recent trend in the United States newspaper business. As seen in Table 5.2, the largest 25 percent of newspaper firms actually accounted for a slightly lower percentage of daily circulation in 1978 than in 1923. A similar breakdown of the largest ten percent and one percent of firms shows a similar stability.

Moreover, in comparison to other developed countries, concentration of ownership in the United States is relatively modest. A study in 1971 found that the 20 largest newspaper firms controlled 43 percent of circulation in this country. Next closest was Spain, with 54.9 percent. Canada had 88.5 percent in this top group and Ireland 100 percent.[2]

Table 5.1   Number of Cities with Daily Newspapers and Number of Cities with Competing Daily Newspapers, Selected Years, 1923 to 1978

Year	Number of Cities with Daily Papers	Cities with 2 or More Dailies*	% of Total Cities with 2 or More
1923	1,297	502	38.7%
1933	1,426	243	17.0
1943	1,416	137	9.7
1953	1,453	91	6.3
1963	1,476	51	3.5
1973	1,519	37	2.4
1978	1,536	35	2.3

*Under separate ownership.

Sources: James Rosse, Bruce M. Owen, and James Dertouzos, "Trends in the Daily Newspaper Industry, 1923-1973," Studies in Industry Economics, No. 57, Dept. of Economics, Stanford University, Table 9, p. 30 and *Editor & Publisher International Year Book, 1979.*

While the 20 largest firms in the U.S. have gained slightly in market share since then, the proportion is still relatively low compared to that of many other nations with a free press.

The desire to own groups of newspapers—for whatever reasons—has long been compelling. E.W. Scripps started his in the 1880s and by 1900, there were eight major chains, including Scripps-McCrae, Booth, Hearst, Pulitzer, and the Ochs papers. In 1908, Frank Munsey's assessment of the newspaper glut was:

> There is no business that cries so loud for organization and combination as that of newspaper publishing. The waste under existing conditions is frightful and the results miserably less than they could be made.[3]

Although the data in Table 5.3 clearly show a steady increase in the number of group owners and the number of dailies they control—with a particular jump during the heavy growth period of the mid-1960s—the average size of the group has not increased much beyond the average of 1933. Much of their activity is merely that of swapping properties. As some chains have grown, others have shrunk or disappeared. The Hearst chain has either bought or established 42 dailies, merging some, selling others, suspending several. In 1940 there were 17 Hearst papers, leading all chains in combined circulation. By 1976, there were only eight Hearst newspapers, the chain ranking eighth in total circulation. At one time, Frank Munsey had six newspapers in New York, Washington, Baltimore, and Philadelphia. These were all merged, sold, or suspended. The trend since the end of World War II has been upward, but of the 167 groups at the end of 1978, over one third owned only two newspapers. At the other extreme, Table 5.4 lists the ten largest

Table 5.2   Percent of Total Daily Circulation Accounted for by Smallest 25% and Largest 25%, 10% and 1% of Newspaper Firms, Selected Years, 1923 to 1978

Year	Smallest 25%	Largest 25%	Largest 10%	Largest 1%
1923	2.2%	82.5%	64.9%	22.6%
1933	2.2	84.2	67.4	23.2
1943	2.2	84.3	66.6	22.4
1953	2.3	83.6	66.6	21.0
1963	2.4	83.0	65.7	22.1
1973	2.8	80.4	66.3	20.6
1978	3.0	78.9	61.3	19.8

Source: Rosse, et al, p. 28. 1978 data added by author.

Table 5.3   Number of Newspaper Groups and Dailies They Control, Selected Years, 1910 to 1978

Year	No. of Groups	No. of Dailies*	Ave. Size of Group	Group-owned Dailies as % of Total Dailies
1910	13	62	4.7	—
1923	31	153	4.9	7.5%
1930	55	311	5.6	16.0
1933	63	361	5.7	18.9
1935	59	329	5.6	16.9
1940	60	319	5.3	17.0
1945	76	368	4.8	21.0
1954	95	485	5.1	27.5
1961	109	552	5.1	31.3
1967	160	817	5.1	46.7
1970	157	879	5.6	50.3
1973	165	977	5.9	55.1
1977	167	1,047	6.3	59.4
1978	167	1,095	6.5	62.5

*Before 1954, number of dailies may be overstated because morning and evening editions of some papers were counted as separate papers.

Source: *Editor & Publisher.*

Table 5.4   Ten Largest Newspaper Publishing Firms by Circulation and Their Total Revenue, 1978

Firm	1978 Circulation (000)	1978 Revenue (000)
1. Knight-Ridder	3,742	$ 878,875
2. Gannett	3,412	690,128
3. Newhouse	3,281	1,200,000[a]
4. Tribune Co.	3,199	897,900[b]
5. Scripps-Howard	2,038	471,900[a]
6. Dow Jones	1,920	363,601
7. Hearst	1,904	556,600[a]
8. Times Mirror	1,880	1,427,854
9. Cox	1,365	400,000[c]
10. Thomson	1,146	306,476
Total	23,887	$7,193,334
% of Total Daily Circulation	38.6%	

[a]Estimate.   [b]1977.   [c]Estimate for newspapers only. Excludes broadcasting.

Sources: Circulation: *Editor & Publisher.* Revenue: Annual reports, except where noted.

newspaper publishing firms. These accounted for more than 38 percent of all daily circulation in 1978, compared to 32 percent for the ten largest in 1971 and 35 percent in 1976.

Effects of Concentration

There is a difference of opinion between those who would agree with Munsey, that concentration of ownership may improve newspapers, and those who believe that chain ownership results in fewer editorial "voices," hence more homogeneous newspapers and a general reduction in quality. This viewpoint is expressed by Oswald Villard, who wrote in 1930:

> It cannot be maintained that the chain development is a healthy one from the point of view of the general public. Any tendency which makes toward restriction, standardization, or concentrating of editorial power in one hand is to be watched with concern.[4]

The conflict may be made more real by reviewing an exchange of opinions in the *Columbia Journalism Review* involving the purchase of the *Honolulu Star-Bulletin* by Gannett. An evaluation of the changes made at that paper after Gannett came in noted that two reporters, including the Washington correspondent, were fired; 12 columns, such as the surfing column and a "Nautical Notes" feature were eliminated, as were two comic strips; the Copley News Service was cancelled; a final edition was cancelled, moving up the final deadline 75 minutes; 30 printers lost their regular positions and were put on a daily basis; three engravers were laid off; and overtime was eliminated. Gannett brought in a new publisher who told reporters that the cuts were needed for economic reasons and that the Honolulu paper was fourth from the bottom in year-to-year revenue improvement in the Gannett chain.

In response to this criticism, the managing editor of the *Huntington* (W. VA) *Advertiser* (which became a Gannett paper as part of the 1971 deal with Honolulu) wrote that the same type of thing happened when the *Star-Bulletin,* an independent paper, bought the *Advertiser.* He claims that when Gannett took over, virtually every member of the news staff got a raise; lingering union problems were settled with three years' back pay; the dingy newsroom was renovated; reporters were given a voice in policymaking and choosing their own editor; there was greater editorial freedom for columnists and reporters; and ad salesmen were given commissions as well as salary. The Huntington papers were encouraged to do investigative reporting, even to the extent of damaging previously untouchable community leaders. The editor also wrote that the paper was opening up communications channels with the community and providing more leadership.

Whether or not group ownership improves or downgrades a newspaper depends on the criteria that are established for making such judgments, the state of the newspaper when the new owner arrives, and, more importantly, which chain is doing the buying. Many will agree that the Knight-Ridder organization has drastically improved the editorial quality of the *Philadelphia Inquirer* and *Daily News* since purchasing them from independent owner Walter Annenberg. Gannett, as just seen, has a more mixed reputation, but generally gets high marks for the quality of its business and editorial personnel. The first priority claimed by management of the Ottaway newspapers is "to improve news content, editorial quality and public service—to reach high standards of excellence. . . ."

On the other hand, the newspapers owned by the Thomson group are frequently criticized. Its late founder, Lord Thomson, once compared newspapers (and television stations) to a license to print money. His creed was to get the most work for the least pay. One Thomson paper is reportedly earning a 45 percent pre-tax profit. "You can't make money like that and still turn out a good paper," warns a West Coast publisher.

To be sure, single newspaper ownership is no guarantee of integrity or quality. Annenberg, when he owned the *Inquirer,* and William Loeb, publisher of the *Manchester Union Leader,* are examples of such owners. One critic, referring to Loeb's use of his newspaper to further his personal causes, writes of the publisher's "florid, virulent style" in attacking those he opposes in his papers.[5]

Summing up the argument for group ownership, John C. Quinn, group vice president for news for Gannett, notes that while each local newspaper can be tailored to the needs of the local market, they also are part of an organization large enough to have their own national news organization—such as the Gannett News Service which includes a Washington, D.C. bureau. Quinn also points out that of the 35 Gannett newspaper editorial boards that endorsed a presidential candidate in the 1976 election, 22 favored Ford and 13 Carter, implying the local autonomy of each newspaper.

Addressing an International Press Institute conference in 1972, Quinn explained:

> Newspaper concentration may multiply the anxiety over evil; it also increases the capacity for good. And a publisher's instincts for good or evil are not determined by the number of newspapers he owns. A group can attract top professional talent, offering training under a variety of editors, advancement through a variety of opportunities. . . . It can invest in research and development and nuts and bolts experience necessary to translate the theories of new technology into the practical production of better newspapers.

> Concentrated ownership can provide great resources; only independent, local judgment can use the resources to produce a responsible and responsive local newspaper. That measure cannot be inflated by competition nor can it be diluted by monopoly.[6]

What Quinn says is not in error. Nor, however, does it prove his case, for it echoes the standard argument supporting concentration of business in general. The real argument hangs on the goodwill of the people in control. And whereas under individual or small group ownership a "bad" publisher has a limited capacity for poor service, a chain which is prone to milking cash from its properties or throwing around its influence can infect numerous localities with poor or destructive journalism.

The potential danger of group ownership lies in the concentration of financial, political, and social power in relatively few people.

The four largest chains—Knight-Ridder, Newhouse, Tribune Co., and Gannett—have 21 percent of daily circulation among them. Of these, the Newhouse chain is frequently mentioned in the same category as the Thomson group. They "chop budgets and staff, hold investment to a minimum, and wring the paper dry of profits," reported one analyst.

Relatively little empirical research has been done on the effects of chain ownership alone. One study, however, did find evidence that, contrary to the assertions of editorial independence on the part of chain owners, "Chain papers were more likely to support the favored candidate of the press in every election." More crucial, however, was the finding that in endorsing presidential candidates in the elections of 1960 through 1972 inclusive, non-chain papers were less likely to endorse any presidential candidate and that the "vast majority of chains exhibited homogeneous endorsement patterns," i.e., 85 percent or more of the papers endorsed the same candidate. The study did add, however, that chains spread out over several regions were "consistently less homogeneous in each of the elections," indicating that the small, personal regional chains tend toward tighter editorial control than the more publicized national groups.[7]

Some examples of chain owners throwing their unified influence in editorial policy includes William Randolph Hearst, Jr.'s demand that his papers support the Johnson-Humphrey ticket in 1964 (though he let each paper make its own decision in 1968 and they split 8-5 in favor of Nixon-Agnew). In 1972, James M. Cox required his nine newspapers, including the *Atlanta Journal* and *Constitution,* to endorse the Nixon ticket.

In a somewhat broader study of both competition and concentration of ownership, it was found that, in the aggregate, there was no evidence that consumers received any benefits from concentration of ownership through chain acquisition of a daily newspaper, at least of those papers which went from independent to chain during the course of the study.[8]

Why the Chains Keep Buying

There are several reasons why independent newspapers are selling out and chain owners are interested in buying more:

• *Profit.* First of all, they can be a profitable investment. Table 2.7 showed that the median profit for the publicly held newspaper groups was 9.6 percent, about twice that of the largest publicly owned manufacturing businesses. It is true that many of the newspaper companies also include revenue and profit from non-newspaper properties, including newsprint and broadcasting properties. But among those at the top of the list—Thomson and Lee—the largest proportion of their revenue is from newspaper production.

• *Scarce commodity.* Second, newspaper properties are attractive because they are a scarce commodity. With a finite market of good, potentially profitable properties, competition to buy them is strong. "Brokers keep calling me on the phone asking, 'Well, are you ready?'" reports John Northrop, publisher of the *Washington* (Pa.) *Observer Reporter* (circ., 3253). But the idea of starting a new paper of any size is not attractive. There just are not that many areas which can support a paper that do not already have one. Cowles Communications spent three years trying to establish the *Suffolk Sun* in competition with *Newsday* on Long Island and gave up.

• *Professional management.* The third reason is that, profitable as a newspaper may be, under the professional management of chains they can be even more so. The objective of a family owned business is often different from one which is publicly owned or professionally managed. Minimizing taxes and maximizing cash in the till, rather than maximizing earnings per share or return on investment, may be the objective of private owners. With the new technology paying handsome returns in labor savings, groups can afford to pay high multiples on a family owned newspaper, expecting to increase profits very rapidly through production savings and other controls.

As a case in point, a newspaper broker tells of a deal in which a South Carolina newspaper changed hands for 60 times earnings, but the new owner doubled earnings in the first year and after two years had increased profits to the point where he had paid an effective 20 times earnings for the property. Robert Marbut, president of the acquisition-minded Harte-Hanks chain, says he would pay "100 times earnings for a newspaper which wasn't making any money," if he thought it had the potential, under new management, to become a profit-maker.

Earnings can also be increased by bringing in professional managers and using the sophisticated business and financial services many of the chains make available. Gannett sends a marketing group to any local paper in the chain to provide in-house consulting to find ways to boost circulation and advertising. Stock analyst Ken Noble explained why this makes a difference:

> I think the motivation of the earlier newspaper groups was essentially to be important people in the cities in which their operations were located. This orientation made them somewhat reluctant to be aggressive in pricing, advertising, and circulation rates. The new managers have no such relationships.[9]

The synergy of group management is perhaps best illustrated in the unique nature of Gannett's Westchester-Rockland Newspaper group. A plant in White Plains, NY prints seven of the dailies in the group, including three zoned editions of one of the papers. The papers, a morning and six afternoon editions, range in circulation from under 10,000 to over 50,000. The papers have some separate news staffers, but share a common building and production equipment and can afford technology which would be prohibitive to any one of the papers alone. Moreover, certain common features and advertising inserts are combined with local news and advertising, enabling each paper to be something more than it might be otherwise. It has what might be termed a "critical mass" needed for certain newspaper economies.

• *Cash.* Newspaper chains tend to generate large amounts of cash, not only from profits but from depreciation and amortization of goodwill. They also carry low debt in relation to invested capital as compared to other businesses. Times Mirror cut its long-term debt by 16 percent between 1971 and 1978 and long-term debt divided by equity dropped from 16 percent to 6 percent, while cash flow per share increased by 107 percent. Knight-Ridder reduced its debt/equity ratio from 18 percent to 8 percent and Gannett realized $25.2 million in cash in 1978 from depreciation and amortization alone. In addition, tax laws allow firms to accumulate undistributed profits to buy other communications properties, and as such are exempt from tax provisions on excess accumulated profits. This encourages further acquisition. Table 5.5 itemizes some recent acquisitions and, where possible, the price paid. (It should be noted that acquisitions are also made through the exchange of stock, especially when the acquirers' stock is traded at a high price-earnings multiple.)

Strategies for Growth in Chains

Newspaper groups have adopted varying strategies for growth. They all recognize to some degree, however, that sizable gains must come through acquisitions, since internal profit growth from circulation, advertising gains and technology savings is slow—after the initial gain from the new technology. Other than this common factor, the chains have several distinct approaches, as seen in the various profiles in Chapter 13.

Some groups, such as Times Mirror, Hearst, Newhouse, New York Times Co., and Capital Cities Communications are multi-product firms, with newspaper revenues sizable, but only part of the total. In 1978, newspaper revenue accounted for only 44 percent of Times Mirror revenues, with other sizable contributions from book publishing (15 per-

Table 5.5   Some Recent Mergers and Acquisitions in Daily Newspaper Industry

Purchaser	Property Purchased	Year	Price
Newhouse	Booth Newspapers	1976	$300 million
Gannett	The New Mexican (Santa Fe) (18,000 daily, 21,000 Sunday)	1976	300,000 shares of stock
	Valley News Dispatch (Pa.) (44,000 daily)	1976	$9.3 million
	Shreveport (La.) Times & Journal (146,000 daily)	1976	$62 million
	Monroe (La.) News-Star World (50,000 daily) + broadcast affiliates		
	Speidel Newspapers	1976/77	$170 million
	Combined Communications	1978/79	approx. $320 million in stock
	Wilmington (Del.) News and Journal (140,000 daily)	1978	$60 million
Combined Communications (acquired by Gannett in 1979)	Cincinnati Enquirer (190,000 daily, 290,000 Sunday)	1975	$55 million
	Oakland (Calif.) Tribune (176,000 daily, 290,000 Sunday)	1977	$13.9 million (plus $2.8 million for Tribune Bldg.)
Rupert Murdoch	San Antonio (Tex.) Express-News (149,000 combined daily, 130,000 Sunday)	1974	$18 million
	New York Post (489,000 daily)	1976	$27-30 million
Dow Jones (Ottaway Group)	Joplin (Mo.) Globe (40,000 daily)	1976	$12.2 million
	Essex Newspapers Beverly (Mass.) Times	1978	$10 million
	Gloucester (Mass.) Times (12,000 daily)		
	Newburyport (Mass.) News (9,000 daily)		
	Peabody (Mass.) Times (4,000 daily)		

Harte-Hanks	Wichita Falls (Tex.) Record-News & Times (52,000 daily)	1976	$15 million (for remaining 72% share)
Knight	Ridder Newspapers (17 daily)	1973	$174 million
Capital Cities	Kansas City (Mo.) Star & Times (626,000 combined daily, 396,000 Sunday)	1977	$125 million
	Wilkes-Barre (Pa.) Times-Leader-News & Record (70,000 daily)	1978	$9 million
Lee Newspapers	Kansas City (Kan.) Kansan (25,000 daily, 26,000 Sunday)	1976	$2 million
	Bismarck (N.D.) Tribune (25,500 daily)	1978	$4.8 million for 53% interest
	Lindsay-Schaub Newspapers (130,000 combined circulation)	1979	$60.4 million
	Decatur (Ill.) Herald & Review		
	Carbondale (Ill.) Southern Illinoisian		
	Midland (Mich.) Daily News*		
	Edwardsville (Ill.) Intelligencer*		
	Huron Daily Tribune (Bad Axe, Mich.)*		
Donrey Media Group	Cleburne (Tex.) Times-Review (9000 daily, Sunday)	1976	N.A.
	Borger (Tex.) News-Herald (7500 daily)	1978	N.A.
	Vallejo (Calif.) Times Herald (30,000 daily, Sunday)	1976	N.A.
Hearst	Midland (Tex.) Reporter-Telegram (20,000) daily)	1978	N.A.
	Plainview (Tex.) Herald (9000 daily)	1978	N.A.
Times Mirror	Hartford Courant	1979	$105.6 million

N.A. Not available.   *Sold in 1979 for a total of $17 million.

Sources: *Editor & Publisher*, compilation of papers and acquisitions, January 6, 1979, January 1, 1977, December 27, 1975, December 28, 1974, plus publicly owned company annual reports and press releases.

cent), newsprint and forest products (16 percent), and magazine, broadcasting, cable, and other business (26 percent). The New York Times Co. has diversified to the extent that newspaper revenues accounted for only 71 percent of the total in 1976, compared to 83 percent in 1968 (and 62 percent in 1978 when a strike shut down the *Times* for three months).

Other firms have stayed much closer to being all-newspaper chains: Gannett, Thomson and Dow Jones among them.

At the same time, some of the chains have long been involved in broadcasting. The Washington Post Co. has four VHF television stations in major markets and one AM radio station, accounting for 12 percent of 1978 corporate revenue—and 23 percent of pre-tax operating income. Lee Enterprises received 27 percent of its revenue from broadcast.

On the other hand, for most of its history Dow Jones, publisher of *The Wall Street Journal*, 19 daily Ottaway newspapers, and *Barron's*, as well as books and other information services, has refrained from diversification into broadcasting. According to president Warren Phillips, it "wanted to stay away from a government regulated industry. Future growth [in broadcasting] is conditional on the government license." Only in 1978 did it change its position to a willingness to consider broadcast properties, perhaps looking ahead to possible easing of government licensing regulations.

Given these various strategies, newspaper groups have also adopted different approaches to newspaper acquisitions. Almost all would agreee with the Times Mirror's Otis Chandler, that, "All else being equal, the choicest property is one that has a market almost to itself." Newhouse, Lee, Gannett, Multimedia, Thomson, Harte-Hanks, Media General, and Donrey Media are among the major chains which have all or virtually all of their newspapers in these "monopoly" markets and generally would not even consider the acquisition of a property that faces head-on competition.

Other firms, however, are more willing to take on the challenge of big city competition, either for the potential big profits it could bring, the prestige involved, or perhaps both. Times Mirror operates most of its largest newspapers in highly competitive markets. Knight-Ridder, although it has numerous monopoly operations among its 33 newspapers, also faces strong competition in Philadelphia, Miami, and Detroit. The New York Times Co. has a chain of profitable, small monopoly market newspapers in Florida, but has many problems in New York. The Washington Post Co. accepted the challenge of competition in purchasing the *Trenton* (NJ) *Times* in 1974. Time Inc., although not a newspaper chain, purchased the ailing *Washington Star* in 1978.

Why Independent Papers Keep Selling

For every purchase, there must be someone willing to sell. Privately held independent newspapers are being pressured to sell for several reasons.

• *Weak management.* Rising costs, including the investment in new technology, wages, newsprint, and presses call for strict controls and profit planning, which small independents cannot always get because they cannot afford the managerial types who can provide this. "The groups are corralling the bright young people and giving them publisher titles," explains one independent publisher. Groups, on the other hand, can have specialists who set up control systems for each paper, without any one having to be burdened by full development costs. Likewise, the chains can utilize production specialists to help in evaluating technology.

* *Family squabbles.* Some family managements are not prepared to deal with the realities of the bottom line. Even at the relatively large *Oakland* (Calif.) *Tribune*, family problems led that paper to sell to Combined Communications in 1977. Both the father and grandfather of the present publisher were former U.S. senators and were interested in politics. With the paper to use as a power base, "business was secondary."[10] Some family members involved in management in 1976 still complained that the paper was being run "more for 'civic pride' than profit." "The idea of a family owned newspaper in the future is not probable," concludes the publisher of the family owned *Louisville Courier-Journal.*

* *Inheritance taxes.* Another factor is the estate tax difficulty. A valuable newspaper property which is privately held is a taxable asset in the estate when the principals die. The estate must pay the tax on the value of the property. If the estate is not well endowed with cash or other marketable securities to sell, the heirs may be forced to sell the newspaper to pay the taxes on it. The 1976 Tax Reform Act, which changed the method of determining the valuation of assets in an estate, may have been an added factor in some sales in 1976. There was some speculation that Dorothy Schiff's sudden decision to sell the *New York Post* to Rupert Murdoch (for a reported $27 million) was because the new law might have put her heirs in a less favorable inheritance tax position.

* *Tax rates.* Yet another aspect of the tax structure encourages selling. Income tax rates are as high as 70 percent, while tax on capital gains is substantially lower. By selling the newspaper in a cash transaction, the seller pays only the lower capital gains tax. If the exchange is for stock in the purchasing firm, then the swap is tax free, until the seller decides to sell the purchasing firm's stock. Moreover, in this case, the seller may then control a substantial block of the buyer's stock. The Booth chain, for example, though already publicly owned and a group owner itself, was still controlled by the Booth family. It was made vulnerable to an outside takeover when it exchanged 17 percent of its stock with Whitcom Investment Co. to purchase *Parade,* the national Sunday supplement magazine. When Whitcom offered this block of stock for sale several years later, Newhouse interests purchased it, giving Newhouse a wedge from which he finally bought total control of Booth in the largest newspaper cash deal ever.

* *High offering prices.* Finally, and perhaps most important most often, independent and small chain publishers are simply being overwhelmed with offers and money. Robert B. Whittington, a vice president of the recently sold small Speidel chain, recalls feeling "like a virgin at a stag party" when hordes of publishers came wooing. The *Valley News Dispatch* (circ. 42,093) in Western Pennsylvania, was sold to Gannett for $9.3

million, or $221 per subscriber. Gannett also bought the *Shreveport* (La.) *Times* (circ., 90,000), along with two smaller papers in Monroe, La. (combined circ., 51,000) for $61 million. When Newhouse bought Booth, the $47 per share offering price compares to the $23 a share the stock was selling for on November 5, 1975 on the Over-The-Counter market about a year before the takeover and about $30 a share about a week before the Newhouse offer in mid-October 1976.

Such sums merely harden the attitude of some of the remaining independent owners. They are so tired of being courted that some have stopped attending publishers' conventions. One such publisher of several small papers deplores the concentration of ownership in a nationwide chain. William Block, whose family controls the *Pittsburgh Post-Gazette*, feels that, "Some chain papers tend to be more cautious about controversy. You tend to play it safe when you don't own the paper yourself."

DECLINING COMPETITION AND THE MONOPOLY NEWSPAPER

Of more concern perhaps than the growth of chains is the decline of newspaper competition within individual markets. Where 502 cities had two or more competing newspapers in 1923, including 100 cities with three or more papers, by 1978 that had decreased to 35 cities, barely 2 percent of total newspaper cities with competing dailies. And only two cities, New York and Philadelphia, had as many as three competing ownerships.

The specter of further elimination of intra-city newspaper competition was the motivating factor behind the Newspaper Preservation Act passed by Congress in 1970 to legitimize so-called "joint agreements" in which two competing newspapers combine their business and production facilities into a single jointly-owned firm, while maintaining separate ownership of the editorial side.

The issue in declining competition is whether it reduces the quality of the editorial product, lessens the diversity of opinions available to the reader, and results in monopoly price structure for advertisers and subscribers.

Effects on the Editorial Product

The most commonly expressed fear is that freedom of the press is endangered by less competition, and hence less diversity of opinion. In fact, most studies have found that readers perceive little difference between competing and non-competing newspapers, and researchers have found little to substantiate the view that lack of local competition itself produces inferior journalism.

Two researchers in a 1956 study found that there were few significant differences in content between competitive and non-competitive newspapers. The one significant difference was in reporting news of accidents and disasters, in which case competing papers carried more such news.[11] Another study found that nine types of news coverage were perceived by readers to be better after mergers than before. Overall, reader attitudes in

Atlanta, Louisville, Minneapolis, and Des Moines were slightly more favorable after mergers eliminated head-on competition.[12]

Yet another study found that competing dailies do not guarantee the marketplace of ideas which some feel justifies the need for competing newspapers. In examining pairs of competing papers in small cities, the investigator found only one pair that showed any tendency to compete by issue, and there the competition was along partisan lines.[13]

A more recent study reaffirmed previous research which has been unable to find significant differences in competing and non-competing newspapers.[14] In one case, the content and reader perception during a period of head-on evening competition in Bloomington, Ind. were contrasted with a time when one of the papers was about to fold (moderate competition) and a period five months after one of the competing dailies closed down. The hypothesis was that under conditions of intense competition, a daily newspaper would devote more of its non-advertising space to local content and sensational and human interest news and features than under conditions of non-competition. Another hypothesis was that readers would perceive no difference in the quality of the two competing papers nor notice any difference in the amount of local news in the remaining non-competitive paper.

In fact, the findings substantiated neither of the hypotheses. Local news content did not decline when competition ended, nor did the proportion of immediate reward items—sports, crime, accidents, etc. And, consistent with previous studies, readers reported no perceived difference in the surviving newspaper. Readers of the two papers were aware, however, of quantity differences in immediate reward items in the two papers. These findings support previous conclusions in similar studies of competing and non-competing newspapers.

Another study, looking only at differences in pairs of competing newspapers, found that, in fact, there are relatively few substantial variations, although leading newspapers in each pair did have some common characteristics.[15] In comparing 46 newspapers in 23 markets, the researchers found:

1. The percentage content in each of 20 editorial categories was almost the same.

2. Leading newspapers have a larger advertising hole.

3. Leaders used more news services.

4. The leader was more likely to be the newer paper.

5. In format, the trailing paper had larger pictures and fewer stories on page one.

Overall, the authors found "few content and relatively few consistent format differences." This dearth of difference among competing and within non-competing newspapers may have several explanations. It could indicate that the constraints of having to sell to a mass market dictate certain formulas which editors have honed over the years. Moreover, since editors often work their way up, moving from paper to paper, they share a common training ground which they all generally follow when they run a newspaper. There may also be the element of media responsibility which editors may feel, particularly when they know they are the only newspaper in town. Publishers also may be particularly sensitive to accusations of abusing "monopoly" power, but they may have also learned that they must meet certain minimum standards to gain subscribers and the advertisers who want a decent circulation and rate. Certainly, it may be a combination of several or all of these or other factors. Perhaps it takes more than even two newspapers competing directly to provide the niche for a paper which can be more specialized, controversial, or otherwise significantly different from its brethren.

Most recently, Hicks and Featherstone studied the amount of content duplication in morning and evening papers in the same city under common ownership.[16] In the literature, the two papers would be considered to be a single "media voice," since it is hypothesized that the single owner would dictate content and editorial policy for both papers. Hicks and Featherstone compared the content of the two Newhouse-owned papers in New Orleans with that of another morning-evening combination owned by a small local chain in Baton Rouge and that of two newspapers in Shreveport, one of which is independently owned and the other owned by the Gannett chain. These two published under a joint operating agreement, however.

The study found no significant difference in the non-advertising space (newshole) of the six papers, all clustering around the national average of 34 percent to 35 percent. The range was from 31 percent to 38 percent, with the independent Shreveport paper having the highest newshole, the evening Baton Rouge paper the smallest.

Perhaps more surprisingly, the study found remarkably little duplication in either news or editorial content among the papers in each city. In no case was there *any* duplication of editorials, columns, cartoons and letters. In hard news and local items, the Baton Rouge combination did have some statistically significant overlap, due in part to joint coverage of state capital news, but the Newhouse papers in New Orleans and the separate Shreveport papers had minuscule duplication. Noted the publisher of the New Orleans papers: "[The reporters on each paper] fight tooth and nail for stories; it is just as competitive as it would be with separate ownerships."

Hicks and Featherstone conclude that the concept of "media voice" might be modified, since in all three cities in their study readers did get two distinct newspapers "in terms of appearance, and no duplicated news. . . ."

Effects on Economic Structure

Economists may describe the newspaper industry as one which conforms to an economic pattern of imperfect competition: stabilization of prices for both advertising and circulation; price discrimination in charging different groups of advertisers or subscribers differing rates at the same time; and non-price competition.[17]

This has led Stanford University economist James N. Rosse to label the structure "isolated" rather than "local monopoly" because:

[A] typical member of the industry, alone in his city market is isolated in the sense that cross-elasticities of demands for his products with respect to prices charged by other newspaper firms or by competing media are certainly finite and generally quite small.

Thus, an isolated form is distinguished from a true monopoly in that "not all demand cross-elasticities are zero." Rosse proceeds to document that economies of scale do indeed exist in newspaper publishing, helping to explain this isolate character. In essence he largely substantiates what is widely known; i.e., the cost of producing 100,000 copies of a newspaper is not ten times that of producing 10,000 copies. Thus, since many costs, such as editorial and composing, are not directly tied to circulation, the cost of production per copy decreases with greater circulation.

This declining long-run average cost curve, however, is balanced by other factors which produce a practical limit on the extent to which a newspaper can expand. First, a large metropolitan daily faces increased transportation costs and other distribution expenses which may actually increase as circulation extends over a wider geographical area. This can be overcome somewhat, but at a cost in fixed plant, through suburban printing locations. The more limiting factor, preventing unlimited national expansion, is the highly localized demand of newspaper content. As the newspaper spreads out, it must become less complete in covering the local news of various communities and serving the needs of local advertisers who are more concerned with agate line rates than overall milline rate. It is this specialization of demand which ultimately offsets the economy of scale effects and determines the geographical extent of local newspaper monopoly.

The "Umbrella" Hypothesis

What has resulted, then, is not intracity newspaper competition, but intercity competition, as developed by Rosse's "umbrella hypothesis."

"The essence of the model," says Rosse, "is the recognition that while few cities have more than one daily newspaper, these newspapers nevertheless compete with each other and with other newspapers." That is, most regions of the country have a metropolitan newspaper whose circulation extends well beyond the central city, perhaps for hundreds of miles. The circulation falls off as the distance increases, but within this circulation area are "satellite cities," each with its own daily whose circulation goes beyond its borders. Dailies in these "level two" cities may have circulation in smaller communities, which in turn may have their own local dailies. Even within the smaller community, there may be weekly newspapers, "shoppers," and other specialized media.

Figure 5.1 illustrates how each level throws an umbrella over the lower levels. The level one papers draw advertising from national and regional advertisers, as well as from local in-city stores. They are also the most subject to competition from broadcast media, since they compete for the major national and international news as well as the advertising revenue. Newspapers at the second and third levels compete with each other only in the fringes of their natural markets, but they must compete with the papers above them and below them.

The second and third level newspapers are the ones which exist because of the needs

Figure 5.1   Rosse's "Umbrella" Model of Newspaper Competition

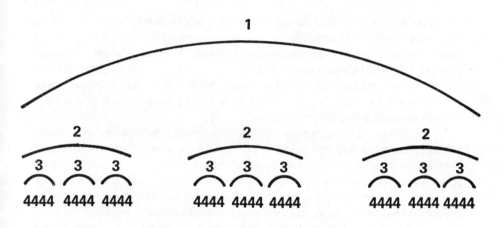

Key:
Level 1 — Newspaper in large metropolitan center
Level 2 — Newspapers in satellite cities
Level 3 — Local dailies
Level 4 — Weeklies and other specialized media

of local readers and advertisers which cannot be adequately fulfilled by the metropolitan daily. Even zoned editions of the big city papers cannot provide the complete coverage of local governments, school boards, and sports teams, or the Main Street shopkeepers in the surrounding towns.

An example of how this works may be taken from the Philadelphia area. The *Inquirer* is available for at least as far west as Carlisle, Pa., 120 miles; east to Atlantic City and Cape May, N.J., 90 miles; south past Wilmington, Del., 49 miles; and north beyond Allentown, 65 miles. Within this area, however, are several "level two" newspapers: the *Harrisburg Patriot, Allentown Call* and *Chronicle,* the *Atlantic City Press,* the *Wilmington News* and *Journal,* the *Camden Courier Post,* for example. At the third level are newspapers in Carlisle and Chambersburg, Pa., also served by the Harrisburg paper; in Bethlehem and Bangor, Pa., competing with the Allentown papers; and similar competition throughout the area.

As already discussed in Chapter 3, metropolitan newspapers suffer more than the smaller papers from the competition of broadcast media. Local suburban newspapers, meanwhile, proliferate and absorb fringe area circulation. Thus, although newspapers may not have the head-to-head rivalries in the central cities that they did 75 years ago, they face more economic competition than the term "local monopoly" implies.

This does not mean that there is no benefit to the owner of a newspaper in the isolated market, especially at the secondary and tertiary levels, where electronic media have less impact. In considering properties for acquisition, owners find that the choicest properties are the ones which have the immediate market to themselves, although Times Mirror Co.'s Otis Chandler may be overstating the case when he says these markets "give you a franchise to do what you want with profitability. You can engineer your profits. You can control expenses and generate revenues almost arbitrarily."

Have the larger firms which result from this natural tendency toward combination and merger been more efficient in practice, especially in light of Paul Samuelson's assertion that, "Imperfect competition may result in wastage of resources, too high price, and yet no profits for the imperfect competitors"? Have consumers of the industry's products—the advertising space for the advertiser and copies of the newspaper for the reader—received any of the potential benefit?

A study investigating this found that consumers receive no benefits from the assumed economies of scale and that consumers pay higher prices under monopoly with no compensating increase in quality or quantity of product. There is some conflicting evidence, however, at least concerning advertisers. The study concludes that, "Concentration of daily newspaper circulation in the hands of a single newspaper does appear to raise the general [national] and classified advertising rates to some extent," but found no statistical evidence of this on retail advertising levels, the area in which the consequences of monopoly power in a market could be expected to be the greatest.[18]

In fact, research suggests that milline rates for advertisers may actually decrease following a merger in a market, due to the dominance of circulation over concentration. That is, any increase in agate line rates is more than offset by the proportionately greater increase in circulation of the combined daily. This comes from the economies of scale: The costs associated with publishing one newspaper with a given circulation are lower than those of two newspapers each with a portion of that circulation. The advertiser also avoids having to pay for duplicate readership of the competing papers.

On the other hand, there is reason to believe that wage rates for newspaper employees tend to be lower in non-competitive situations.

Cross Media Ownership

The effects of non-competitive newspapers in a particular market are mitigated not only by the existence of competing media, i.e., television, radio, and magazines. What is potentially more insidious for readers and advertisers would be the situation in which more than one medium in a locality is under the same ownership. This is reflected in concern over cross-media ownership.

In a landmark project, Guido A. Stempel studied the effects of a complete media monopoly in one small city, Zanesville, Ohio.[19] There, the city's only newspaper, radio station, and television station were under the same ownership. Comparing Zanesville's residents with those who lived in similar cities with greater media diversity, Stempel found that:

(1) Zanesville residents used the news media less and were less well informed than residents in comparison cities.

(2) Zanesville residents got less news than residents in two comparison cities with competitive media.

(3) Despite this, Zanesville residents used less non-local media than those they were compared with.

(4) Nonetheless, public acceptance of the media was high.

Other studies yield conflicting findings on the effects of newspaper/broadcast affiliations.

Although the effects may be in dispute, as a result of both FCC regulation and the general growth in the number of available broadcasting outlets, the number of distinct voices, i.e., separately owned newspapers, AM, FM, and television outlets, actually increased between 1950 and 1970 by 25 percent, overall press control in the top 100 markets having peaked in 1940. In that year, 23 percent of the broadcast voices were owned by newspapers in the same market. By 1950, the percentage had dropped to three percent.

Table 5.6 shows the decline in situations where a newspaper owned the only radio and/or television station in a community. Instances where a community had only one television station owned by the only newspaper dropped by two-thirds from 1967 to 1971. In 1973, newspaper-affiliated television stations still accounted for 16.1 percent of all TV stations in the top 100 markets. Under current FCC rulings, newspapers are prohibited from constructing or purchasing any broadcast facilities which would overlap their newspaper market. Moreover, in March 1977 a U.S. Court of Appeals overturned an FCC ruling and ordered that even existing newspaper/broadcast combinations must be forced to split up. This affected over 230 such combinations.

Although Christopher Sterling warns that the trend of decreasing concentration may have reached its peak, he concludes:

> There appears to be a multiplicity of voices to be heard and read providing news and entertainment daily. When one adds in other media originating within most of these SMSAs, plus the many information and entertainment sources received but not originating in each market, the variety of voices and points of view is almost numberless.[20]

Actually, ownership of several broadcast properties is seen by some of the smaller publicly owned newspaper firms as a tactic in forestalling unfriendly takeover attempts. Before Speidel joined Gannett, there had been an unwanted intrusion in the market for its stock from the Thomson organization. Newhouse was initially opposed by Booth

Table 5.6 Commercial Broadcast Stations by Affiliation with Newspapers in Same Community, 1967, 1971

	1967			1971		
	Radio Only	TV Only	Both TV & Radio	Radio Only	TV Only	Both TV & Radio
Stations Not Affiliated with Newspaper in Same Community	884	254	N.A.	890	294	N.A.
Stations Affiliated with Newspaper in Same Community (Majority Ownership)	230	15	201	194	16	183
Only Station in Community	104	2	13	77	1	12
Percent of Total	45.2%	13.3%	6.5%	39.7%	6.3%	6.6%
Non-Affiliated Stations in Same Community	839	215	N.A.	798	264	N.A.
Communities with Only One Daily Newspaper with Ownership in:						
Only Commercial Radio Station	76	N.A.	N.A.	53	N.A.	N.A.
Only Commercial Television Station	N.A.	29	N.A.	N.A.	10	N.A.

N.A.   Not available.

Source: U.S. Bureau of the Census, *Statistical Abstract of the United States, 1978.* (99th ed.), Washington, D.C., 1978, Table No. 985, p. 594.

management in that buyout. Groups such as Lee and Harte-Hanks must have similar concerns.

But since the FCC has to approve the transfer of ownership of licensed broadcast facilities, a potential unwanted suitor faces this added obstacle. Moreover, there is a greater likelihood that the buyer may run into cross-media ownership hassles in merging existing properties with the acquired ones. Thus, the broadcast properties are a profitable hedge in the acquisitions game.

ANTITRUST AND LEGISLATIVE ACTIVITIES

As part of the only industry specifically mentioned for protection in the Constitution, the newspaper has been largely, although not completely, immune from judicial and legislative tampering. One important case which did affirm the government's ultimate right to insure freedom of expression was the Associated Press case in 1945. The AP, a cooperative financed by member newspapers to provide news accounts to all, had a policy of restricting competition by making it extremely expensive to buy a new membership in a city where there were already newspaper members. The government sued the Associated Press on antitrust grounds, and the AP's defense was the First Amendment, as well as the theory that newspapers were not covered by the Sherman Act since they were not engaged in interstate commerce. More important than the substantive ruling against the AP's restrictive practice, the Supreme Court's ruling clearly placed newspapers within the jurisdiction of antitrust legislation. It is surely in the government's power to preserve the free dissemination provided for in the First Amendment:

> Freedom to publish is guaranteed by the Constitution, but freedom to combine to keep others from publishing is not. Freedom of the press from governmental interference under the First Amendment does not sanction repression of that freedom by private interests.

With the rights of the government firmly established, the Justice Department brought an action against the two newspapers in Tucson, Ariz. which had formed a joint operating company to handle advertising, business, and production matters, leaving editorial staffs and policy in the hands of the separate owners of the two papers. Forty-two other newspapers in 21 cities had similar joint operating agreements.

Using Tucson as a test case, the government charged the two papers with price fixing, profit pooling, and market allocation. In 1969, the Supreme Court upheld a summary judgment supporting the government's charge. This ruling brought action on a bill which had been introduced in Congress in 1967 to protect such arrangements. So the Newspaper Preservation Act was passed in 1970, in effect exempting the 22 joint agreements from antitrust prosecution. The Act does, however, limit the right of future agreements, which must be approved by the Justice Department on a case-by-case basis. There are also sanctions for abuse of the legalized combination to prevent further competition in the market, but these have not been applied. Table 5.7 identifies cities with agency shops, as well as those with totally competitive newspapers.

The proponents of this legislation argued that two separate editorial voices were a better alternative than the single voice which would exist if an otherwise marginal paper was merged into a single ownership. The opposing view, held by some independent newspapers, mostly small dailies, as well as *The New York Times* and the American Newspaper Guild, was that prosperous suburban dailies and weeklies were replacing these failing metropolitan newspapers. The joint operating agreements could therefore lessen competition within the city and promote an unfair advantage over existing or potential rivals.

Critics of the Act welcomed a lawsuit by the *Anchorage Daily News* to dissolve a joint operating agreement it had with the larger *Anchorage Times*. The litigation was the first such attempt to break an agreement and the *Daily News'* owner charged the *Times*

Table 5.7   Cities with Competing Newspapers, 1979

Competitive Newspaper Cities		Agency Shop Cities
Anchorage, Alaska		Birmingham, Alabama
Little Rock, Arkansas	New York, New York	Tucson, Arizona
Los Angeles, California	Cleveland, Ohio	San Francisco, California
Sacramento, California	McAlester, Oklahoma	Miami, Florida
Colorado Springs, Colorado	Oklahoma City, Oklahoma	Honolulu, Hawaii
Denver, Colorado	Philadelphia, Pennsylvania	Fort Wayne, Indiana
Manchester, Connecticut	Scranton, Pennsylvania	Evansville, Indiana
Washington, District of Columbia	York, Pennsylvania	Shreveport, Louisiana
Champaign-Urbana, Illinois	Chattanooga, Tennessee	Lincoln, Nebraska
Chicago, Illinois	Cookeville, Tennessee	Albuquerque, New Mexico
Slidel, Louisiana	Austin, Texas	Cincinnati, Ohio
Baltimore, Maryland	Dallas, Texas	Columbus, Ohio
Boston, Massachusetts	Houston, Texas	Tulsa, Oklahoma
Detroit, Michigan	San Antonio, Texas	Pittsburgh, Pennsylvania
Columbia, Missouri	Seattle, Washington	Knoxville, Tennessee
Fulton, Missouri	Green Bay, Wisconsin	Nashville, Tennessee
St. Louis, Missouri[1]		El Paso, Texas
Las Vegas, Nevada		Salt Lake City, Utah
Trenton, New Jersey		Charleston, West Virginia
Buffalo, New York		Madison, Wisconsin
		Spokane, Washington

[1]The St. Louis papers have a common printing plant but sell all advertising and circulation independently. In February 1979 they announced they were considering combining these functions as well and thus would become an agency shop.

Source: *Editor & Publisher International Yearbook, 1979,* plus additional reports.

with "monopoly, mismanagement, and breach of contracts," all of which, it claims, have lessened competition between the two newspapers and injured the *Daily News.*

The *Daily News* formed the agreement with the *Times* in 1974, the first new agreement approved by the Justice Department since the Newspaper Preservation Act had been made law. It had to be judged "failing" to get that approval, and statements showed it to be losing $500,000 a year since 1969. Under the joint operating agreement, losses continued at about the same rate. The *Times*, with three times the circulation of the *Daily News*, sells advertising at one-half the milline rate of its competitor. In late 1978, the two papers agreed to dissolve the joint agency and the *Daily News*—purchased by the McClatchy chain—was able to resume publication on its own in 1979.

Another issue, involving the *New Orleans Times-Picayune*, concerned the legality of a morning/evening combined advertising rate offered by the owner of the two papers. Do not such rates, which may actually be cheaper in combination than for a single paper, invoke price discrimination to the disadvantage of a competitor of one of the combination's papers? The Supreme Court ruled the practice legal, thus making it that much more difficult for a single newspaper to compete with a morning/evening edition operation offering low combination rates. Advertisers would tend to go into the morning/evening combination at a rate much lower than using a morning and evening from competitive firms.

Another antitrust suit involving a similar issue was filed in early 1977 by the owner of the *Sacramento* (Calif.) *Union* against McClatchy Newspapers, owner of the *Sacramento Bee, Fresno Bee,* and *Modesto Bee* (all California) as well as several radio and TV stations. The suit contended that McClatchy Newspapers was illegally monopolizing the market by offering joint ad buys between the broadcast stations or discounts for ads in all three newspapers.

Newspaper groups do have to show some sensitivity to antitrust laws, however. So far, the Justice Department has shown little activity concerning concentration of ownership, even as Gannett hits the 80 newspaper mark. For the most part, the chains have been careful not to buy papers that have overlapping distribution and thereby lay themselves open to charges of controlling all papers under the umbrella.

For example, although Gannett's Westchester-Rockland Newspapers provide the basic local papers for a large contiguous area in suburban New York City, they all compete under the dominating influence of the large metropolitan papers which are widely available in their territory.

On the other hand, Times Mirror was forced to sell its *San Bernardino* (Calif.) *Sun* and *Telegram* in 1970 because of an antitrust ruling based on the predominance of the *Los Angeles Times* in Southern California and the lessening of competition which would result if the relatively nearby San Bernardino papers were brought under the same ownership. The point that geographical proximity is the key, not overall size of the chain, is underlined by the ready acquisition of the San Bernardino papers by Gannett.

There was some talk among industry analysts that Gannett's merger with Speidel Newspapers, announced months after Newhouse bought out Booth Newspapers, would provoke interest on the part of Congress or the Justice Department in the increased size of the chains. Separately, but simultaneously with these activities, Rupert Murdoch, the owner of a chain of Australian and British newspapers, received considerable visibility by following up his purchase of the *San Antonio News* with a $27 million purchase of the *New York Post,* and ten days later the acquisition of the company that publishes *New York Magazine* and the weekly *Village Voice.* In fact, the Justice Department did announce a "preliminary inquiry" into possible violations of antitrust statutes in Murdoch's New York purchases, but nothing further happened. The Federal Trade Commission held a public hearing on concentration of ownership of all mass media in 1978 and in Congress, Rep. Morris Udall (D., Ariz.) has been outspoken in his criticism of media concentration.

SUMMARY

The evidence clearly points to a continuing trend of mergers and acquisitions consolidating newspaper owning in fewer hands. Since 1970, more than 50 percent of daily newspapers have been owned by newspaper groups.

Only 35 cities now have truly competing newspapers. Nonetheless, research has shown at best clouded evidence that group ownership or a single ownership of newspapers in a community has caused any disservice to readers or advertisers. In most cases, subscribers report no perceived differences in papers following the demise of competition. Content analysis also has shown few significant differences between competing and non-competing newspapers.

There are cases where some have complained of deterioration when a chain buys a local newspaper, but there are also cases of noticeable improvement when certain chains buy a newspaper. The difference seems not so much determined by group or independent, competing or non-competing, but by the motives and interests of the owners. A group owner may offer a local newspaper access to better national reporting and features, as well as help in advertising sales. On the other hand, a chain controlled by those interested in squeezing out all possible profits from their acquisitions can do widespread harm to good journalism.

Some independent newspapers may be selling out because of problems heirs may have in paying taxes on inherited properties, but they are also enticed by the high prices acquisition-minded buyers are willing to offer.

Competition may come from sources other than directly competing newspapers. Small town papers have some competition from larger city papers, and all face other media or weeklies and "shoppers" for gaining the advertisers' dollars and the readers' attention.

The Newspaper Preservation Act was supposed to help maintain competition in cities and was passed by Congress to overcome a Supreme Court ruling which had banned such "joint operating agreements."

FOOTNOTES

1. Frank Luther Mott, *American Journalism,* 3d ed. (New York: MacMillan, 1962), p. 635.

2. Raymond B. Nixon and Tae-Youl Hahn, "Concentration of Press Ownership: Comparison of 32 Countries," *Journalism Quarterly* 38:13, Spring 1971.

3. John Tebbel, *The Compact History of the American Newspaper* (New York: Hawthorne Books, Inc., 1963), p. 242.

4. Oswald Garrison Villard, "The Chain Daily," *The Nation,* CXXX, 1930, pp. 595-597, cited by Gerald L. Grotta, "Changes in the Ownership of Daily Newspapers and Selected Performance Characteristics, 1950-1968: An Investigation of Some Economic Implications of Concentration of Ownership" (unpublished doctoral dissertation, Southern Illinois University, 1970).

5. Peter Nichols, "Check It With Bill," rev. of Eric Veblen, *The Manchester Union Leader in New Hampshire Elections* (University Press of New England), *Columbia Journalism Review,* November/December 1975, p. 53.

6. Robert L. Bishop, "The Rush to Chain Ownership," *Columbia Journalism Review,* November/December, 1972, p. 21.

7. "The Big Money Hunts for Independent Newspapers," *Business Week,* February 21, 1977, p. 59.

8. Gerald L. Grotta, *op. cit.*

9. Robert E. Dallos, "Bidding Sends Prices Higher in Newspaper Acquisition Binge," *Los Angeles Times,* January 9, 1977, Sec. VI, p. 5.

10. " A Bitter Family Squabble Put Oakland's *Tribune* on the Block," *Business Week,* February 21, 1977, p. 60.

11. Raymond B. Nixon and Robert L. Jones, "The Content of Non-Competitive vs. Competitive Newspapers," *Journalism Quarterly* 33: 299-314, Summer 1956.

12. Raymond B. Nixon, "Changes in Reader Attitudes Toward Daily Newspapers," *Journalism Quarterly* 31:421-433, Fall 1954.

13. Gerald H. Borstell, "Ownership, Competition and Comment in 20 Small Dailies," *Journalism Quarterly* 33:220-222, Spring 1956.

14. John C. Schwitzer and Elaine Goldman, "Does Newspaper Competition Make a Difference to Readers?" *Journalism Quarterly* 52:706-710, Winter 1975. Galen Rarick and Barrie Hartman, "The Effects of Competition on One Daily Newspaper's Content," *Journalism Quarterly* 43:459-463, Fall 1966.

15. David H. Weaver and L.E. Mullins, "Content and Format Characteristics of Competing Daily Newspapers," *Journalism Quarterly* 52:257-264, Spring 1975.

16. Ronald G. Hicks and James S. Featherstone, "Duplication of Newspaper Content in Contrasting Ownership Situations," *Journalism Quarterly* 55:549-554, Autumn 1978.

17. Royal H. Ray, "Competition in the Newspaper Industry," *Journal of Marketing* 15:444, April 1951.

18. John Henry Langdon, "An Intra Industry Approach to Measuring the Effects of Competition: The Newspaper Industry" (unpublished doctoral dissertation, Cornell University, 1969), p. 2.

19. Guido H. Stempel, III, "Effects on Performance of a Cross-Media Monopoly," *Journalism Monographs,* No. 29 (June 1973), pp. 10-28.

20. Christopher Sterling, "Trends in Daily Newspaper and Broadcasting Ownership, 1922-1970," *Journalism Quarterly* 52:247-256, Summer 1975.

6

The New Technology
of Newspaper Production

Undoubtedly, the most exciting topic in the newspaper industry during the 1970s was the revolution in the technology of newspaper production. As recently as 1973, it was still accurate to call Linotype-produced galleys the "present, but rapidly fading, method of newspaper production." By 1979, the "rapidly fading" description proved to be perhaps conservative, as the large city dailies joined their smaller cousins in adopting the electronic machines which have speeded up the production process and resulted in great cost savings to the industry.

There are actually three areas of the newspaper operation in which new technology has had a visible impact. First, computers have aided in handling many of the business functions of newspapers, including billing, payroll, inventory, and other such bookkeeping services. In this respect, newspapers are using the technology in much the same way as any other large institution.

The second area in which technology has changed the newspaper is in the back-shop operation, that is, the composing room, where the newspaper copy has been transformed from words on paper into type and then plates for the press. It is in this process that newspapers have achieved their most dramatic cost savings in the 1970s.

Finally, technology has greatly changed the nature of the newsroom, classified, and advertising operations through advances in front-end systems, the means for entering information into the system that eventually sets the type. This is the world of VDTs (video display terminals), OCRs (optical character readers or "scanners"), floppy disks, and computer storage. The front-end changes, though not responsible for cost savings or improved productivity, have had a noticeable impact on content of the newspapers and have developed as the natural extension of the requirements of the back-shop technology.

Future developments in the use of electronic technology appear to be in the areas of circulation and marketing, the latter part of the "total market concept" being adopted by many daily newspapers.

This section describes what the new technology is, what it replaced, and why it is so significant in the evolution of the newspaper business.

PRODUCTION TECHNOLOGY—A QUICK HISTORY

Until early in the 19th century, print technology had not progressed much beyond where Gutenberg left it in the 15th century. The basic machinery was a converted wine press, type was set by hand (though metal type did replace wood), and 200 pulls per hour by a husky man was considered good work. The cost of a press and enough type for a small newspaper in the years immediately following the American Revolution was a modest $200 to $800.

It took 350 years beyond Gutenberg for the first major advance in print technology—Frederick Koenig's invention of a steam-driven rotary press. The first one in the United States was at the *New York Daily Advertiser*, installed in 1825 and capable of turning out an astounding 2000 papers per hour. The impact of this breakthrough was great, because it not only decreased the time to produce a four-page paper by 1100%, but it opened the way for multiple cylinder presses, such as Hoe's in 1832, which in turn made possible the mass circulation papers.

By 1847, Hoe was producing a steam-driven rotary press capable of 8000 impressions per hour, and soon thereafter he added as many as ten impression cylinders to bring impressions per hour to 20,000. However, these improvements did have a price. Hoe's big presses cost $20,000 to $25,000, making it increasingly difficult for a small printer to start up a paper in the large cities. In the country, on the other hand, the mid-1800s still found the prevalence of the old hand presses.

The rotary press did stimulate the need for a further innovation, stereotyping. Unlike the old flat-bed presses, where the type was placed flat on the press, the rotary press required the type to be formed around the curved cylinders. In the stereotype process, a mat is molded from the made-up page of type and this in turn can be used to produce a type form which is curved to fit the cylinder. It also means that many stereotypes can be made of any page. Though stereotyping itself was used previously in book printing, the first newspaper press which made use of it did not appear until 1861.

Between Koenig's invention and 1886, however, newspaper production technology improvements consisted of extensions of what already existed: Presses were made faster, rolls of paper replaced sheet fed presses, and cylinders replaced the flat bed. The bottleneck in production remained in the laborious hand setting of type, which limited the size of the newspaper and the speed with which news could be gotten into print.

But in 1886, Ottmar Mergenthaler introduced his Linotype. Instead of setting type one character at a time, at the rate of one newspaper line a minute, the Linotype operator, sitting at a keyboard, would press the desired key and a mold for that character would fall out of a storage box located on the top of the machine. As the letters fell into the designated form, the operator would add spacers and hyphens so that the words formed a line of the desired length. Molten lead was then shot through it to make a metal form of the line. The individual molds were then mechanically returned to the storage box at the top of the machine.

An experienced Linotype operator could set five lines per minute, a significant improvement over the manual method.

As far as metropolitan newspapers were concerned, this was the second and final technological breakthrough in production until the 1960s. Having the Linotypes driven by punch-paper tape cut on separate machines eliminated human slowdown and enabled the Linotypes to work at closer to six lines a minute. Computer-justified and -hyphenated tapes were added in 1960, raising line-casting speed to 14 lines per minute. But by this time, smaller dailies and weeklies were already familiar with the technology which had been perfected and accepted throughout the industry as the central change in the production process: photocomposition, providing the essential interface between the speed of the computer and the capacity of the modern presses. Table 6.1, which summarizes the developments in typesetting since Gutenberg, highlights the decreasing time periods between each innovation.

The new composition process has also provided impetus for a different type of printing process, offset. In this process, a thin photosensitized plate is mounted on the press cylinders, instead of plates with raised letters as in letterpress. Offset had been used by smaller papers since the end of World War II. But a number of problems had to be overcome before it became economically feasible for use on metropolitan dailies. Offset will be discussed further later in this chapter.

NEWSPAPER PRODUCTION—THE OLD WAY

The use of the Linotype to cast hot metal lines, which are then arranged into a page form and sent through the stereotyping process, has almost disappeared from all news-

Table 6.1   Typesetting Speeds for Newspapers

Year	Newspaper Lines Set/Minute	Innovation
1454	1.0	Movable type
1886	4.9	Linotype
1932	5.6	Punch-paper tape driven Linotype
1960	14.0	Computer-hyphenated & justified paper tape driving Linotype
1964	80.0	Photocomposition
1966	1,800.0	RCA typesetter
1967	15,000.0	CBS-Mergenthaler Linotron for specialized publications

N.B.   The fastest typesetters in regular use by daily newspapers in 1978 were machines utilizing cathode ray tubes at 4,000-5,000 lines per minute.

Source: Ben H. Bagdikian, *The Information Machines* (New York: Harper and Row, Harper Torchbooks, 1971), p. 95. Bagdikian derived this information from William D. Rinehart, "Technological Developments in Newspaper Printing," American Newspaper Publishers Association Research Institute, Inc., 1967.

paper operations, with the exception perhaps of a few of the largest papers which are in the process of doing away with the last of their old machinery. A survey by the American Newspaper Publishers Association found that by the end of 1975, 94 percent of its members' plants used photocomposition for all or some of their type. The Mergenthaler Linotype Co., the primary supplier of the hot metal machines, stopped producing them in the United States by 1970 and sells none to newspapers today.

The creation of a newspaper page ready for printing, utilizing the hot metal and obsolete production method, is the subject of Figure 6.1. Note in the following description that it is highly labor intensive, often redundant, cumbersome, and error-prone.

1. Reporters, wire service and syndicated features, classified ad takers, and display advertising salespersons all create copy on paper. This copy is generally hand-carried or mechanically transported to copy editors and ad managers for corrections, changes, and headlines. They send finished copy to the composing room.

2. A routing desk in the composing room farms out pieces of the copy to various teletypesetter operators, often with several working on pieces of the same story or ad. Headlines are similarly routed.

3. The operators punch the stories on typewriter keyboards which feed into a computer that produces a punch-paper tape which includes coded instructions for hyphenation and justification.

4. The paper tape is then fed into a mini-computer attached to the Linotype, causing the machine to operate in much the same way as a scroll controlling a player piano. This hybrid of automechanical devices results in a casting speed of about 14 lines per minute.

5. The various parts of the story or ad now set in metal slugs must now be assembled in the proper order and taken to the proof press, where a proof is taken from the galley. The type is sent to a storage area while the proof is corrected.

6. Proofreaders must carefully read each line and make correction notations. The corrected proof is returned to the composing room, where lines with errors are manually recast. These are sent, along with the proof, to the storage area where a composer must pull out the bad lines and substitute the corrected ones. The juggled or repeated lines which the reader of the paper often finds result from the wrong line being tossed out or the new line being put in the wrong place at this stage. The type, as set in metal, is a mirror image of the actual characters, making error all the more likely. If time permits, a new proof is pulled and sent through a repeat process.

7. The corrected galleys of type are then sent to make-up, where they are assembled, along with photographs, which have been screened, and other art work which have

Figure 6.1   The Old Newspaper Production Process

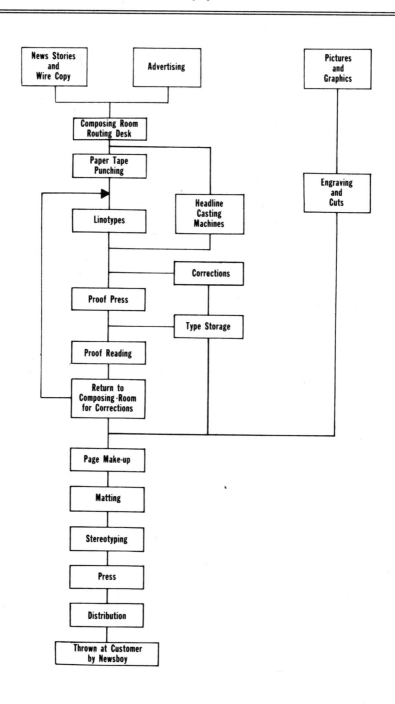

been converted into zinc cuts. Copy and art work, plus advertisements, are assembled into page forms. Making everything fit exactly is often a matter of trial and error, with lead spacers added to make columns of type longer, or with parts of stories pulled or pictures cut down to make it all fit. Typically, composing room personnel and the make-up editor, not the news or department editors, make the decision on what is cut. Advertisements, of course, cannot be trimmed. When everything fits, the page form is locked up so nothing falls out when it is moved. A standard size page, almost all lead, is quite heavy, which in part accounts for the large-sized men who have been compositors.

A proof is made of the entire page to make sure that pictures and captions, headlines and stories go together.

8.   The finished page is now matted. A wet, thick piece of artboard is placed over the metal page and inserted into a machine which exerts great pressure on the mat, resulting in a cardboard impression of the raised characters and dots of the pictures on the mat.

9.   The mat is curved and dried, making it ready for the stereotype machine. Molten lead is injected at high pressure into the mat. On large papers where several press lines print the newspaper at once, multiple lead plates are made from the mat for each page. The resulting lead plates, each of which weighs about 40 pounds, are properly curved to fit the cylinders of the press.

10.   The stereotype plates are attached to the cylinders of a letterpress, which is then ready to run at a speed of up to 60,000 to 70,000 papers an hour, with the relief of the plate making an impression with each revolution of the cylinder.

THE NEW TECHNOLOGY

Cleaner, quieter, more efficient, and less costly are the attributes of the new technology now prevalent in the newsrooms and back-shops of the nation's newspapers. All around the country, the clanging of the hot metal machines within the dark caverns of composing rooms has been replaced by carpeted rooms with two or three phototype-setters, doing for printing today what Gutenberg did 500 years ago—revolutionizing a slow and tedious production process. Gone are the noise and dirt, the heat of molten lead, and the odor of lead vapor. In their place are artists' make-up tables in quiet, brightly lit, and carpeted rooms; cool, breathable air; fewer and less highly skilled workers; and substantially higher productivity. But the change has been accompanied by some union and human relations problems, rapid technological obsolescence, and a general dose of future shock.

The New Hardware

In the back shop, the Linotype and stereotype machines have been replaced at most newspapers by phototypesetters and cameras and new plate-making equipment. The heart of the operation is the phototypesetter, a compact device that projects and prints the images of letters, numbers, and related characters on photographic paper at up to 5000 newspaper lines per minute. More typically, the phototypesetters are designed to produce 60 to 500 hyphenated and justified lines per minute, with machines for large newspapers, such as Mergenthaler's Linotron 606, rated at 1850 11-pica lines of eight point type per minute. Thus, the phototypesetter, controlled either by a small internal computer or a larger central processing unit, has increased typesetting speed to four to 123 times faster than the punch-paper tape-fed Linotypes—and with fewer errors as well.

With machines which can set type so quickly, it is essential to get the copy into the processing system rapidly. This is accomplished with input through an optical character reader (OCR) or video display terminal (VDT). An OCR is a device that uses light rays to scan a printed page and convert the typed characters or bar codes into electronic impulses. This electronic language can be stored in one of a variety of ways, including in computer memory. It is then processed into hyphenated and justified form by photocomposition.

OCR copy must be more carefully and cleanly prepared than in the old process, because the scanners are very susceptible to stray marks. Although routine corrections can be made on the paper with relative ease, major changes or additions may require retyping the copy, unless editing is done on a VDT. OCR input speeds vary, depending on the sophistication of the machine—as fast as 4000 words per minute with an Autologic, Inc. OCR, but more typically 225 to 1000 words per minute, with predicted errors of .01 percent to .004 percent (or 2.5 to 1 error per 25,000 characters).

Used for original input as well as editing, the VDT has rapidly become the most popular input device for newsrooms. The VDT consists of a television-like display tube, actually a cathode ray tube (CRT). Input is by means of a typewriter keyboard. In using the VDT, the reporter or ad taker effectively substitutes the video display for paper. The copy is typed out on the keyboard and the results appear on the screen. Some terminals have elaborate function keys which allow editors to make all the corrections they formerly made with a pen. Reporters' terminals have less editing capability.

As with the OCR, output from the VDTs can be onto a punch-paper tape or to floppy disk for storage. At more sophisticated systems, output from either system goes directly to storage in a central computer or mini-computer for later editing or typesetting.

Figure 6.2 provides a simplified graphic representation of a typical production process using the new technology.

1. Input is through OCR or VDT. Editors or ad managers call up a stored story or advertisement on a VDT and make appropriate corrections, add a headline, specify type style and size, and either send the story to be set on the phototypesetter, stored for later use, or spiked—killed—and thus purged from the storage queue. All this is through code instructions given on the VDT.

2. The computer and phototypesetter become the composing room. The two may be separate units, such as the high speed APS line from Autologic, the large Mergenthaler

Figure 6.2   The Current Newspaper Production Process

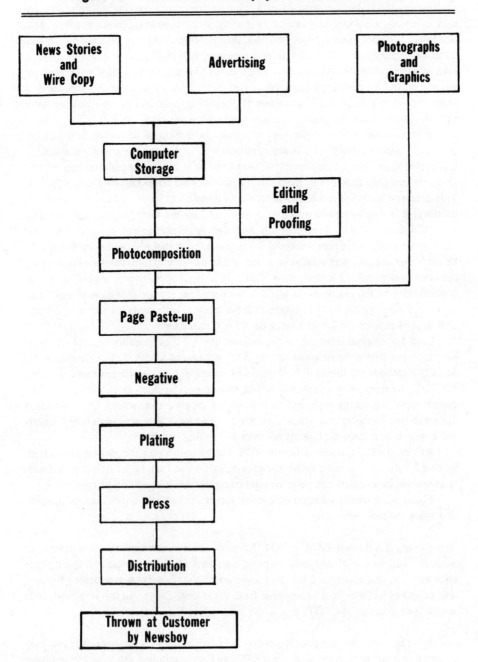

Linotrons, or the systems from Digital Equipment Corporation (DEC). Smaller papers can use typesetters with internal mini-computers for hyphenation and justification, such as those from Compugraphic or Mergenthaler's V.I.P. line. Input can be directly from a separate computer, from paper tape, from computer-prepared magnetic tape, or directly from a keyboard attached to the typesetter, such as Compugraphic's Compuwriter.

Since the photocomposition machines can create columns of varying widths and of mixed type styles and sizes (as large as 72 points), they have to a large extent eliminated the problem of bringing together separate batches of type and headlines. Both headline and body copy are typeset on a single galley.

Furthermore, since they are nearly error-proof, almost all mistakes are human. So if errors can be eliminated during the editing phase, they can be virtually eliminated by the time the type is set, thus ending the need for the cumbersome proofreading of galleys and making corrections after typesetting.*

3.   The photocomposed columns go to make-up, where they are pasted onto a page the size of the full newspaper page. Photocomposed advertisements, art work, and glossy photographs are also pasted onto the page, thus eliminating the unwieldy metal galleys and engravings. This pasted-up page looks and reads much the same as will the final printed page.

4.   The mat molding process is replaced by the camera room. Here, a photograph is taken of the whole page. The resulting negative is sent to plate-making.

5.   To make an offset plate, the negative is sandwiched between glass and a thin photosensitive metal plate. The plate is exposed to bright light and developed by rubbing it with a chemical solution. The result is a plate with two areas: those which were exposed to light, i.e., wherever there was a letter or character or dot, and the rest of the plate, which remains unchanged.

Some papers, still using their old letterpress presses, use a similar process, but instead produce a lightweight plate, coated with a layer of photosensitive plastic. The exposure to the negative results in a raised surface or relief for the printed area, so the end product can function much as a stereotype plate. Many of the largest newspapers, which need multiple copies of each page, are using the negative to make an engraved plate and then stereotypes, as in the old process.

6.   The plastic relief plates or stereotypes are attached to the cylinders of a letterpress and run traditionally. The offset plates are mounted on the cylinders of an offset

---

* The elimination of the proofreader is one area in which newspapers have been able to cut expenses as a result of the new technology. It also means that editors and reporters can no longer blame the compositors for "typos." Charles Hauser, executive editor of the Providence (R.I.) *Journal* and *Bulletin* suggests that typos should now be called "newsos" to indicate the new locus of responsibility.

press. Unlike the letterpress, in which the plate prints directly onto the paper, the offset plate is immersed in the oil-based ink and sprayed with a water mist as it revolves. Only areas which were exposed pick up the ink. The ink-coated areas are transferred to a rubber-blanketed cylinder which in turn makes the actual contact with the paper, thus offsetting the ink impression to the paper.

FUNCTIONS OF THE TOTAL PRODUCTION SYSTEM

The new front-end and production systems have basically had the primary goal of permitting the original keystroke to be captured electronically, whatever its source or purpose. That is, instead of everything first having to be typed or written on paper, then retyped for the line casting machines, the original entry of the reporter, editor, classified ad taker, or display ad designer becomes the basis for setting the type. The computer serves as both an intermediary and a processor, storing information as well as hyphenating and justifying it for photocomposition. Moreover, the information so stored can be sorted and arranged by the computer, as in collecting classified advertisements into categories. At the same time, billing and accounting procedures can use the information initially entered by an ad taker.

The nature of the total system varies according to the size and needs of each individual newspaper. Hardware has been developed which permits even small dailies to economically share in the electronic benefits. But all the systems have the same goal of capturing and building from the initial keystroke.

A system is a series of people and devices arranged to work together in a highly predictable pattern leading to the accomplishment of a common objective. Although newspaper production has always been a system in this sense, the new technology makes two significant changes. First, it increases the emphasis on devices, thus greatly eliminating the chance for human error. Secondly, it makes the newspaper product more reliable, so rather than worrying about just getting the paper out on deadline, greater attention can be given to uniformity of the day-to-day product and, more importantly, the accuracy of the daily news content.

Hardware

A newspaper production or front-end system consists of both hardware and software aspects. The former includes the actual machinery and electronics—the machines. The latter is the programming or instructions which make the machines work in a desired manner. For the most part, the state-of-the-art in hardware exceeds the capabilities of the software. For example, Mergenthaler Linotype Co. showed a 505TC-100 photocomposition machine at an industry trade show in June 1973 capable of setting a full 100 pica-wide newspaper page, eliminating the usual paste-up galleys. But the software to allow a newspaper make-up editor to give a computer instructions for full page make up was still in the prototype stage in 1979.

The basic hardware components of newspaper systems are:

Input Devices
- Optical character readers (OCRs) (including bar code readers)
- Video display terminals (VDTs)
- On-line (to a computer) keyboards
- Off-line keyboards (for floppy disk or paper tape)

Storage Devices
- Central computers (CPUs)
- Floppy disks
- Punch-paper tapes
- Distributive units (mini-computers)

Processing Devices
- Central computers
- Mini-computers

Editing and Make-up Devices
- Video display terminals
- Electronic layout boards

Output Devices
- Phototypesetters and CRT typesetters
- On-line typewriters
- Line printers

At some large newspapers, a single control computer is being replaced by a number of mini-computers, each a "distribution unit" or "input processing module." This procedure allows many input devices to be built into the system, without slowing down access time for each user and thus eliminating the dependence on a single expensive computer which, should it break down, could slow or stop the entire newspaper operation.

The System at Work—A Generalized Case
The actual system depends on the unique needs of each newspaper. What follows is a synthesis of how a total system might work at a typical metropolitan newspaper. A graphic representation of the components of this system is illustrated by Figure 6.3.

- *Editorial.* A reporter writes a story at a keyboard, but instead of the characters appearing on a piece of paper, they appear on a CRT. If there are any typing errors or if the reporter wants to add or delete some words or sentences, keys on the keyboard permit the changes without affecting the rest of the story. The reporter will also add some other

Figure 6.3   An Electronic Copy Processing System

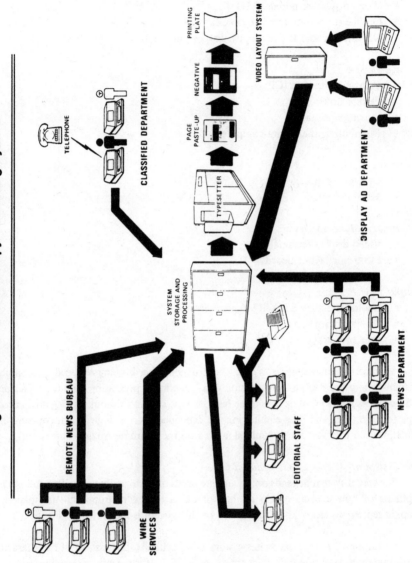

simple information, such as whether it is local news, sports, a Sunday feature, or whatever, all or part of her or his name, and a one- or two-word title for the story. If close to deadline, the writer can send each screen-sized take to computer storage so that an editor can begin the next step. Otherwise, when the reporter is satisfied with the story, a single key command puts the story in an appropriate computer queue or electronic storage bin.

A desk editor then has available a list of all the stories waiting in each queue, such as sports, local news, national news, business, etc. The editor accesses these through a simple request on his or her VDT and the first page appears on the screen, along with a notification of how many more pages are stored. Editors can then scroll the story on their screens backwards or forwards, using keyboard commands to make normal editing changes.

Next, the general editor may call the edited story to the screen of his VDT. Many newer programs will automatically compute the story length and display the hyphenated and justified form. The editor adds a headline via the keyboard, as well as a designation as to where the story should appear in the paper.

The story is then directed, via keyboard instructions, to a typesetting queue where it is ready to be set for production. The only major modification of this process is where the initial story is typed by the reporter on an electric typewriter, with the resulting paper read into the system by an OCR. This is the process used at the *Atlanta Journal* and *Constitution*, among others. But once in memory, editing is carried out the same as if entered on a VDT.

Most syndicated features now arrive at the newspaper in OCR-readable format. Stories from the Associated Press and United Press International are processed by the wire services in a similar manner at their many bureaus, but the teletype machine has been replaced by direct high- and low-speed transmission from the wire services' own large computers to the wire service queue in the computer at the subscriber newspaper. Most newspapers have included the capability of obtaining a hard-copy printout of anything stored in the computer on a high-speed (200 lines per minute) line printer.

Articles from reporters in remote bureaus, previously transmitted by the old teletype, may now be sent one of three ways. The *Detroit News* uses OCR in each bureau to read in stories over telephone lines to the newspaper's computer. One problem with this approach is that reporters can't tell if there were any minor scrambles in the transmission. The *Miami Herald,* a Knight-Ridder paper, is one that has VDTs in the bureau, making it literally an extension of the main newsroom. A third alternative is to use a Teleram terminal, a mini-VDT which stores the reporter's story on a cassette tape which can then be transmitted over a telephone hook-up at 1000 words per minute to the computer just like a wire service story. The *Austin* (Tex.) *American-Statesman* is using this approach. The Teleram is particularly attractive because it is a portable unit and can thus be carried to the scene of breaking news or sporting events.

• *Display advertising.* As with editorial copy, display advertising copy is entered into the system through OCR, VDT, or perhaps direct keyboarding. Actual ads can now be made up on the forerunner of the device which will eventually be used to make-up all pages, including editorial. Using a CAM—composition and make-up terminal—the make-up artist calls up copy on a large CRT screen (200 square inches in the case of the popular Raycomp-100 and Raycomp II, or 23 inches round for the Camex 135). The operator also has a make-up easel which represents the advertising space and an electronic pen which is connected to the unit. Thus, while the board represents the space of advertisement, the actual copy is displayed on the VDT. By touching the stylus to the board, the operator can pick up copy displayed on the VDT and move it around to the correct position for the ad. The pen can also be used to draw in representations of eventual graphics. The operator also specifies type size and style, which is generally reflected on the VDT representation.

  • *Classified advertising.* The ad taker, sitting at a VDT, accepts a caller's phone-in ad, typing it out as dictated by the caller, and seeing it displayed on the screen. When the copy is completed, a simple instruction displays the copy in justified and hyphenated form, along with actual linage and charges for the operator to give the customer on the phone. All ads are then stored by the computer, along with ads being repeated from other days. The system automatically deletes an ad after its predesignated final run. Existing ads may be called up on the VDT for modification, or instructions may be given for that ad to be skipped on certain days. The system allows late corrections or changes to be called in, and these modifications are made as easily as when the ad was first placed. Ad copy may alternatively be entered by the ad taker typing copy on OCR forms, but with subsequent changes made on VDTs.

  The system can be designed to provide an immediate credit check, in the case of VDT entry, or a delayed credit check if OCR entered. In the case of the former, the operator would be able to tell a caller immediately if there were an outstanding balance for previous ads or the current status of a contract account.

  Using key words or text, the computer sorts the ads by classification, with full newspaper columns, justified both horizontally and vertically, generated by the phototypesetter. Reports for management on total linage or expiring ad compilations can be accessed on the VDT or printed out on a line printer.

  • *Accounting.* As classified and display ads are entered into the system, information regarding invoices and billing goes into the computer. Information on ad cancellations, space charges (including premiums for special location or discounts), contract fulfillment data, and the like can be stored and generated for management use in hard copy or for VDT access. Thus, accounts may be updated as they are changing in real time. Accounts can be posted daily and advertisers who use several names can be readily billed under a master contract. All information is added at the time the ad is entered, thereby reducing paperwork and bookkeeping. The new system thus links with previous automated accounting systems by capturing the original keystrokes in advertising production.

Systems for Smaller Papers

  In the early stages of the technological change at newspapers, the complete system as described above was economically feasible only for medium- and large-sized dailies. By

1976, low priced mini-processors, floppy disks (compact plastic storage devices which have reduced reliance on punch-paper tape), and less sophisticated but less expensive VDT and OCR units, either controlled by standardized software packages or hard-wired, have brought to the small daily papers many of the same basic features that the big city papers can enjoy.

THE CONFIGURATION OF LARGE PRODUCTION SYSTEMS

One of the bottlenecks in developing full-scale systems for large newspapers with the volume of material they must process each day has been the limitations on the storage capability and real-time access burdens put on the big central processors which were required to allow the many VDT terminals a metropolitan newspaper required. By 1976, however, manufacturers had developed distribution systems which handle large numbers of terminals.

Thus, instead of a single large computer, with all its programming problems and the need for another similar, expensive computer for back-up, the new systems depend on small computers which serve a cluster of terminals—editorial, classified, or display ad—which are in turn tied into a large data base. This approach minimizes the demands on any single computer and greatly reduces the difficulty if any single computer goes down when it is needed, since the mini-computers serve as back-up for one another.

This is the essence of the front-end system ordered by Knight-Ridder's Philadelphia Newspapers, Inc., publishers of the *Philadelphia Inquirer* and *Daily News.* This editorial-only system, provided by System Development Corporation (SDC), has 164 VDTs connected to six 64K Hewlett Packard mini-computers and 35 microprocessors. The video terminals, moreover, are intelligent, meaning that they have the storage and control capability to perform most writing and editing functions virtually instantaneously, with no need to access the central processing unit (CPU). When the CPU must be relied on for these functions, the reaction time can be almost three seconds.

Perhaps the most ambitious electronic system using this approach is the one announced for the *New York News*, the largest daily circulation newspaper in the United States. Figure 6.4 shows the configuration of 239 VDTs with 12 mini-computers (here called "input processing modules"). In addition, two processing modules are to be reserved for page make-up terminals and control of the phototypesetters. The entire system feeds into and draws from an 80-megabyte (80 million character) random access disk storage file. In using such a decentralized distribution system, data will be able to be transferred between input modules and the data base at 40,000 characters per second. Hyphenation and justification, controlled at each of the mini-computers, is accomplished at a rate of 2000 characters per second. Although implementation was begun in 1977, by early 1980 all parts of the system were still not operational.

The *Atlanta Journal* and *Constitution,* on the other hand, is an example of newspapers which rely on control from a large computer, a Tal Star T-1000. The Atlanta papers use OCR input for most copy, which routes the material to a T-4000. After editing,

Figure 6.4   Proposed New York News/Mergenthaler Mini-Processing Computer System

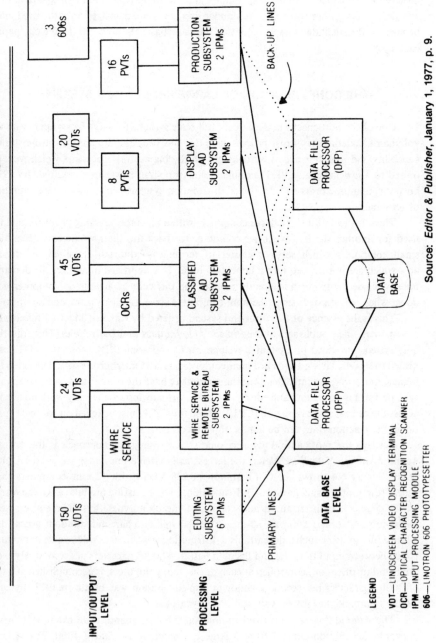

Source: *Editor & Publisher*, January 1, 1977, p. 9.

LEGEND

VDT—LINOSCREEN VIDEO DISPLAY TERMINAL
OCR—OPTICAL CHARACTER RECOGNITION SCANNER
IPM—INPUT PROCESSING MODULE
606—LINOTRON 606 PHOTOTYPESETTER

the story is sent to the T-1000, which drives the Autologic APS-4 phototypesetters. Atlanta management claimed to be satisfied with this approach, but it does place a greater burden on a single system and results in a response time for editors at their VDTs of two to three seconds during periods of heavy usage.

Converting from Old to New Systems

The transition from the Linotypes and hot metal to electronics and photocomposition has come to the industry with startling speed—perhaps to make up for the relatively slow rate of change chronicled at the beginning of this chapter. In 1973, a Knowledge Industry Publications, Inc. study of newspaper technology found that "the totally computer-oriented, cold-type newspaper system was not fully operational anywhere" in the United States. Within five years, major newspapers such as the *Chicago Sun-Times* and *Daily News* and the *Baltimore Sun,* medium-sized papers, such as the *Atlantic City Press,* and small ones—like the *Pittsburg* (Kan.) *Sun* had complete front-end systems operational.

Still other papers are in the midst of converting. The first step for many large papers was to move to cold type production of classified and display advertising, using small, special purpose components such as the Harris 2500 or Raycomp-100 make-up terminals and DEC PDP/8 computers. Editorial front-end systems need involve little more than converting to OCR input, with punch-paper tape output fed into a phototypesetter, such as the operation at Richmond Newspapers, Inc. This installation, which represented the state of the art in 1973, had no central data base or distribution system, but simply ran typewriter-corrected copy through scanners to paper tape, then into Photon phototypesetters.

By the end of the 1970s, newspaper companies were ordering complete systems, such as the Harris systems ordered in 1976 by *The New York Times* and *Washington Post,* the Mergenthaler system specified by the *New York News,* or the SDC system installed at the Philadelphia newspapers. The rapidity of the changeover can be seen in Table 6.2, which summarizes the inventory of hardware in use at daily newspapers. The number of phototypesetters had increased 179 percent in the 1971 to 1978 period, as the number of hot metal line casters fell by 88 percent. OCR and VDT devices barely existed for newspapers in 1971.

PRESSES AND PLATES

Despite all the new electronics on the front-end, however, many newspapers have experienced some difficulty in adapting the finished product—a pasted-up newspaper page—to the traditional method of printing, the letterpress. This is the same basic design which has been around since Hoe married the rotary press to the stereotyping process in the mid-19th century. The making of a stereotype was based on having the original page made from metal with raised characters, from which the mats were molded and molten metal injected to form the curved stereotype plates.

Table 6.2   Trends in Equipment at Daily Newspapers, 1971 to 1978

	Number in Use			Percent Change 1971-78
Device	1978	1975	1971	
Computers	1,982	971	632	214%
Offset Editions (M.& E.)	816	544	267	206
Photo-or CRT Typesetters	3,090	2,898	1,107	179
Direct or Pattern Plate Plants[a]	379	286	31	1,123
Video Display Terminals	15,841	3,896	155	10,120
Optical Character Reader Units	712	538	16	4,350
Typewriters for OCR Input	22,237	18,778	N.A.	—
Hot Metal Linecasters (Manual or TTS)	1,158	3,451	9,465	− 88
Total Plants Reporting	1,069	942	869	23
Total Newspapers Represented	1,321	1,128	1,052	25

[a] Includes direct lithography.

N.A. Not Available.

Source: "Specification Data," 1971, 1975, 1978, eds. R. I. Bulletin, (Easton, Pa.: American Newspaper Publishers Association Research Institute).

The photocomposition process, on the other hand, results in a flat, two-dimensional prototype of the finished page. It thus lends itself to the offset printing process.

But newspaper presses, the single most expensive piece of equipment the publisher has, have long lives—25 to 40 years is typical. Replacing a five- or ten-year old letterpress with an offset press is not to be lightly considered. In 1972, the Graphic Systems Division of Rockwell International estimated that a new offset press for a 50,000 to 100,000 circulation daily newspaper would cost $1.2 million. The 320,000 circulation St. Louis Post-Dispatch spent $12 million for new offset presses in 1973, while the Philadelphia Inquirer and Daily News spent a reported $15 million for nine new letterpresses in 1972. Even a 10,000 circulation daily would have spent $75,000 for an offset press in 1972. By 1976, the cost of new presses had increased an estimated 40 to 50 percent and the escalation continued at about 10 percent annually to 1979.

What this means is that those newspapers with newer letterpress units had to have some way of getting the benefits of the photocomposition process, yet still use the letterpress, at least until it wore out, which would be many years.

Plate Alternatives
Several technological compromises have been worked out with the development of the plastic shallow relief plate, the improved performance of direct lithography, plastic, zinc, and magnesium pattern plates, and plastic injection molding, all of which foster the interface of the new cold type production with the old letterpress.

The first breakthrough came in 1969 with the shallow relief plastic plates or thin metal plates. Developed as a joint research venture of the American Newspaper Publishers Association Research Institute and several private companies, the plate has been marketed by W.R. Grace Company's Letterflex, Hercules' Merigraph, Dyna-Flex, and the most successful, the NAPP plastic plate, among others. The distinguishing characteristic of all these is that they permit the full use of cold type photocomposition and use the final page paste-up to produce a negative, just as in the offset process. But the negative is then used to produce a lightweight plate with a relief similar to the stereotype plate.

Typical of the plastic plates is the NAPP system, the result of a joint venture between Lee Enterprises, Inc., a small newspaper chain based in Davenport, Iowa, and Nippon Paint Co., Japan. The plate is an aluminum-backed polymer coated combination. When designed to be used for direct printing, the polymer coating is .020 inch thick on a .010 aluminum backing, and thus the depth of the relief is .020. The plate can also be used as a pattern plate. In this mode, the plate replaces the hot lead page in the stereotype process. A mat is rolled from the pattern plate.

In either case, the process works the same way: A plate is removed from its sealed package and placed in an exposure unit beneath the page negative which has been made from the newspaper page paste-up. After a 45- to 70-second exposure, it is put through a wash-out unit which uses water and a small amount of biodegradable defoaming agent to remove the non-exposed polymer areas. The plate is then dried and polymerization is completed, leaving a raised printing surface. The plate is then curved. If it is being used to print directly, it must be locked onto a saddle which is mounted on the press' cylinder, since the press was designed for a thick, 40-pound stereotype, instead of this thin plate.

The advantages of using a direct printing plate system are:

1. It permits benefits of all the cost savings of photocomposition.
2. It preserves the publisher's investment in letterpress equipment.
3. It is easier to handle: a few ounces compared to the 40-pound plate.

There are some drawbacks, however:

• *Plate costs.* In stereotyping, once the mat is molded, duplicate plates for multiple press lines can be made for about six cents each, after the first plate cost of $.66 (plus engraving costs). Shallow relief plates cost $2.00 to $2.50 depending on manufacturer, volume, and depth of relief desired.

• *Equipment expense.* The cost of the processing equipment is relatively modest, but a capital outlay nonetheless. The expense varies depending on the speed and volume needs of the newspaper, and thus may range from $20,000 plus installation for the manual Dyna-Flex system to $250,000 for an EOCOM Laserite. In addition, there is the investment in the saddles needed to adapt these plates to existing press cylinders. Richmond Newspapers, Inc. spent a reported $200,000 on saddles for presses which handle a maximum run of 200,000 Sunday papers. There are additional costs which are frequently necessary to improve the mechanical tolerances of the presses to achieve acceptable print quality from these plates.

• *Time*. The time to produce the first copy of a page from a stereotype mat is about nine minutes, but once the mat is made, duplicate pages needed for second or third press lines take one minute each. The EOCOM Laserite takes three minutes per page, the Letterflex 135, four minutes, the Dyna-Flex, 6.5 minutes. Thus, for small papers with only a single press line, the direct process may be quicker. For papers which need multi-page capability, it is still slower than stereotype.

• *Printing quality*. This is still an area of considerable disagreement among production people. The shallow relief plates have produced uneven results. Tests conducted by the American Newspaper Publishers Association Research Institute (ANPA/RI) and various newspapers report on quality of an acceptable level, especially with the NAPP plate which has over half the market for direct plastic plates. Leon Hooper, in charge of plate production at the *Springfield* (Mo.) *News-Leader* rated the results of NAPP "much better than hot-metal stereo" and generally "excellent." The *Cincinnati Enquirer* reported that it was "pleased" with NAPP as a direct plate. But some executives of the Ottaway chain bemoan the "poor quality of converted letterpress," although it finds that the NAPP plate is the best. The ANPA/RI summed up the responses to its investigations of Letterflex and NAPP installations by emphasizing that "careful quality control practices in all stages leading up to (and including) the preparation and use of photo-imaged letterpress plates" are the key to successful use of these processes. Alternatives to printing with shallow relief plates are:

Pattern plates. Pattern plate is the term for a plastic or metal plate which is used to produce a mat for production of a stereotype plate. Thus, instead of rolling a mat from a hot metal page, the mat is made from a plate produced through the photocomposition process. The process of making a pattern plate is identical to making a shallow relief plate, but since a mat must be made and then a stereotype, the plate must have a deeper relief than a direct printing plate to insure acceptable printing quality.

Thus, by coating their plate with a thicker layer of photopolymer, NAPP, Letterflex, Merigraph, and others can be used as a pattern plate. Dow Chemical and Ball Metal Company are two of several firms which market an all-metal plate process, using photoengraving to produce magnesium (in the case of Dow) or zinc (Ball Metal) plates which can be used for direct printing but are usually used as pattern plates.

The use of pattern plates to produce conventional stereotype plates overcomes several of the disadvantages of the direct printing approach, while retaining the primary objective of joining photocomposition to existing letterpress. For example, a major metropolitan newspaper needs many plates of each page for its many press lines. The *Los Angeles Times* sometimes makes 18 to 20 plates per page and *The New York Times* uses an average of 3000 plates per day. If printing direct from shallow relief plates, the cost, at a minimum $2.00 per plate, would be $6000 per day for *The New York Times* and $58,000 per week for *The Los Angeles Times,* for plates alone.

The material cost for a pattern plate is about $3.00, and for stereotype plates made from these about six cents each. So *The New York Times,* for example, requiring 200 original pages (counting remakes of some pages for different editions), would only need 200 pattern plates, at $600, plus 2800 stereotypes, at $168, or a total of $768—a materials savings of $5232 per day. (This calculation ignores labor expense, which in this example is considered to be equal for both processes.)

Among the large newspapers using a pattern plate, either plastic or metal, are *The Houston Post* and *Newsday* (both use NAPP plates), and *The Boston Globe* and *Detroit Free Press.*

The Los Angeles Times, unsatisfied with the costs of any of the systems on the market, has developed its own recyclable plastic plate. The process involves taking the negative made from the photocomposed page and making a magnesium engraving from it. A mat is rolled from the engraving. However, instead of using the mat to make a metal stereotype, it is placed into an injection molding machine and polypropylene plastic is forced into the mat. The result, 20 seconds later, is a plastic plate .10 inch thick, with a relief of .040 inch. The cost of the material for a single plastic plate is about 30 cents, but since the plastic can be recycled 18 to 24 times, the average cost is under two cents. The *Times* feels the new system not only reduces plate costs, but "upgrades quality."

Overall, the *Times* estimated that its own costs per plate have dropped from $1.86 for lead, to 39 cents, including materials and labor. Estimated annual savings on the complete system will be $900,000 in materials and labor. However, capital equipment costs are substantial, with a single line costing an estimated $205,000, a second line an additional $165,000, plus $170 for each aluminum saddle.*

Direct lithography. In the direct lithography process, a letterpress is modified to print directly onto newsprint from offset plates. The page negative is exposed to the plate, except it is burned in reverse, with the emulsion side of the negative up. The resulting plate has mirror image characters (unlike a regular offset plate, which is a readable facsimile of the page paste-up). The key to the process is dampers which control the amount of water flow onto the plates. Thus, an existing letterpress must be converted by adding water to the press units, as well as saddles to the cylinders. As in offset, the oil-based ink and water is passed over the plates, but instead of printing onto a blanket, the plate prints directly onto the paper. The first installations were at relatively small newspapers, such as the 16,000 circulation *Oil City* (Pa.) *Derrick* and the *Trenton* (N.J.) *Trentonian.* The largest installation at the end of 1976 was the *Kansas City Star* and *Times,* with over 300,000 daily circulation.

The *Star* changed to DiLitho in 1976 primarily through a process of elimination of alternatives, but based on a 100 percent conversion to cold type. Besides enabling the paper to take full advantage of photocomposition and keep their letterpress equipment, executives expect that ink consumption will be down and the life of the press will be increased. They have also gotten rid of the heat and acid from the engraving and stereo departments.

* The *Times* spent about $225,000 for 1500 saddles.

The cost of converting to DiLitho is about $25,000 per press unit, or about $1.1 million for a paper with the 45 press units converted at Kansas City. This is considerably higher than the cost of equipment and saddles for the shallow relief plate alternative. On the other hand, once the modifications are made, the newspaper can use offset plates, which cost about 80 cents each, considerably less than the $2.00 or more for the direct printing plates. Nor is the newspaper tied to a single supplier, as is the user of one of the plastic plate systems. Furthermore, if a plant gradually wants to convert to offset printing, DiLitho is very compatible, so the newspaper can run both systems during the changeover with little confusion.

There are several criticisms of the DiLitho system, however. First and most important, paper waste is considerably higher than with conventional letterpress—it generally runs closer to the three to four percent waste common to offset than the one percent of letterpress. At the *Star* it was running 2.5 percent to three percent. Second, it takes considerable training to make a good letterpress operator into an accomplished DiLitho pressman. Kansas City held training classes for press operators, one hour per shift each week. Third, there are some questions about press maintenance, since direct lithography involves adding a water input to a press which was not designed to have water. Finally, obtaining quality color is a problem, since the ink/water balance must be set separately for each color and many letterpress color inks emulsify and bleed in water. Kansas City had to limit its use of editorial color to concentrate on advertising color.

Nonetheless, DiLitho is becoming an increasingly popular conversion, in part because of its acceptance at the Kansas City newspapers. An ANPA/RI production specialist expects that the added newsprint waste will be compensated for by the plate savings. Quality approaches that of offset and is superior to letterpress, especially with color. In 1976, 53 newspaper plants had one or more DiLitho units and the *Boston Globe*, after a trial, decided to make the conversion. Not only are seven press manufacturers offering conversion kits, but a Japanese manufacturer has put on the market a new, built-from-scratch DiLitho press. The process may become the primary alternative for large circulation newspapers that desire improved quality without writing off their letterpress investment.

The Switch to Offset

Letterpress has been the printing mechanism of record because of its long marriage with the hot metal typesetting process. The offset press, on the other hand, has been in use for daily newspapers since 1961, and its development has closely paralleled the development of photocomposition. By the end of 1978, however, 1283 daily newspapers, out of 1778, were printed on offset. For the most part, these are smaller papers, with the *St. Louis Post-Dispatch* (circulation 263,994) the largest circulation daily printed totally offset at the beginning of 1977. (The *Wall Street Journal* printed more of its papers on offset, but at several separate printing facilities around the country.)

Table 6.3, showing the number of offset-printed newspapers and the percentage of circulation they account for, indicates a steady increase in the number of offset newspapers. Moreover, while the number increased by 73.1 percent from 1971 to 1978, the proportion of total circulation these newspapers accounted for more than doubled, indicating

**Table 6.3   Growth in the Number of Offset Printed Daily Newspapers,
1971 to 1978**

Year	Offset Newspapers	Total Daily Newspapers	Offset as % of Total	Circulation of Offset Printed Papers as % of Total Circulation
1971	741	1,748	42.4%	14.0%
1972	868	1,749	49.6	18.8
1974	1,110	1,774	62.6	27.1
1976	1,217	1,779	68.4	29.8
1978	1,283	1,778	72.2	36.6

Source: 1971, 1972, 1976 and 1978: ANPA/RI, "Daily Newspapers Printed by Offset,"
annual; 1974: *Editor & Publisher.*
Figures by *Editor & Publisher* are taken from ANPA/RI computations. Until 1974,
ANPA/RI figures include only ANPA member newspapers. Starting in 1974, statistics include non-ANPA members. Compilation also includes college, business, financial, and foreign language daily newspapers. *Editor & Publisher,*
counting only general circulation dailies, lists 1,183 offset papers in 1976, out of
1,762 total papers, or 76.1 percent, so the discrepancy is not great.

that larger newspapers are making the conversion. Still, the great bulk of offset-printed
papers are in the under-75,000 circulation category, as seen in Table 6.4. Using a somewhat different base of ANPA member papers only (which tends to underrepresent smaller
offset papers), the table shows that over four-fifths of papers under 25,000 circulation are
printed offset, but only 23.2 percent of the largest papers.

In 1973, both the *St. Louis Post-Dispatch* and the *Portland Oregonian* and *Oregon
Journal* switched to offset, accounting for the large jump seen in Table 6.3 in offset-
produced circulation. But by 1977, even the largest papers were making commitments to
offset. *Newsday* (1976 circulation, 466,635), the Long Island, NY daily owned by the
Times Mirror Co., ordered five eight-unit Goss offset presses, for installation by 1979.
This was done despite the plastic injection mold plating methods which the *L.A. Times,*
another Times Mirror paper, had developed. *Newsday* had been using NAPP pattern
plates on letterpress.

Almost simultaneously, Knight-Ridder's *Detroit Free Press,* with 620,541 daily and
714,121 Sunday circulation, announced that it had ordered 36 Goss Metro offset units as
part of a $19 million order. This also indicates the speed with which offset has become ac-
cepted by large newspapers, for as recently as in 1972, the *Philadelphia Inquirer,* another
Knight-Ridder paper, committed over $15 million to new letterpress units. But Rockwell-
Goss, the largest manufacturer of presses in the United States, has had no domestic orders
for letterpresses since 1973. *The New York Times* has put offset presses in its new
Carlstadt, N.J., printing plant.

Table 6.4   Daily Newspaper Publications Shown by Method of Printing and Circulation Size, 1978

			Printing Method					
	Offset		Letterpress Stereotype		Letterpress Direct Plate*		Total Newspapers	
Circulation Size	N	%	N	%	N	%	N	%
Under 25,000	620	84.7%	12	1.6%	100	13.7%	732	100.0%
25,000 to 75,000	147	38.9	11	2.9	220	58.2	378	100.0
Over 75,000	49	23.2	28	13.3	134	63.5	211	100.0
Total Newspapers	816	61.8	51	3.9	454	34.4	1321	100.1

* Includes direct lithography.

N.B.   Percentages all total across. May not equal 100.0 percent due to rounding.

Source: *Specification Data, 1978,* ANPA Research Institute; based on reports from 1,321 member newspapers printed in 1,069 plants.

Thus, with the continued movement of the newspaper industry to photocomposition, it appears likely that as existing letterpresses wear out, they will be replaced by offset presses at the largest newspapers. The reason for the sudden interest in offset by the large newspapers has to do with the further development of controls for the presses which appear to have overcome the biggest drawback—the two or three times increased newsprint wastage over letterpress operation, an added waste which threatened to be quite serious in light of inflated newsprint prices (see Chapter 9).

The traditional advantages of offset can be summarized as follows:

1.   Quality. Besides being completely designed to interface with photocomposed pages, the undisputed advantage of the offset printing process is the look of the finished product. Pictures in particular are reproduced with detail and contrast far greater than that available with any letterpress operation. This becomes even more evident when comparing color reproduction.

2.   Shorter set-up time when using color. The *St. Louis Post-Dispatch* claims that there was a 15 to 20 minute front-end saving in makeready for color as compared to letterpress.

3.   Cleaner operation. Letterpresses are known for the ink mist they send flying into the air, coating the press room and pressmen—a cause for concern given federal Occupational Safety and Health Act (OSHA) requirements. This situation is virtually eliminated in offset printing.

4. Cheaper plates than direct printing plates. As discussed in the previous section on direct lithography, offset plates cost about 80 cents each, from a variety of suppliers. Direct printing plates are as much as $2.50 each and must be purchased from the firm that markets the entire processing system.

5. Commercial printing opportunities. Particularly at smaller papers, offset conversion may provide the opportunity to generate additional income through development of commercial sales. By adding special commercially oriented folders or color units, the press can be utilized over a greater period of the day, instead of sitting fallow after a print run of an hour or less.

Among the potential problems with offset are:

• High operating costs. Greater care must be taken to keep the rollers of the press clean, which means a wash down at the end of each day's press run—a maintenance schedule almost unheard of in letterpress plants. However, the experience at the *St. Louis Post-Dispatch* is that this extra clean-up and maintenance is about equal to time saved on the front-end, so the total time and cost is not much different.

• A greater waste of newsprint. Although a three percent waste is common (compared to one percent for letterpress), tight controls can reduce that figure. The St. Louis paper expected to get wastage to within one to two percentage points of letterpress waste and Rockwell-Goss predicts an overall two percent wastage or less is feasible. To this end, Goss has developed a computer-directed system using its Press Control System (PCS) and Page Area Reader (PAR). These devices help preset compensators and ink feed prior to start-up, resulting in less start-up waste. They also allow a single press operator to make all changes in the running press from a single console. Nonetheless, even one percentage point greater waste at today's newsprint prices could cost a big city newspaper an added $280,000 a year in newsprint expense compared to letterpress.*

• Although offset plate costs run about a third less than shallow relief plates (which are essentially offset plates with the photosensitive polymer coating), this is still considerably higher than the cost of a stereotype plate.

• Making an offset plate takes slightly longer (25 minutes from paste-up, compared to 20 minutes for stereo), but total throughput speed is not critically different. Moreover, the *St. Louis Post-Dispatch* found that it was able to reduce its production force by 45 former stereotypers, making the offset process economically competitive with the letterpress.

---

* Based on newsprint costs for a 260,000 circulation daily using approximately 75,000 tons of newsprint a year at a cost of $375 per ton. Obviously, as prices increase, the gap widens.

As in changing to any printing process which interfaces with cold type make-up, conversion to offset requires plate-making and camera equipment. Similar equipment is required for DiLitho. But costs are comparable to relief plate equipment. The *Post-Dispatch*, which also prints the evening *Globe-Democrat* spent $80,000 on darkroom equipment and $30,000 for three automatic plate processors in 1973.

The letterpress should not be given up for dead, however. The ANPA Research Institute has been experimenting with a lightweight press designed specifically to use the plastic direct printing plates. Lee Enterprises, in conjunction with a Japanese manufacturer, has built a prototype of a similar press and expected to have it in operation at its *Quad City Times* newspaper in mid-1980. Existing letterpresses were designed to move the old, heavy lead stereotype plates. Such massive gearing has been eliminated in these new presses, which are expected to be competitive with offset presses in operational specifications.

Dry Offset

The rapid increase in the cost of newsprint has caused some users of offset presses to look for ways to reduce newsprint waste, especially smaller papers who might not be able to afford the PCS-PAR type system described above. The ANPA Research Institute has thus begun experiments in dry offset: using shallow relief plates on offset press. The hoped for advantages, besides reduced paper waste, include "a savings of chemical cost . . . [and] reduced press maintenance." Although it seems to be a step backward for those who hold offset as a higher quality process than a raised surface process, ANPA/RI did find it to be "a valid technical process," though not without "some headaches and problems." The process was tried at two Gannett newspapers, the *Bridgewater* (N.J.) *Courier-News* and the *Beaumont* (Tex.) *Enterprise* and *Journal*.

Press and Plate Summary

Given the inevitability of 100 percent photocomposition in composing rooms across the country, newspaper managers with letterpress plants face one or two basic decisions. First, if printing is still done on letterpress, the question is whether to switch to offset—a major investment—or use one of the hybrid systems to salvage a few more years from existing presses. If the choice is the latter, then a decision must be made on which plating alternative: direct, plastic injection, molding, stereotype from a pattern plate, or direct lithography.

The decision may be made on purely economic grounds, or quality standards may be included. The management of the *St. Louis Post-Dispatch*, for example, claimed that, "There is no doubt about it, we are willing to pay a price for higher fidelity and readability" in their decision to go offset. The Ottaway newspaper group (a unit of Dow Jones) spent $15 million between 1971 and 1975 on capital improvements, justifying the investment in new offset presses for most of its papers pragmatically: "We think the sharper printing quality of photos and text and the higher quality of color reproduction on offset presses justify this heavy investment in printing quality."

In making the final decision on letterpress systems, these guidelines are suggested:

1. Decide if the paper is committed to letterpress in the short term (one or two years) or the longer term (five to ten years). The answer to this may determine the capital investment a company is willing to make. If a paper hopes to squeeze a few more years out of its presses, an inexpensive NAPP or Letterflex system may be worthwhile. But if the press has too many good years left, a more expensive DiLitho conversion might be appropriate.

2. List all the alternative letterpress plate systems, taking into account:

    a. equipment costs
    b. manning levels
    c. material costs
    d. equipment productivity
    e. single page processing time—this determines how long it will take to get the last page on the press
    f. ecology problems the system may create (acid or other hard to dispose of chemicals)

3. Test the alternative plates on the existing press and determine the printing quality of each. Are any particularly good? Just suitable? Unacceptable? The test should ideally be made with the saddle equipped with the recommended lock-up.

4. Calculate the payback, return on investment, discounted cash flow, or present value of each system. Then the subjective values of other requirements, such as print quality, pictures, makeovers, and deadlines can be factored into the economic evaluation.

A similar analysis can also be done for the alternative of switching to offset. To summarize each of the printing systems:

• *Shallow relief plates (direct).* These are typically thin metal sheets coated with a photopolymer. One plate must be made for each page from a negative. They are then mounted on saddles, which build up the press cylinders to make up the difference between the thickness of the stereotype plates and these fraction-of-an-inch thick replacements. Among the major suppliers are NAPP, Letterflex, Hercules Merigraph, and Dyna-Flex. Plates cost $2.00 to $2.50 each and capital equipment for processing, $20,000 to $150,000, even higher for laser systems. Saddles cost $200 each.

   Major advantages: Relatively lower equipment costs, rapid payback, thus salvages existing letterpress while allowing conversion to photocomposition. Retains basic letterpress skills. Eliminates stereotype.

   Major drawbacks: Expensive if many plates are needed for each page. Less flexibility for makeovers. Quality varies, but at best equals stereotype. Somewhat slower than stereo for multiple pages.

• *Pattern plates.* These use the same technology as the shallow relief plate, but make use of a deeper relief (at a slightly higher cost per plate) to use as a form for making a molded mat, from which a stereotype is made. Thus, only a single plate is processed, with the actual printing still being done by stereotype plates. Cost per pattern plate is $2.50 to $3.00. Major suppliers of processing equipment are Ball Metal (for magnesium plate), NAPP, DuPont, and Dow Chemical (latter two produce both types of metal plates).

Major advantages: Permits use of stereotype—low plate cost, fast multiple plates, quality. Minimal investment in new equipment.

Major drawbacks: Still uses heavy stereotype plates, hot lead operation. Denies many of the benefits of photocomposition.

• *Direct lithography (DiLitho).* This is a process for using offset plates on a letterpress. The press is modified with dampener units and water fountains and added controls, at a cost of $10,000 to $25,000 per press unit. Offset plates, at $.70 to $.80 each are used. Suppliers of conversion packages are Dahlgreen, Inland Newspaper Machinery, Harris, and Rockwell-Goss. A Japanese firm, Tokyo Kikai Seisakusho, Ltd., is offering a press built expressly for DiLitho.

Major advantages: Salvages letterpress investment, and increases quality, especially of color, closer to that of offset. Plates are one-third cost of shallow relief. Can mix offset and DiLitho units in the same plant, even on the same press line, making conversion easier. As flexible as offset for transmitting plates to satellite printing locations.

Major drawbacks: Requires new press skills which may result in temporary lowering of quality during learning period. Substantial conversion expense. Plate costs higher than stereo. Paper wastage likely to be two to three percent, compared to one to two percent for letterpress.

• *Offset.* This is the process most compatible with photocomposition. Thin metal plates are exposed and treated so that when run on the press, using oil-based ink and water, only those areas with characters transfer ink to a blanket on another cylinder, which in turn offsets the ink to the paper. This involves using a new press for those plants with the old letterpress. Major manufacturers include Rockwell-Goss, Harris, Wood-Hoe, and Crabtree-Vickers. Prices run about ten percent higher than an equivalent letterpress, ranging from $260,000 for two units plus a color unit to print eight full-size pages, to $20 million or more for large metropolitan installations. Plate costs are $.70 to $.80 each and investment in processing equipment is relatively minimal.

Major advantages: Best quality reproduction, especially color. Simplest interface with photocomposition. Adaptable for use with facsimile transmission to satellite printing plants. Will be further refined as laser plates and computer-to-plate composition becomes perfected. Lower plate cost than plastic relief plates. Much cleaner operation.

Major drawbacks: Higher newsprint wastage (see DiLitho). Requires more maintenance and clean-up. Slightly lower press speed than letterpress. Requires unusual investment if scrapping a letterpress which still has years of life remaining.

DECISION-MAKING CRITERIA FOR THE NEW TECHNOLOGY

As with many business decisions, criteria for the selection of capital equipment for modernizing newspapers are limited by (1) the particuilar needs and circumstances unique to each operation, and (2) the dynamic technological environment which makes many choices outmoded by the time they are implemented. This latter point has been dubbed "analysis paralysis" by ANPA/Research Institute's Peter Romano, and his suggestion for handling it is to simply set a cut-off date for the decision and consider no alternatives which become available after that date. The first limitation, therefore, is the one which each newspaper management must understand before the decision-making process moves very far.

Undertaking a Study

The place to begin is with a careful study of the newspaper's operation, answering first the question: "Why are we contemplating this change?" It may be as a result of existing constraints of the operation, such as the needs of Media General, Inc. to generate rapid output of financial data to make its *Financial Daily* (now *Weekly*) feasible. A strike by the typographers' union in Richmond, Va., shortly after the *Daily* started up forced Media General to come up with a system which would allow it to publish its two Richmond newspapers (the *News Leader* and *Times-Dispatch*) without the skilled composing room personnel. The needs were not to improve news handling, but to provide for continued production with unskilled workers. Another constraint might be a limitation of present capacity, which indicates the acquisition of some new machinery.

More frequently, however, the answer is that the changeover is being made by choice: It is an opportunity to expand the data base, extend deadlines, or reduce composing room expense. For example, the composing room at the *Allentown* (Pa.) *Call* and *Chronicle* had been understaffed at the time management was considering buying into the new technology. Therefore, its objectives included speeding up the production process while reducing the strain of getting the papers out on time each day.

Once recognizing whether the decision is one of choice or constraint, management can then answer further questions to refine its analysis:

- How does it wish to operate in the future?

- What constraints does it wish removed from the process?

- How close to deadline does it wish to produce? How large is the news hole?

From the response to these and perhaps other questions, come the final decisions:

- How much equipment is necessary to do all this?

- What equipment is available?

Each newspaper and management will have its own answers. Even within a news-paper chain, various papers will identify unique needs. A West Coast one-edition after-noon paper has far different needs than does a four-edition East Coast morning paper.

The bottom line, in sum, is the need for each paper to determine its objectives. Needs come first, design of the system to fulfill these needs next. If the study is well done, the equipment which can implement the system almost falls into place given the specifications already arrived at.

An example of this process is the case of the *Baltimore Sun*. Management there began with an evaluation of their operation which yielded three objectives:

1.   Reduce the error factor of the news and editorial pages (totaling 1070 in a five-week period using hot metal).

2.   Meet the existing deadline schedules, which had been averaging 25 minutes late on the first two editions.

3.   Achieve a rate of return which would provide a three-year payback on their capital investment.

Following these objectives, the paper decided to begin its conversion in the newsroom—contrary to a typical pattern which starts with the classified or display adver-tising departments. The result was an orderly conversion and the attainment of all the goals on or ahead of schedule.

Who should be responsible for undertaking this study? The most successful results appear to come when management involves representatives from all affected departments. This not only improves attitudes of personnel toward the change, but assures that the final decisions result in a balancing of the needs of news, classified, display, and production operations. The *Call-Chronicle*'s plan was the product of such an approach, as was the Baltimore plan. Nevertheless, one official must be responsible for resolving conflicts and coordination, to be sure that the final system is cost effective, and that compromises do not result in a system which conflicts with the overall objectives.

Choosing the System and Hardware

Having analyzed the objectives of the newspaper, management must make basic system choices: OCR or VDT input? Floppy disk, paper tape, or computer storage? Pen-cil or VDT editing? Letterpress or offset? DiLitho, stereotype, or direct plates? At this stage, the economics of technology first become a serious consideration. For an evaluation of OCR or VDT input, management must consider the number and capability of the OCRs themselves, compared to the cost of VDTs. There must be sufficient numbers of in-put terminals in either case to handle peak loads, but VDTs, at $3000 to $6000 each, are less readily justified sitting idle at non-peak times than are far less expensive electric type-writers. On the other hand, can the newspaper afford to have a reporter sitting around near deadline waiting for a VDT to be available?

For VDT editing, a decision must be made on the number of terminals. Should there be one for each editing position, or can they be scattered around? How many controllers are required? What size data base is necessary? If reporters will be using VDTs for input, will they be stand-alone units, output onto paper tape or floppy disk, or will they be hard-wired to a computer? Copy volume from correspondents and syndicates may affect the OCR/VDT input equation.

There appears to be little pattern among small, medium, and large size papers favoring OCR or VDT. Some large papers, such as the *Atlanta Journal* and *Constitution* and Richmond newspapers have used OCR input and VDT editing. In Atlanta, *Journal* assistant managing editor Robert Lott expects to "stay with reporter OCR for the future. There's no need to change to VDT so long as OCR is still required for entering outside copy." Joseph Ungaro of the Westchester-Rockland Newspapers agrees, adding that "OCR may be more than an intermediate step" between the old way and VDT entry. He adds that OCR may still be economically justified for many applications until the early 1980s. Westchester-Rockland Newspapers, however, is using the Hendrix 6500 system VDTs for editing.

But at the Allentown daily newspapers, with a combined daily circulation of 125,000, all local copy is OCR-written and pencil-edited, with only wire service copy, which comes in directly to a computer, VDT-edited. "Terminal editing discourages editing," complains executive editor Edward Miller. The management at Allentown looks on the electronic system as a means for copy management, not as an editing procedure.

At the even smaller *Pottsville* (Pa.) *Republican* (29,000 circulation), publisher Uzal Martz, Jr. eschews "bells and whistles" for a basic system of OCR input, with floppy disk storage and transfer to stand-alone VDT editing terminals, without a central computer. The disks also provide for the photocomposers, at a reported savings of over $125,000 over a more sophisticated—but in Martz's view, unnecessary—Harris 2500 alternative.

On the other hand, there are managers of newspapers of all sizes who have decided that going all-VDT, even at a greater initial expense, is the better long-range strategy. The first large-scale installation was that of the *Detroit News* in 1973. Although the *News* had 250 local reporters, it figured it needed only 72 Hendrix 5700 VDTs, since not all reporters and editors are on duty at the same time. Only stories from remote bureaus are typed and fed through scanners for entry into the central computer, then VDT edited at the main plant.

The *Milwaukee Journal* and *Sentinel* had a total of 108 Hendrix terminals installed originally, in a system similar to Detroit's. The *Washington Post, The New York Times, The Philadelphia Inquirer* and *Daily News* and the *New York News* are among the large city dailies that have installed hundreds of VDT editorial systems from Harris, Mergenthaler and others.

In each case, management made its choice based on well articulated criteria. In Milwaukee, the system had to give editors complete control over the editing process in the newsroom, making sure to adapt the system to their editing requirements, not the converse. Planning began three years before installation and management interviewed representatives of nine manufacturers and visited several vendor plants and other newspapers before deciding on a supplier. At the *Post*, a strike in the fall of 1975 forced a switch to cold type using OCR, and the Harris system came from a desire to keep as much of the paper in cold type after the strike ended by purchasing an interim, off-the-shelf system.

The general manager of Philadelphia Newspapers, Inc. reported that the company chose System Development Corporation's Text II because it was "the most flexible system we found after a year-long search." The editor of the *Daily News* looked to the system to enhance the quality of the news operation and the *Inquirer*'s executive editor, Gene Roberts, added that it will return control of the copy to the editors (rather than typesetters) and that "the end result will be greater accuracy, greater copy control, and better deadlines."

"Better editorial control" was also the primary objective at the much smaller (circulation 72,000) *Atlantic City Press,* where two years of planning went into the decision to switch to an all-VDT Digital Equipment Corporation Typeset-11 input and editing system using 24 terminals. And with costs being driven further downward by advancing technology, there are now all-VDT systems economically available for even small dailies, such as the *Pittsburg* (Kan.) *Sun* (1978 circulation, 13,000).

In late 1973, the *Sun* had converted to photocomposition and bought a new offset press. Its need then was to find a front-end system that would have the advantages of the new on-line storage and retrieval systems, but that did not require expensive programming and capital costs. In 1974 it found one of the first low cost systems, manufactured by Computype (now part of Harris Corp.). The system that the *Sun* uses emulates many of the characteristics of the systems being ordered for the metropolitan dailies, but at a fraction of the cost. It does this by using hard-wired rather than programmable components, and floppy disk storage instead of a more expensive central processing system memory.

Cost of Conversion to Front-End Photocomp Technology

The investment in the new technology is thus dependent on not only the size of the newspaper, but its editorial, advertising, and business needs, as well as the financial and human constraints that are unique to each operation. As just one further example, in determining the number of VDTs which must be ordered to handle peak period demand from reporters, the *Atlantic City Press* decided on a ratio of two reporters for each terminal. At *The New York Times* the ratio varies from department to department, but its initial plans specified an overall rate of two terminals for every three reporters, with some departments where reporters frequently must write close to deadline, as in financial, having a ratio of one to one.

With the advent of the low cost front-end VDT systems that use floppy disks and that are hard-wired, the capital cost for a small newspaper already using photocomposition can be as little as $50,000. A more sophisticated system, having random access memory (not available on floppy disk systems) and programmable functions, is available for under $100,000. At the other end of the range, costs are open ended, as more terminals, controllers, program features, and advertising and business package options are developed.

For the small papers, with circulations of 10,000 to 20,000, or even less , several vendors offer alternative packages for under $150,000.

The all-VDT system installed at the *Pittsburg Sun* is a Computype package, a hard-wired, nonprogrammable system using floppy disk storage. Based on the manufacturer's list prices (in 1976), the installation costs about $60,000. The basic equipment consists of:

6 CompuEdit VDTs with 4K memory at $3195 each	$19,170
1 CompuStor with 750K storage on three floppy disks	23,000
1 Model 120 Universal Data Communications interface with installation and 2-way switch box	3,745
1 AP six-level slow speed wire interface to CompuStor	2,000
1 Model 150 paper tape reader and interface	1,500
1 Extel line printer and interface	2,500
Total	$51,915

In addition, the paper must add the cost of connecting cables ($.75 to $1.50 per foot), spare parts kits ($1495 for VDTs, $3995 for CompuStor, $850 for 120 Universal Interface) and perhaps optional disk gauges, to measure memory left on each disk, at $1295 each.

The *Sun* already had a photocomposition capacity with its Compugraphic 2961 (was $9000, now discontinued). Headlines were made on a Compugraphic 7200 (about $4500) and display advertising is set on a Compugraphic ACM 9000. It also had a Hendrix 5200 VDT for a small amount of off-line corrections of some paper-received wire service and advertising copy. The *Sun* printed for a short time on its letterpress using a Dyna-Flex direct plate, but purchased a five-unit Goss Urbanite press in 1973.

The next step up in front-end systems is a programmable unit with greater expandability, more memory, and a random access memory which, unlike the floppy disk configurations, allows direct access to any story or ad in memory regardless of when it was entered.

The ONE System's ONE/10 package, at a base price of $166,000 includes:

- 2 mini-computers with two 32K memories

- 10 million character disks

- 1 newswire interface

- 2 photocomposition machine interfaces

- 1 high-speed (300 LPM) line printer and interface

- 15 ONE/eL4 4K character memory VDTs (additional terminals $3400 each, up to 30 total)

- Basic software

Some newspapers with this system include the *Carlisle* (Pa.) *Sentinel* (circulation, 15,000), *Casper* (Wyo.) *Star-Tribune* (24 VDTs, circulation, 33,000), and *Delaware County* (Pa.) *Times* (25 VDTs, circulation, 44,000).

The larger papers, with more sophisticated needs—and with greater financial resources—are spending $1 million and more for their complex systems. The *Milwaukee Journal* and *Sentinel* spent $1.5 million on their 108 VDT Hendrix 3400 system—actually four systems, each capable of handling up to 32 VDTs. The output is on four APS-4 phototypesetters made by Autologic, Inc. As is the case in large newspaper operations, the software is written or supplemented by in-house programmers, an ongoing expense which is easy to overlook in calculating conversion expenses. Milwaukee wrote all their own production software packages and the Atlanta newspapers have five programmers and systems people exclusively for editorial and hyphenation/justification work, in addition to their ten staffers for business applications.

Although smaller systems can use VDTs that cost $3000 to $4000, the larger papers demand greater flexibility and more options in their reporter and editor VDTs. In addition, the large papers include VDT make-up of display advertising in their systems, a piece of technology which is still economically beyond the smaller systems.

The display ad make-up terminals, described previously, are relatively expensive pieces of equipment. The Raycomp-200 and Camex 135 each cost about $200,000 for a controller and two work stations, plus proof printer and some common options. (The newer Raycomp II, with fewer features, is slightly less money.) Adding two more work stations brings the total costs to $257,000 and $350,000, respectively.* A large city daily would need about six Raycomp-100 terminals. The Harris 2200 system is another popular competitor for this market.

Reporter and editor terminals in use or ordered for *The New York Times, Baltimore Sun,* and other large papers cost about twice that of the simpler and least expensive models. The basic Harris 1520 terminal is about $6000. An even more sophisticated reporter or editor terminal is the 1700 series at $7500, with up to 32 special functions which can be programmed into it. With a dual screen or column capability, an editor can compare two stories for quicker and better editing. For the added money, with either

---

* These are base prices and do not include printers, interfaces, magnetic tape drives, and other popular options.

model, the newspaper also gets an Edit-Trace feature which permits an editor to see exactly what changes have been made by which sub-editors.

The Harris 2560 system, which the company claims is designed for newspapers with 50,000 to 200,000 circulation might have the following configuration for about $1 million:

- 72 VDTs—36 1520 models
  36 1700 series models

- Model 2560 dual processor and disk drives each with 132 megabyte storage

- Peripheral equipment and input/output interfaces

Such a system could support an editorial staff of up to 250 persons, with four news bureaus and eight wire service lines, 25 pages of classified advertising, and Sunday editions of 200 pages or more.

For a newspaper with circulation approaching 400,000 daily, Harris estimates a cost of around $1.7 million for the customized 2570 system. This price would include 150 VDTs (up to a maximum of 348 terminals can be accommodated), a dual controller and three peripheral controllers, plus 50 other peripheral devices.

Photocomposition hardware itself is a relatively small part of a cold type production system. For a small newspaper, the bottom of the line Compugraphic CompuWriter II or Mergenthaler Linocomp machines, with typesetting speeds up to 60 lines per minute, are available at a cost of under $10,000. Compugraphic's Unisetter, at $18,000, does 80 lpm and the Videosetter Universal, setting 450 lpm, is $35,000.

At the higher end, the CRT typesetters such as the Harris Fototronic 7400 series, rated at 1000 lpm, the Mergenthaler Linotron 606, which can technically set up to 3000 six-point nine-pica lines a minute and Rockwell's Metro-Set 1000 lpm units cost $100,000 and upwards. Also in this category are the APS-4 or APS-5 of Autologic, Inc. These machines are available in sizes of up to 100-pica (a full newspaper page) widths. One difference in prices is the existence and size of the built-in computer which some units have, while others depend on a separate computer for typesetting commands.

Optical character readers also have a wide range of prices. Compugraphic offers a model for $25,000. A higher speed reader, such as Rockwell's Metro-reader II with a maximum speed of 1050 words per minute, starts at $37,500. ECRM, Dymo Graphics Systems, CompuScan, and Mergenthaler are other major producers of OCR equipment.

EFFECTS OF TECHNOLOGY ON COSTS AND PROFITS

Although the cold type production process is cleaner, quieter, and in the case of offset printing, of higher quality than the hot metal method, the primary benefit to publishers is its speed and efficiency. The initial conversion to electronic typesetting has produced dramatic reductions in the composing room force. Minor cost benefits include the great reduction in typographical errors in display and classified advertising that would otherwise result in having to reprint the ad for free, higher employee morale, and in at least one case, a lowering of insurance premiums when the cold type composing room was reclassified from a publishing to a clerical operation. Among some of the reported results are these:

- In Richmond, Media General Corp. estimated that in its first year of photocomposition, payroll expense was $1.2 million lower than what it would have been had unionized composing room employees accepted Media General's final offer during a strike. The union didn't, but with the lower skill requirements, the newspaper was able to replace the composing room personnel of 192 persons with 140 employees at considerably lower pay scales.

- The *Worcester* (Mass.) *Telegram* and *Gazette* spent $89,000 for an OCR for input, replacing 12 paper tape keypunchers who were paid $120,000 a year.

- In 1974, for the first time in its history, the Ottaway Newspaper group spent more for news and photo staff salaries and expenses than for composing room mechanical costs. During 1974 and 1975, composing room employees dropped 19 percent (from 407 to 330), while editorial employees increased slightly to 350.

- At Lee Enterprises' *Quad City Times,* new systems reduced page make-up time from eight man hours per page in 1968 to 48 minutes in 1975.

Composing Room Economics

The big saving has come through the reduction in the number of highly skilled and paid typographers, often members of the International Typographers Union (ITU) (see Chapter 8). In many cases, the ITU continues to represent what is left of the composing room, primarily paste-up functions, plus the keyboarding of some outside copy or corrections. But, as at the *Quad City Times* and in Atlanta, attrition rapidly lowers the work force. In a few cases, such as Richmond, the $200 to $250 a week ITU typesetters were replaced by a smaller number of non-union workers at half the ITU pay scale, since the skills for which the compositors had been paid were no longer required.

This increased efficiency can be readily seen by comparing the time it would take to set in hot metal a 2500-word news story with the time via photocomposition. Using a computer-assisted punch-paper tape to operate a line caster, at 14 lines per minute, it took about 35 minutes to set the story, with several errors. A photocomposition machine of modest speed could set the same article (from the original keystrokes) in about one minute, with no machine errors.

This efficiency is now showing up in composite newspaper industry income statements. Although overall newspaper expenses have been increasing along with revenue, composing room costs have fallen. Table 6.5 compares composing room expense for a typical 34,000 circulation and 260,000 circulation newspaper for the years 1971 and 1978.

Table 6.5   Composing and Editorial Expense at Daily Newspapers, 1971 and 1978

Expense For:	Circulation Category			
	34,000		260,00	
	1971	1978	1971	1978
Composing Room	$542,300	$271,296	$1,976,287	$1,716,949
% Change		− 50.0		− 13.1
% of Total Revenue	15.4	4.6	9.1	7.0
Editorial	$444,300	$740,319	$2,040,851	$2,893,970
% Change		+ 66.6		+ 41.8
% of Total Revenue	11.4	12.6	9.4	11.7

Source: *Editor & Publisher.* Compiled by Newspaper Analysis Service, Cincinnati, Ohio. Calculations by the author.

For the smaller paper, the table shows that composing room expense as a percentage of total revenue has decreased substantially, from 15.4 percent to 4.6 percent. In absolute terms, expense has fallen 50.0 percent, despite an increase in the number of printed pages. This can be compared with other expense categories in Table 2.10 and is consistent with the experience of specific newspapers.

For the larger newspapers as a group, change has come less visibly because of their need to move more slowly in making the vast changeover required, their greater fixed investments in equipment, and labor contracts which frequently inhibited their ability to effect maximum cost savings. Nonetheless, composing room costs actually decreased 13 percent between 1971 and 1978 while overall expenses were up more than 53 percent in that period. The number of man hours per page fell from 9.4 in 1971 to 5.7 in 1978, down 65 percent, and overtime hours decreased 61 percent.

On the other hand, there has been no comparable labor savings in the editorial department due to technology. The front-end systems help get the copy into the production system faster, in fact shifting part of the production process—entering the keystrokes into the production system—from the back-shop to the newsroom. As a result, editorial expense, primarily labor, continues to increase, in absolute dollars and in percentage of total revenue, as the editorial staff assumes greater responsibilities.

Return on Investment

Standard measures of comparing savings from alternative uses of money in purchasing capital assets include simple payback or annual rate of return calculations, as well as more sophisticated computations such as discounted cash flow and present value, both of which consider the time distribution as well as net cash earnings of an investment. Given the depreciation factor in calculating true investment returns, newspapers are well-advised to use the latter two techniques for making choices in capital investment decisions.

Most newspaper publishers still speak in terms of the relatively easily computed and understood payback method, in which the expected average annual net savings attributable to the investment is divided by the cost, the result being the period of time in which the publisher recoups the investment. Although not as sophisticated as other techniques, it is particularly useful when technological change is occurring so rapidly that near-term obsolescence of equipment is a major factor. From this point of view, newspapers have been finding that savings generated by the new systems are great enough to result in very rapid payback. Uzal Martz, Jr. of the *Pottsville* (Pa.) *Republican* suggests a maximum five-year payback. James Ottaway, Jr. says his newspapers must look for a three-year payback, "exclusive of added depreciation costs, cost of money, or the write-off of old equipment." Many managements look to a one to two and a half year payback on investments in the new technology.

Dow Jones calculated that a $1.5 million investment it made in production automation between 1969 and 1973 paid for itself in pre-tax profit every nine months. The *Baltimore Sun* conservatively estimates that its $3 million modernization project would be repaid in three years, based solely on the estimated attrition rate of seven percent of its typographers per year. *Sun* management did not include in this the projected reduction in overtime, and also omitted the added one-time expense for early retirement incentives. (At $10 per hour, the *Sun* averaged between 2100 and 2400 hours of overtime per week in the second half of 1974. During the same period in 1975, with the system operational, the paper had "virtually eliminated overtime," for a $550,000 saving in that six-month period alone.)

A more detailed example can be seen in the experience of the News and Observer Publishing Co., which publishes *The Raleigh* (N.C) *Times* and *The News and Observer* (combined daily circulation 162,000). The papers have a total of 40 reporters and 31 editors. They invested $800,000 in a VDT front-end system and another $200,000 in photocomposition conversion, for a total $1 million investment. Table 6.6a summarizes the results. Composing room staff dropped 44 percent, proofreaders by over two-thirds. Payroll savings were $628,500 in 1976, increasing to $724,500 by 1978, exclusive of any salary increases.

Table 6.6b shows the return, taking a seven-year straightline depreciation, with no salvage value. The payback is just over two years, the ROI is 52 percent in year one and 42 percent thereafter. It should be understood, however, that some other expenses may be incurred that are not calculated here, such as maintenance for the electronic equipment and in-house or contracted programming assistance. Rarely included in figures such as these given by the Raleigh papers are training costs and lost time for both editorial and production people to master the new instruments. Many newspapers may run the old and new systems together while bugs are ironed out. Nonetheless, enough experience has been accumulated in these conversions to know that the savings indicated in this section are real; and the magnitude of the savings makes this aspect of the new technology a sought-after, significant cost reduction investment, in addition to the other editorial and quality advantages which just add to its attractions.

Table 6.6a   Impact on Editorial and Composing Room Staffing from Newsroom and Photocomposition Conversion at Raleigh News and Observer Publishing Co.

	1971	1976	Percent Change
Composing Room Staff	100	57	− 43%
Editorial Staff	78	81	+ 4
Full-Time Proofreading Staff	14	4	− 71

Table 6.6b   Hypothetical Payback and ROI Calculation on Raleigh Investment

Investment		$1,000,000
Average Annual Net Payroll Savings (at 1976 wage rate)	$676,500	
Less: Increased Taxes Net of Investment		
Tax Credit and Depreciation*	156,149	
Net Savings, First Year		520,351
Net Savings, Subsequent Years		420,351
Payback Period	2.2 years (26 months)	
Annual ROI	52.0%, first year;	
	42.0%, additional years	

*Assumes 7 year straight-line, no salvage value.

Sources: *Editor & Publisher*, May 8, 1976; Knowledge Industry Publications, Inc.

NEWSPAPERS AS A MARKET

Table 6.2 dramatically illustrates the tremendous market which newspapers constitute for suppliers of hardware and related services for the new technology. The number of VDTs increased by 307 percent between 1975 and 1978 alone. Besides purchases of copy processing systems, newspapers have had to replace stereotyping equipment with cameras and darkrooms, plate-making equipment, saddles for their letterpress presses, or direct lithography conversion equipment. Moreover, it is difficult to assess how many newspapers have purchased new offset presses earlier than they would have because of their natural combination with the cold type process.

The number of firms supplying newspapers has proliferated with the growth in the market. In 1977 there were at least 28 firms which offered VDTs and keyboards for input, with 20 of these firms specialized enough to offer separate VDT editing models. Fully 42 firms promoted typesetting "systems," ranging from Harris, Mergenthaler, Rockwell International, and Hendrix down to companies like Imlac Corp., Optronics, and Fototype. About 28 firms provided computers of various sizes and functions to the industry and at least 13 major firms and perhaps 15 others marketed photocomposition machines. Ten firms sold press saddles.

It was not until 1976 and 1977 that many of the largest newspapers began to announce multi-million dollar contracts for their newsrooms: $13.5 million for the *New York Daily News,* about $8 million for the *Chicago Tribune,* $3 million in Baltimore, $1.5 million in Milwaukee, plus large systems announced for the *Washington Post, The New York Times,* and *Philadelphia Inquirer* and *Daily News.*

Foreign newspapers are also becoming more involved in adopting the latest equipment. Besides the 1500 or so daily newspaper plants in the United States, there are an estimated 1400 plants in Europe and approximately 1000 others in the non-Communist world.

One industry source estimates that total expenditures for electronic copy processing equipment, exclusive of presses, was $350 million in 1976, with the leader, Harris Corp., writing orders for at least $50 million in phototypesetting equipment alone. Overall, about $182 million was spent on photocomposition, almost $100 million on copy processing, primarily VDTs, and the remainder on other electronic equipment, such as platemakers. Of the $350 million total, however, almost half came from commercial and in-plant printing operations, with newspapers accounting for about $180 million.

OTHER TRENDS IN NEWSPAPER TECHNOLOGY

Full-Page Composition
The next step in the composition technology is full pagination, which will result in the final elimination of the composing room in newspaper plants. In the 1977 process, columns of news copy coming from the phototypesetters are merged with the advertisements and all this material is pasted to a sheet of paper to make up the original newspaper page. Pictures and graphics are added to make a camera-ready positive from which the negative and then plates are made.

Technology has reached the stage whereby the typesetters will instead produce newspaper pages already fully composed. The actual make-up is done on large VDTs. The make-up editor will call the articles and ads (and eventually digitally stored photos and graphics) from computer memory. Pages will be made up on the screen, much as advertisements can now be composed on the Raycomp, Harris, or Camex machines. The editor blocks out the space for all elements of the page and then gives the computer instructions to have the entire camera-ready page printed out, hyphenated, and justified as a complete page, eliminating any paste-up.

From this stage, it is only a short step to bypassing the positive page altogether. Instead, the computer controls a laser plate-maker, etching an offset or plastic plate directly, ready for the press. Thus, the composing room, camera room, and plate-making are all combined into one operation, from editor to plate. Both processes have been demonstrated, and some in the industry expect the first stage—full page phototypesetting—to become commonplace in the 1980s.

IBM had been working on a full-page composition system with the Newspaper Systems Development Group, a consortium of eight newspaper organizations formed in 1970. The project's plan was to have IBM develop the software and a separate contractor develop the hardware to produce a complete pagination system, including graphics. However, at the end of 1976, NSDG terminated the project with IBM, reportedly because of the "additional millions" which participants felt would be needed to complete the system but would be difficult to cost justify.

Another system has been demonstrated by Mergenthaler Linotype Co., which has sold its Page View Terminal system as part of the *New York News'* electronic system. The Mergenthaler system is not designed to include graphics, but will typeset tabloid pages, with windows for graphics, at a rate of a page in 22 seconds. A mid-1978 completion date had been anticipated for the system, but it was not achieved.

A prototype interaction system called NEWSHOLE was demonstrated at the ANPA/RI Production Management Conference in 1976, the result of a master's thesis at the University of Toronto. Media General, Inc. and Mead Corp. announced a joint pagination development project in January, 1975, with an 18-month targeted completion date, but called it off when progress proved slower than expected.

With the exception of an acceptable graphic scanner needed to translate graphics into computer-storable digitized information, the basic hardware for these systems was in existence in 1979. Autologic, Inc., winner of a contract with NSDG to develop the scanner, had prototypes developed when the project was abandoned. The first of the two main obstacles that remained appeared to be the software which would allow make-up editors to have real-time access to all the information stored in the computer with an acceptable response time. The second problem was the cost of the large data base which would be necessary to accommodate the digitized storage of graphics. It is likely that only large newspapers with back-up central computers will have the capacity for this storage at first.

Plate-making

As noted above, the final step in streamlining the production process will be the complete elimination of the camera room, which now receives the page paste-up (or fully phototypeset page) and takes a picture of it to make a negative of the page, which is then used to burn an offset or relief plate. This step will be complete when the system is capable of storing and assembling page ingredients including all graphics. The hardware is available.

Thus, the system of the future will go from a page composed on a VDT and stored in the computer, directly to a plate. This would save the newspaper the equipment, materials, and labor costs involved in generating a camera-ready positive and making the negative. In the meantime, an intermediate step is being used by EOCOM with its Laserite plate-making system, which takes the positive page, scans it with a beam from a low-wattage laser, and uses the information to drive a more powerful laser to expose a photo-sensitive plate (offset or relief). The cost of a complete EOCOM unit is $165,000 and the *Los Angeles Times* is using four units in transmitting 80 pages a day to its Orange County satellite plant. Since each unit is run by one person and will eliminate a five-person camera room crew, the *Times* will be saving $500,000 annually with the $1 million system. EOCOM calculations show that the expected 12 minutes from paste-up to plate under the existing process is reduced to three minutes by omitting the camera/negative step. In its intermediate stage, the Laserite is making a negative which must then be conventionally processed.

Gannett wrote off a $9.8 million investment in Laser Graphic Systems Corporation in 1975 when it decided to abandon the development of a laser-produced letterpress plate. This resulted from Gannett's analysis that technology had already passed by a letterpress plate, given the rapid advances being made in offset presses and plate-making capability, as demonstrated by the EOCOM venture.

Dow Jones, which uses facsimile transmission from its production facilities to its satellite plants, has been working with Test Data Corporation to develop a laser plate-maker. It was demonstrated in use by receiving a page transmitted by satellite from Chicopee, Mass. to Las Vegas, directly as an offset plate. The system can also be used to produce a page negative.

Other firms working on laser plate-makers are LogEtronics, Inc. and Image Information, Inc. Use of direct positive page-to-plate is expected beginning in 1980, with complete computer-to-plate capability not practical until later in the decade.

Plateless Printing

Eliminating the 300-ton printing press will not come quickly. First, full-page computer make-up and storage of all elements must be perfected, proven to be reliable, and shown to be economical. Then may come the final step in producing an ink-on-newsprint newspaper: plateless printing. This may take one of two technologies. One possibility is ink-jet printing, in which an ink gun sprays ink in the form of letters as the paper moves below it. In its initial application, this process is being used to print mailing labels. In one trial, the Internal Revenue Service provided a magnetic tape with a million names and addresses on it. The tape was fed through a small computer, which in turn activated an A.B. Dick ink-jet gun, producing a stream of ink which was broken ultrasonically into 66,000 droplets which formed the required characters on the mailing labels. A German newspaper, the *Frankfurter Rundschau,* has installed an ink-jet addressing system to be used with inserters, but the Muller-Martini Ink Jet Addressing system has been designed to address newspapers or other mailing pieces on-line at press speeds.

However, before this process could actually be used to print an entire newspaper, it would have to demonstrate its reliability on a wider scale, greatly improve its image quality, as well as increase its operating speed over four times.

An alternative technology is the electrostatic process being pursued by Stanford Research Institute and the Massachusetts Institute of Technology. In this process, computer-driven lasers burn millions of microscopic impressions onto the surface of wet newsprint, into which dry printing powder is machine wiped, creating visible type and pictures.

Under either system, the elimination of plates and pressures would permit the use of simplified presses and reduce paper waste. More significantly, the computer-controlled plateless press would permit editors to insert late-breaking news as the press is running. Printing at satellite plants could be controlled from a central computer at the main plant, and the potential exists for refined applications of zoned editions, with both editorial and advertising copy specialized by area.

Plateless printing is technologically unlikely before the mid-1980s and probably is even further away. In a 1970 survey by the RAND Institute, specialists in technology did not give electrostatic plateless printing more than a 50 percent chance of being "widespread" until 1995. Another specialist warns that it "may never happen" at all unless the industry makes a major funding effort in research. But if and when it does come, it will signal the end of the reign of the last holdover from the 18th century in the production of the "new" newspaper.

Facsimile and Satellite Transmission

Widespread use of facsimile reproduction of the newspaper at the subscriber's home or office has been on the horizon at least since 1938 when a *Newsweek* article talked about the *St. Louis Post-Dispatch* being the first facsimile newspaper to be experimentally delivered to the home. In 1948, RCA's David Sarnoff was talking about transmitting the complete Sunday edition of a newspaper to a subscriber's home via radio in one minute. In 1966, RCA was still predicting facsimile news service to the home, but has since abandoned such expectations.

The concept of transmitting the pages of the finished newspaper directly to subscribers is intriguing because it would eliminate many of the more cumbersome aspects of newspaper publishing: printing and delivery. Printing a newspaper still requires a 300-ton press to spread a fifth of an ounce of ink over 64 pages of newsprint, with the final product delivered to the customer by a newsboy. However, with a facsimile machine in every home, both the press and the boy would be obsolete.

But this aspect of facsimile—Homefax—is still distant at best for two reasons:

1. Print facsimile still needs paper in the machine.

2. It requires a substantial capital investment on the part of each household, plus maintenance and supplies.

Perhaps the most ambitious experiment in home facsimile is being conducted in Japan by *Asahi Shimbun,* an 11-million circulation daily newspaper. Cables have been provided in a new town development near Tokyo for 100,000 potential subscribers. But although the technology is ready, the newspaper has found several drawbacks. First, the current cost per sheet of facsimile paper is six cents, much too dear for commercial use. Second, even in mass production, the paper estimates a telenewspaper receiver will cost as much as a color television set. Third, officials have perceived widespread apathy, as people believe that this form is not necessary. As a result *Asahi Shimbun* may reserve facsimile for "hot" news, while conventional editions carry the bulk of news, features, and advertising.

The cost of paper and capital can be overcome by using existing television sets and cable or telephone systems to send and display the news. Three systems have been field tested in Great Britain for several years. These are CEEFAX, ORACLE, and Prestel (viewdata). CEEFAX and ORACLE send their information along with the broadcast signal over the air and at any one time are capable of providing up to 800 screen size pages of up to 150 words each. Prestel, among the most promising of the approaches, is sent over telephone lines. It is capable of thousands of pages.

The cost of decoders for CEEFAX and ORACLE is expected to be about $100 (in great volume), while Prestel is paid for by a metered telephone call, plus a charge per "page" viewed. The systems are still limited, however, in their presentation of graphics, which are crude, thus limiting the appeal to advertisers as well as to those who view this as a true replacement for newspapers. Among the North American experiments are Telidon in Canada and Viewtron (a joint venture of Knight-Ridder and AT&T) in the U.S.

Reuters News Service and United Press International have cable news information services. But whether via broadcast or cable, television display as a substitute for newspapers has some disadvantages which may hinder its widespread acceptance.

First, it cannot be clipped out or stored for handy reference. Second, viewers in a household must all watch the same presentation simultaneously—one cannot see sports while another reads the editorial page. Third, it is not portable—it can't be read on the bus, airplane, or a park bench. Fourth, it is not adaptable to random access and scanning. Fifth, there is a limit to how much a TV screen can display, which is far less than a newspaper page. Sixth, advertisers may not find it suitable for their needs.

The RAND survey predicted about a 50 percent probability that direct electronic transmission of the newspaper to the home would be widespread by 1995. Many of those in the forefront of technology in the newspaper industry find even this lead time too liberal. Joseph Ungaro expects the ink-on-newsprint newspaper to be the prevalent form by the end of the century. Jules Tewlow, as ANPA's director of special projects, concluded his analysis on the subject by saying:

> It would appear unwise, if not patently foolish, to bet on the facsimile technology which offers only a limited potential for future growth as a principal carrier of information into the home. . . . Sheer bulk of product, logistics, and limited selectivity capabilities preclude this.

A study conducted for the White House Office on Telecommunications in 1975 found that, "Of the mass U.S. television audience, less than ten percent would have sufficient interest to purchase home facsimile or other similar ancillary information systems."

The study also indicated that not until the middle of the next decade will commercial ancillary information systems, which would provide "pages" of information on the television screen, become commercially viable. Even this may have been optimistic for the home consumer market.

While facsimile as a replacement for the daily newspaper has a questionable future, it does have a useful and productive function as a means of page and document transmission. The *St. Louis Post-Dispatch, Los Angeles Times,* the *Christian Science Monitor,* and the *Wall Street Journal* are among major dailies using facsimile pages at satellite production plants for plate-making.

There are three methods for transmitting facsimile pages: microwave, broadband telephone lines, and earth satellite. For short distances, telephone lines are most frequently used. *The Post-Dispatch* is using this method to transmit 30 to 40 standard newspaper pages an hour between their downtown composition and printing headquarters and their suburban printing plant 20 miles away.

Microwave, which is line-of-sight transmission only, becomes expensive over long distances. The *L.A. Times* is using microwave to transmit its page paste-ups to the EOCOM Laserite in Orange County, 30 miles away, at the rate of two minutes per page.

Dow Jones, with 12 printing plants around the country, has used land lines and microwave, but now is making use of earth satellites for some of its transmissions, at great savings. In 1970, Dow Jones began using leased video grade microwave to send facsimile pages of the *Wall Street Journal* from Palo Alto to Riverside, Calif. and from Chicopee, Mass. to Princeton, N.J. at the rate of one page every 3.8 minutes. Technological improvements in bandwidth compression helped cut costs 78 percent. But the big savings came with satellite.

The cost of sending microwave facsimile pages from Chicopee to Princeton was $10,000 per month. Sending the same pages to Dow Jones' new production facility in Orlando, Fla. would have been $75,000 monthly by microwave or $25,000 by telephone land lines. However, when the Orlando plant opened on November 20, 1975, Dow Jones beamed its pages to the WESTAR I satellite 22,300 miles above the Atlantic and back down to a receiving station at the Orlando plant. Not only is the resultant cost only $2000 monthly for Dow Jones, but the Princeton plant can receive the same signal at no additional charge, and thus save the entire $120,000 yearly microwave charge. Transmission time is 3.5 minutes per page.

Ground stations were as much as $2 million several years ago, but small receiving stations had dropped to $70,000 by 1976. The forecast was for a $5000 price tag for a mass-produced, four-foot receiving dish in 1980, making the receipt of satellite-transmitted communications from wire services and others economically feasible on a large scale. Thus, the use of satellites for communication between newspaper operations is still in its infancy.   •

Data Banks

As newspapers automate, they are acquiring the capability for the storage of vast sums of information, most of which never ends up in the newspaper. At present, the cost of storage is such that much of the accumulated data base must be purged, often as frequently as every 24 hours. However, it is not a great leap from the present systems to one which will have the capacity to save all or most of what is in the newspaper, plus much of what was deemed useful enough to enter the system in the first place, but never found its way in the paper.

The most ambitious attempt to provide a live, on-line real-time data bank is The New York Times Information Bank, a computerized information retrieval system which contains article abstracts from 60 sources. With the addition of 20,000 new items each month, the Information Bank had over 2.0 million abstracts by the beginning of 1980. The system allows the subscriber to query the data bank from a VDT connected by telephone lines to the central computer in New York. The response is in the form of an abstract of an article, which can also be printed on a high-speed printer. The full text of articles from the *Times* is available on microfiche.

At a cost of $45 to $50 per hour of computer time, plus terminal and line charges, the Information Bank's use is still primarily restricted to government, business, and educational institutions, including the three major television networks. But it may serve as the prototype for newspaper-marketed information services for the home.

A similar, though less ambitious information system is sold by Dow Jones, in a partnership with Bunker Ramo Corp. The Dow Jones-Bunker Ramo News Retrieval Service provides subscribers, frequently stock brokers and analysts, with news which appeared in the *Wall Street Journal, Barron's,* the Dow Jones ticker, and several other publications. A customer, again using a VDT and telephone connection, can key in the stock symbol of a company, an industry code, or a government agency code and the system will respond with a list of headlines, most recent ones first, of all filed news stories on that subject. Any entire story can then be called to the screen. Alternatively, a customer can request a list of all headlines from the ticker for the day, or key in "Hot News," which provides only bulletin-type ticker news. In many ways, the system functions as a video facsimile medium, but because it stores items for 90 days back, it provides a more expanded service.

IBM Corp. is promoting a packaged version of The New York Times Information Bank for newspapers to use internally as an electronic morgue. The newspaper would have to create its own data base, using IBM's "STAIRS" program. The main problem is again economic rather than technological, since information has been stored on a randomly accessible disk. IBM estimates that a large city daily newspaper would have to store about 1 billion characters a year. At a cost of current $.50 per million characters per month, current costs for storage alone would be $6000 for each year of data base stored on-line. This is exclusive of all other hardware and operating costs.

Mead Data Central, which has been successful with Lexis, providing full text on-line VDT presentation of legal decisions, now offers Nexis, a similar service for business offering many newspaper and magazine articles on-line. In 1980 the *Boston Globe* began offering an easy-to-access data base of abstracts of its daily publication.

RATE OF ADOPTION OF NEW TECHNOLOGY

The rate of introduction and widespread use of much of the new production technology has proceeded at a pace much faster than had been anticipated as recently as 1970. In that year, the RAND Institute asked about 25 individuals in fields relevant to the future of communications to make predictions about the widespread adoption of specific innovations. Figure 6.5 compares their 1970 assessment with the consensus of nine specialists in the newspaper field who were asked identical questions in a special survey in February, 1977.

Survey Results

In the 1977 survey, respondents were simply asked whether a particular innovation was widespread by 1976 or, if not, the year they felt held a 50 percent probability for widespread adoption. (A copy of the survey and the list of respondents is included in Appendix A.) As in the RAND survey, "widespread" was not defined. The specialists in this panel are all involved in the newspaper industry, so their results were contrasted only with those in the RAND study who were specialists in the industry's technology.

On the RAND panel, there were several developments that never reached a 50 percent probability of widespread adoption. One of these involved the keyboarding of material onto paper tape for entry into computer. The reason may be that even in 1970, technologists expected developments to quickly supplant paper tape technology. In fact, eight out of nine of the 1977 panel considered this mode already widespread by 1976 and added comments such as "a dying mode" or "but declining rapidly." The ninth participant wrote "never."

The RAND survey also failed to reach a 50 percent level for use of machine-readable hard copy as computer input—OCR utilization. But by 1977, two-thirds viewed it as widespread, two more by 1978, while another wrote "certainly by 1979 if not already." The widespread use of portable reporters' terminals is somewhat ahead of the schedule anticipated in 1970, when a 1980 target was reasonable. In early 1977, the common use of these devices was seen as very close by, with one respondent adding that he did not view the 200 Teleram terminals "in the field now" as being "widespread," although others might.

Using VDTs to key material directly into the computer in digital form barely reached the 50 percent probability for 1985 according to the RAND experts, but 1977 analysts expected a more timely common usage, given the various systems which already existed, including the Hendrix, Harris, Mergenthaler, Raytheon, N.E.W.S., ONE/Systems, and Computype (now part of Harris) packages described in this study. Digital storage and retrieval (statement five) is an extension of digital entry, or as one respondent explained, "Most front-end systems combine [statements] three and four into five." A third of the panelists considered this already widespread, with the consensus of the rest being 1979.

Many editors are already making editing and format decisions on the VDT (or CRT as the older study called it), but the "mutual interaction" qualification to statement six may have resulted in the strong 1980 consensus, compared to a 1985 expectation by RAND.

Despite the existence of prototype VDT full-page composition systems and laser plate-makers, the experts in 1977 foresaw statement seven technology as far off as the mid-1980s, although one said "never" and another wrote that, "Due to *present* high cost, 50 percent use is improbable." (His emphasis). The previous panel felt that widespread adoption would not come before 1990.

A third of the 1977 respondents declined to speculate on the advent of electrostatic or

Figure 6.5   Prediction of New Technology Adoption
(Year of 50% Probability of Widespread Use)

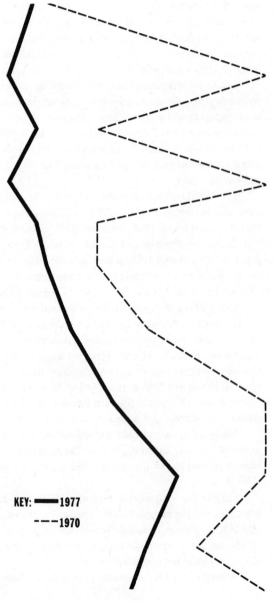

1975 | | | | 1980 | | | | 1985 | | | | 1990 | | | | 1995 | | | | NEVER OR BEYOND

1. Reporter's portable keyboard for direct input to local new headquarters with transmission via acoustic coupler or portable radio.

2. Inside headquarters, keyboarding of all material into computer via paper tape.

3. Inside headquarters, keyboarding of all material into computer directly in digital form.

4. Inside headquarters, machine reading of typed hard copy for entry into computer.

5. Storage in digital form of gross input for later callup and editing.

6. Editing and decisions on format by CRT and/or light pen with capacity for mutual interaction by two or more editors at their own consoles.

7. Composing of whole page designs on a CRT and direct production from this of printing surface for some form of pressure printing.

8. High speed electrostatic or ink jet printing with capacity for changing content electronically without interrupting production.

9. No hard-copy production of final paper but large amount of text and graphic material stored in computer and available for selective retrieval by the computer.

KEY: ━━━1977
---1970

10. Facsimile capable of rapid reproduction of newspaper-like content to the home.

11. High-resolution CRT for home video reading with capacity for making selected hard-copy.

ink-jet printing or replied "never." But the remainder expected it as early as 1983 or as late as 2000, with 1989/1990 being the middle ground. The RAND statements dealt with electrostatic rather than ink-jet printing as a possibility and the specialists did not see any greater than a 46 percent chance of its widespread use by 1995.

Similarly, the RAND survey found only a 45 percent probability of general use of a system which eliminated hard copy reproduction of the newspaper in favor of selective retrieval, presumably by consumers at home, of text and graphics. Fewer than half of the 1977 specialists wished to make a firm prediction, with 2050 being one outside estimate. Although one respondent again said "never," another wrote "sooner than one might guess," while a third, even more optimistic, estimated 1980.

The RAND wording for statement ten did not include "to the home," although it was in a context which made home facsimile the clear intent. The previous group did not anticipate such usage on a widespread basis before 1995, but of the six panelists in 1977 who estimated a date, the early 1990s predominated. One of those who did not pick a year added "other alternatives more feasible."

Finally, the use of home video facsimile with a hard copy option for selected material was considered unlikely by the RAND group, reaching a 49 percent probability by 1995. The latter day prophets were willing to predict a 1985 to 1995 realization of this, with 1989/1990 the most likely time. One of the respondents may have been speaking for the unwritten thoughts of the others in writing that statements nine, ten, and 11, all alternative methods of distribution, are "not necessarily mutually exclusive. Nor are they necessarily totally in lieu of printed product." This participant's expectation is that the 1995 to 2000 period "will probably see a shakedown of these alternatives."

The six or seven years between the time of the two surveys bridged a major gap between what was only technologically feasible in 1970 and what had already been proven by 1976. Full page make-up on a VDT and direct plate-making were still not in regular use, but unlike a mere six years previously, there were working prototypes of both. Other input and storage and retrieval systems made the glimmer of 1970 the near reality of 1977.

An important qualification to the analysis of the RAND findings adds that, "An innovation can have a significant impact on society long before it has a fifty-fifty chance of 'widespread' use or before it is used by half of all the population." It notes that it was not until the 1940s that half of the homes in the U.S. had telephones, although their impact on communications had been felt long before.

On the other hand, a comment on the 1977 survey warns that, "Technologies will not become widespread in use just because they exist. Monopolistic aspects of newspapers plus cultural biases will slow technology which does not produce a high rate of return." The respondent is saying that neither newspapers nor their competitors will introduce a specific technological innovation merely because it is feasible. The technology which did away with the Linotypes has been shown to have a sizable return on investments. Front-end VDT editing systems are less readily justified and have been slower to gain acceptance, at least until the price became more attractive. New forms of page make-up and plate-making beyond existing technology may not yield savings or produce revenues that would support the required investment.

For example, in referring to adoption of electrostatic or ink-jet printing, one newspaper executive in the 1977 survey anticipated a 1990 "production capability," but added that, "Implementation [is] a function of press investment in 'old' processes and cost of new, as well as [a] mode of supplying subscribers with [an] information package." Figure 6.6, the technically feasible production process of 1990, should be compared to Figure 6.2, the current process.

Thus, those who wish to predict the future of the newspaper must be diligent in separating the technological horizon from the economic reality. Certainly the future holds the expectation for continued gains in the speed at which information can be gathered and processed, as well as in the quantity of information which can be stored and held for access. The potential exists for the consumer to have greater selectivity in the type and form of the information which he or she can retrieve. Newspaper owners are left with making

Figure 6.6   Technologically Feasible Production Process of 1990

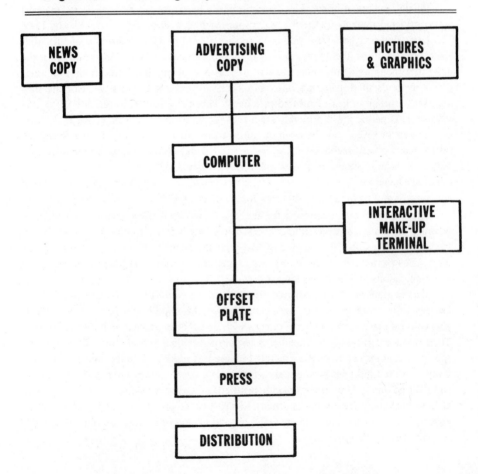

the marketing decisions regarding the utility of offering alternative methods of production and distribution of their product. And one question that they will have to deal with is how these new forms, should they involve non-print methods of distribution, would affect the service they perform for advertisers. It is their function for this constituency, above all else, which may be the determining factor that may keep the newspaper of 20 years hence at least looking much like the newspaper of 1980.

SUMMARY

Changes in the technology of newspaper production have drastically modified the nature of the news and composing rooms. The hot metal linecasters which dominated the composing room since the late nineteenth century have given way to phototypesetters which work 20 or more times faster, cleaner, and quieter—with fewer errors—than the old method.

The cold type process has been only the cutting edge of the new system. Total systems have affected the way display, classified, and news copy are entered into the channel which eventually feeds into the typesetting machines. Video display terminals and keyboards and optical character readers are new input devices, with the terminals replacing paper and blue pencil for editors. Because what is seen on the screen is what gets set, proofreading of galleys can be eliminated.

The more sophisticated of the new systems include large-screen make-up terminals for display advertising composition and complete merge, sort, and billing subsystems for classified advertising.

To accommodate the cold type process, newspapers have turned to a variety of modifications of their letterpresses. For all but the largest newspapers, direct printing plastic plates have replaced the stereotyping process. Other papers are producing pattern plates to use as the basis for stereotyping. The major trend, however, was the continued switch to offset presses, first for just the smaller papers, but by the mid-1970s for even the largest of metropolitan dailies. There have been gradual improvements in the DiLitho process, enabling papers to use offset plates on their letterpress equipment. Newsprint waste is still a significant drawback to both offset and DiLitho; but new computer-based controls have been designed to reduce this problem. Offset produces a higher quality reproduction of pictures and color than letterpress.

The new technology has been rapidly adopted because of its proven cost effectiveness. The photocomposition conversions have yielded complete paybacks in as little as one year, and rarely more than three years. Front-end newsroom systems are less cost effective, but are naturally compatible with the new composing room components. Most of the savings comes through reduced labor requirements, although other savings come as the result of fewer errors, improved printing quality, and byproducts of computer technology.

Further innovations may include video terminal make-up of the whole paper, with plates made directly from laser-etching machines, bypassing the entire typesetting and paste-up process. This step has not yet been shown as being cost effective, however. Plateless printing presses, using computer controlled ink-jet or electrostatic processes, are just being developed. Their use on a widespread basis is unlikely before the end of the 20th century.

Figure 6.7 summarizes the state of current newspaper composition systems and adds the expectation of Lee Enterprises, Inc. for the rate of continued evolution.

Facsimile reproduction of a hard copy newspaper to the home has been possible for 40 years, but is dismissed as uneconomical. Video facsimile, such as CEEFAX or Prestel, is in the experimental stage, but may be used more as a supplement than a replacement means of distribution.

Facsimile has been successfully adopted by several newspapers for sending pages or plates from one point to a remote printing plant, either in the suburbs, or, in the case of the national *Wall Street Journal,* thousands of miles across the country. Transmission has been through telephone lines and microwave, but earth satellites have been successfully and economically used by the *Journal.*

A 1977 survey of experts in the area of newspaper technology indicates that many technological innovations are moving more rapidly into use than a different group of ex-

Figure 6.7   Newspaper Composition Systems Evolution

	INTRODUCED	WIDELY USED
PROOFING AND CORRECTION WITH PHOTOTYPESETTING	1970	1972-1982
AREA COMPOSITION/TEXT INPUT & EDITING SYSTEMS - FRONT END TO PHOTOTYPESETTING	1972	1974-1990
MODULAR EDITORIAL MAKE-UP AUTOMATIC CLASSIFIED MAKE-UP	1977	1977-1990
EDITORIAL PAGE LAYOUT (TEXT ONLY)	1977	1978-1990
FULL PAGE LAYOUT WITH GRAPHICS AND PLATEMAKING	1979	1980-1990

Source: Lee Enterprises, Inc., Davenport, Iowa.

perts predicted in 1970. Nonetheless, there is a recognition that there remains a crucial gap between those improvements which are technically possible and those which are economically feasible.

Overall, the data on the new technology tend to substantiate the position that newspapers are using more electronics and will continue to improve in this area, but all with the end result of producing a product which will look similar and be distributed much the same way as the newspaper of 1977.

7

Effects of Technology on the Newsroom

New machines have invaded the newspaper. The routine of the newsroom has been disturbed by the arrival of equipment which makes the long-time tools of reporting and editing—typewriters, pencils, and paper—obsolete. The noisy clatter is being replaced in many newsrooms by the drone of fans cooling the innards of the VDTs.

In the production departments, the burly compositors have lost their real control over the composing process. The jobs which once required a six-year apprenticeship can now be handled by high school graduates fresh off the school bus—and at half the pay. Most significantly, control of production has passed from the composing room to the newsroom, as computers and VDTs enable editors to keep track of their copy and layout up to the point it is ready for plate-making.

Thus, the new electronics have given editors greater flexibility than they have ever had. They have the control over copy and editing that the journalist/printers had over their product before the age of mechanization.

Nonetheless, there have been some problems in changing over to the new technology. But planning in advance of the changeover has enabled many publishers to minimize the disruption.

There has been little systematic study of the effects of the new technology in the newsroom and on content, but this chapter may serve as a sampling of the reactions and experiences at several of the newspapers which have had some time to digest their new environment.

EFFECTS ON WORKERS

Introducing many changes in a short period of time, in an industry which has seen little basic innovation in 100 years, was bound to cause some problems. As has been the case in industries which have previously undergone automation, the addition of computers and electronics in the newspaper production process has resulted in the following potential for human problems:

• Isolation of workers, through the creation of new jobs and loss of old jobs, as well as geographical displacement.

• Anxiety at all levels. This is particularly true in cases where active rumor mills and grapevines spread stories of impending changes.

• New skill requirements. Retraining of employees is required for the operation of new devices. Fair pay scales must be established for these new requirements.

• New forms of organization. Along with changes in process and function, parts of the organization may disappear, new departments and positions evolve.

• Ability of supervisors to adapt. They must be able to help others make the transition, so their own attitudes toward change are critical.

• Motivation. As more processes become machine-controlled, determination of the work pace passes from people to machines. Such functions as feeding OCRs are boring and lack much opportunity for worker satisfaction. Management is thus faced with the challenge of finding new approaches to motivation, such as job rotation.

Effects on the Composing Room

Most attention has been paid to effects on the people in the newsroom and on the news content itself. But the workers in the composing room have been hit most fundamentally by the change. From the high skilled needs of expensive typesetters who work the complex Linotypes or the TTS terminals, then skillfully make up pages from lead slugs and turn over the locked up forms to the stereotypers, the skills which are now required are no greater than those of an ordinary typist or a minimally trained commercial art student. Metal forms are replaced by paper galleys and a glue pot. (And soon, when make-up is done on a VDT and the entire page is set at once by the large phototypesetters, even this function will be gone.)

The careful and neat now have priority over the strong and hearty. After resisting the inevitable change for many years, the International Typographers Union has finally yielded to the times, exchanging lifetime positions for its current members for withdrawing their opposition to full implementation of the electronic process.

As a result, the nature of the composing room is changing. Certainly there are fewer people. At the Richmond, Va. newspapers, where a strike eliminated the ITU shop, the average of the composing pay fell proportionately.

However, along with the lower age came less stability in the work force. The turnover rate jumped from seven or eight percent with the ITU to an initial 25 percent with the younger work force. Yet, even this lack of stability need not be a limiting concern, for where it took six years to train a new printer, the lesser skills of today require barely a week of apprenticeship. The turnover rate also moderated in later years.

Richmond executives found the new workers adapted better to change, since they were not as set in their ways. One young paste-up man with a commercial art background conceded that his work was not very artistically fulfilling. Most of his colleagues did not view what they were doing at the newspaper as a career, he admitted, but were "just passing through.'' Nonetheless, he did relate to the excitement of laying out the news, adding a visual identity to otherwise lifeless print.

But the experience of displaced workers in the composing rooms really is not much different from the changes which have affected many other manufacturing industries previously. In the newsroom, however, the reporters and editors have had to face change in their jobs, which have an even longer tradition than have the printers.

Effects on the Newsroom

In newsrooms where all copy is entered and edited on VDTs, the change is obvious and total. In situations where local copy is produced for OCR, the change for reporters may be as relatively minor as substituting new IBM electric typewriters for old Underwood manuals. Under the former circumstances, one newsroom executive believes he has identified a ''code of behavior'' which news staffers go through in the process of switching to an all-VDT processing system. Charles Tait, when assistant to the managing editor at the *Baltimore Sun* saw: (1) anticipation with fear; (2) disbelief; (3) dissolving into a ''high'' on the technology after a brief period with the new system; (4) then some disillusionment; (5) partial rejection; and finally (6) an ultimate enthusiasm for the new approach.

Jim Day, a staffer at the *Sun,* reported in an interview that a year after full conversion to all-VDT, there were only a few unhappy holdouts. ''The new machines were easier to operate than we thought,'' he explained, but then he admitted that the older staffers were scared at first. After a period of time, however, they found the system was more flexible than the old way, since it makes self-editing easier. ''The reporter is more aware of what his finished product looks like,'' Day said, but the reporters at first tended to overwrite, since to see what they had written previously took more effort to bring back than a sheet of paper. But this was balanced by increasing experience, and the slug line tells the length of the story immediately. ''What's on the screen is what gets set in type,'' notes Day, and thus a writer must be more careful about typographical errors and accuracy. ''You can't blame the mistakes on the composing room any more.''

At other papers, where OCR input is used, the change is less pronounced because reporters are still using the same basic process. At the Richmond papers, executive editor John Leard tried to keep electronics out of the newsroom as much as possible. Copy was typed on scannable font electric typewriters, but reporters edited their own copy with non-scannable ink pens. Leard wanted the staffers to put their emphasis on content, so he required them only to put two simple pieces of coding on their stories. A separate operation, the ''news processing unit,'' was responsible for other coding and typing in scannable correction. The OCR output was on paper tape which was then fed into the photocomposition machines. Leard sees the new technology merely as a way to get in later news with fewer errors and feels that the system basically accomplished this.

When the *Kansas City Star* converted to OCR input in 1973, it too set an objective of keeping typing for the scanners on IBM Selectrics ''as close as possible to typing on the old manual typewriters.'' At the time, city editor Tom Eblen found some reporters significantly slower, but improvement came with practice. There was some initial resistance to the change, as one reporter good-naturedly wrote: ''To hell with the electric typewriter machine. . . . They'll slow down production, cause morale reduction and turn us into blithering boobs. . . ." But the old manuals were sold to the reporters for $10 each when the Selectrics arrived and the switch was made with seemingly little trouble. Eblen does recommend, however, that reporters and editors be taken to the composing room to see the scanner operate, as those who understand the system make it work better.

At the small (10,917 circulation) *Troy* (Ohio) *Daily News,* the reporters got more involved with the whole system. There, the Selectrics were hardwired to a Star-Xylogics computer. The copy went into the computer as typed, so corrections had to be made with coded symbols. Then, the reporter goes to a VDT to call a story via a file number and edit it further on the screen. As a small paper, the staff was used to frequently acting as both reporters and their own editors. Nonetheless, general manager Roger Stilwell commented:

> Some of our people felt originally that the system would inhibit creativity. But we pointed out that they really weren't doing anything now they didn't do before. . . . The difference was that now they weren't communicating instructions to other people via pieces of paper. They were doing it themselves via electronics.

The degree of training and preparation for a changeover to any type of electronic system varies substantially, ranging from the 11 hours of formal classroom sessions that the Baltimore newspapers provided for its members on the desks to the almost *ad hoc* session arranged in Kansas City after the Selectrics were installed. Lee Enterprises, whose flagship *Quad-City Times* (Iowa) was one of the first papers to move to an all-VDT newsroom, has found that a management philosophy stressing decentralization and human development has worked successfully: "New machines will always be coming along, but people are what really matter."

PREPARING FOR CHANGE

In getting newsroom personnel ready for the new systems, the news executives have considered the following:

• Create some pre-conversion benchmarks—like how long it takes to do specific jobs or where the weak spots are, to provide a basis for comparison with the new system. This includes having an idea of the quality of the editing.

• Whatever the system, explain it thoroughly to all employees before it is operational.

• If there is to be an increase in newsroom workload, be sure to plan for added personnel.

• Schedule some dry runs with the new system before it becomes operational. Gannett requires the manufacturer to set up the system at the manufacturer's plant and sends some news staffers to check it out before it will accept delivery.

• Some actual work should be run on the new system parallel with the old system. Put in some errors for copy editors to correct. Include time tests.

• Several hand-picked news staffers should be sent for intense advanced training at the manufacturer's school. They can then return and help prepare a staff manual and be resource persons in helping to train the rest of the staff.

• Once the system is operational, several newsroom people should be designated liaison with the data processing and production departments, since the newsroom system will interface with these others.

• Use those pre-established benchmarks to follow through on the quality of work after the system is operational.

Enhanced Responsibility for Editors and Reporters

Overall, the trend in the electronic newsrooms has been to put the entire production process into the hands of the editors. Generation of phototypeset news copy and its paste-up is assigned to the news editor. The keyboarding, mark-up, and paste-up of advertising material is the responsibility of the advertising department. Thus, the newsroom has greater control following from its involvement with the production process. What is written by the reporter and corrected by the editor is what gets set—there is virtually no chance of misplaced lines or dropped letters in typesetting to change or obscure the meaning of an article. Hence the "typo" has given way to the "newso."

At least, this is what is claimed. However, copy which is fed into the computer through OCR is still subject to the vagaries of the scanners, and careless VDT editing can lead to as much gibberish as the best of the old days of misplaced slugs.

The advertising department, controlling its own production, also has responsibility for its errors and for seeing that proofs are ready on time. Locating this responsibility in the advertising department has reduced charge-offs for ad mistakes by two-thirds in Richmond.

Editors seem unanimous in that the greatest single advantage of their new systems is the added flexibility they provide. What they are really saying is that the electronics gives them more time and fewer restrictions. Dan Hayes, managing editor of the *Quad-City Times,* explained that their VDT input and editing system makes it a better edited paper with fewer production restrictions. Previously, editing often found copy written close to the deadline was inferior due to time pressures. This is less of a problem given the added time provided by a system which can set the edited story instantly.

Hayes elaborated: There is less permanence on the screen, making it easier to polish than pen and pencil stories. Using a typewriter, the reporter might write a lead, rip it out of the typewriter, and have to type 80 percent of it over again in the new lead. Now they can "attack, get words on the typewriter [VDT] quicker" and find it easier to massage the story, moving around sentences and paragraphs, producing better writing. Hayes tempers this, however, with the admonition that this capability is not always used to its best advantage.

Jim Day in Baltimore echoes Hayes' experience, adding that the result has also been that the earlier editions are cleaner, with fewer typos.

At the *Allentown Call* and *Chronicle,* editor Ed Miller asserted that he noticed less editing on the VDTs than with pen under the old system. But this may be merely part of the adaptation process. In Atlanta, *Journal* assistant managing editor Robert Lott can recall no particular problems with editors when they switched to all-VDT editing after a brief training period. Nor did the paper need additional copy editors.

Dan Hayes could not say if there was any change in the amount of editing in his newsroom, but he did acknowledge that using the terminals takes at least as much time as before. On the other hand, "There are just so many things which fit into triple-spaced copy" on paper, which can itself limit editing. Such is not the case with the VDT capability.

Reporter Jim Day has not noticed any less editing, but if there is he would attribute it to the cleaner copy the reporters are producing on the VDTs. Day does believe that the copy desk is somewhat slower; one editor has been added. The reporters' deadlines have been moved up to allow for more editing time at the *Sun.* John Leard needed extra help at the editing desk when the Richmond papers moved to VDT editing. The Raleigh, NC newspapers added two copy editors and a clerk after the change to VDTs.

IMPACT ON CONTENT

Although the consensus seems to be that a cleaner final product with perhaps better layout is the most visible result of the new technology, reporters at some papers have noticed the ability of the machines to get late stories set in type quickly, providing no doubt a personal gratification in being able to break such news.

One of the most encouraging developments, however, comes from Davenport, where part of the savings from the production process has been funneled into the editorial side. Since the paper went electronic, Hayes claims that it has added correspondents in two cities, an assistant librarian to expand the library, and a full-time investigative reporter. These additions are no doubt reflected in the content of the paper and are among the most positive signs that the new technology may go beyond adding to the bottom line of publishers, and actually contribute in a meaningful way to the substance of the newspaper.

For the most part, however, introduction of VDTs has been accompanied by attempts to adapt them to existing editing habits. Reports of more innovative uses are just beginning to drift in from the field:

• At the *Kansas City Star,* news editor Bob Busby produced a daily, page one two-column package which included an index and the weather, a witty sentence or two, promotions of major inside stories, and a categorized summary of major news stories. This was compiled from items fed him from terminals on city, telegraph, sports and other desks.

He did the final edit, determined headlines, boldface, and tabulation, and gave a single terminal command for production of the column on a single piece of photocomposed film.

• At the *Kansas City Times,* an assistant editor produces a highly popular column reporting on oddities and people in the news. Each item has a headline and many include thumbnail pictures. A five- or six-character command allows the editor to designate headlines, body type, and indents for the pictures. A character count provides accurate copy fitting.

• When he arrives at his desk early in the morning, the editor of the small (circulation 5800) *Paragould* (Ark.) *Daily Press* goes through all copy, deciding not only on what to run and where, but making immediate decisions on column width and type size for each story. For two decades, most small dailies like the *Daily Press* have been locked into a single column width on wire service copy which came over the teletypesetter systems. Setting odd-width columns was expensive. Thus, these papers tended toward monotonous layout. But the wire stripping and format functions of the *Daily Press'* editing system makes odd-width columns readily available. Two-digit codes call up formats containing spacing, column width, type size, and other information. Not only is every page now tailor made and layout planned better, but each staffer is able to carry his assignment through to the printed page.

From these examples, it is clear that the vague promise of greater flexibility is being applied in specific and sometimes creative ways to improve the content and appearance of newspapers of all sizes.

Thus, among the points of consensus among editors are:

• VDT systems do add much flexibility in editing and copy handling.

• They do not significantly alter the deadline structure or allow for cutting back on newsroom personnel; in fact, in many cases more editors are needed. But they do help get late breaking stories in the paper because they are tied to high-speed typesetters.

• In some cases, certain jobs must be downgraded, with lower level of skills required; hence a cost savings.

• Using VDTs requires more editing time, but they encourage more heavy editing, combining, reworking between editions, inserting, etc. One reason for taking longer is the added time it takes to move the cursor across the screen.

• There is often a drop in editing quality at first, while editors are still uncomfortable with coding or the nuances of the VDTs. But once these factors become familiar, the editors regain their former speed.

SUMMARY

Newspapers have not approached the human element in the conversion process with any consistent pattern, but effects of the new technology on people appear to have been minimal. Some composing room personnel have been retrained for other functions, such as paste-up, and in most union shops, personnel reductions have been largely through attrition. Some reporters and editors were apprehensive about the new equipment, but have quickly accepted and adopted the innovations.

There have been no dramatic changes in newspaper content, but there are reports of expanded flexibility to create new formats. If deadlines have not been generally extended, editors do claim the ability to get late breaking items into the paper closer to press time. Some publishers have funneled a portion of their production savings into expanded editorial budgets.

Overall, the new technology is credited with putting more control—and responsibility—for the final product in the hands of the editors.

8

Labor and Unions in the Newspaper Industry

The previous chapters mentioned some ways in which technological changes at newspapers were affecting personnel and showed how new production processes often result in the need for fewer workers in some positions. This chapter takes a more specific look at the labor situation in the newspaper business, especially at how organized labor has reacted to the changes. It touches on employment levels, wage rates, and the outlook for future manpower needs.

Production departments of newspapers have had union organization since before the Civil War, although editorial and business employees were not generally organized until after 1933, when Heywood Broun started the American Newspaper Guild. In 1979, four national or international unions represented workers in the newspaper and kindred printing professions: The Newspaper Guild (representing editorial, clerical and advertising personnel), the International Printing and Graphic Communications Union (the result of a 1973 merger between the Pressmen and Stereotypers), the International Typographical Union (ITU, representing mailing room and composing room personnel), and the Graphic Arts International Union (formerly the Lithographers and Photoengravers). The International Mailers Union merged into the ITU in 1979.

Although some large city newspapers may have to deal with these as well as other unions, such as the Teamsters who might represent delivery truck drivers, the types of labor problems which often make headlines are not necessarily widespread in the industry. One tabulation found that fewer than 25 percent of U.S. dailies had any union representation at all. The most pervasive union, the ITU, represented fewer than 470 papers, albeit almost all of the major ones.[1]

At many papers, the ITU local was a major obstacle to the introduction of labor-saving new technological equipment to composing rooms in the 1960s and 1970s. At issue was who would have jurisdiction over the input to the phototypesetters: the reporters and editors who prepared OCR scanner copy or used VDTs for writing and editing, or the typographers, who traditionally and by contract had jurisdiction over preparing copy for the Linotypes. In many cases, copy provided on paper tape from wire services or which was otherwise camera ready would have to be reset by typographers as bogus—duplicate type which would be set, then eventually discarded. As will be seen, this issue has been largely settled, but new problems face newspaper workers and management.

GENERAL EMPLOYMENT SITUATION

Newspapers are highly labor intensive, with direct wages accounting for about a third of all expenses at a typical large or medium-sized daily. Understandably, there must be considerable emphasis on the part of the publishers to keep tight control over wages. At the same time, the publisher knows that any difficulty with one union may result in the shutdown of the entire operation, since members of a nonstriking union may refuse to cross the picket line of the strikers.

One overriding characteristic of the employment situation in the newspaper industry is the declining number of jobs in mechanical and production departments. Table 8.1 shows that total employment at newspapers increased in 1978, as did employment in all manufacturing. But whereas the trend for all production workers has been generally upwards since 1965, these employees in the newspaper field have been declining since 1970, a natural outcome of the labor-saving devices being introduced. By 1978, total newspaper employment was more than 393,000, but production employment was down to 165,000.

Table 8.1   Employment in Newspaper Industry and All Manufacturing Industries, Selected Years, 1965-1977 (Index: 1965 = 100)

Year	Newspaper Employees (000)				All Manufacturing (000)			
	Total	Index	Production Workers Only	Index	Total	Index	Production Workers Only	Index
1965	345	100	175	100	18,062	100	13,434	100
1970	372	108	181	103	19,349	107	14,020	104
1973	382	111	181	103	19,820	110	14,575	108
1974	385	112	176	101	20,046	111	14,613	109
1975	379	110	168	96	18,347	102	13,070	97
1976	383	111	167	95	18,956	105	13,625	101
1977	393	114	165	94	19,554	108	14,066	105

Source: U.S. Bureau of Labor Statistics, *Employment and Earnings,* monthly.

Employment Outlook

The U.S. Labor Department reports that in 1976 there were 152,000 composing room employees in the United States, one third of whom worked in newspapers. The outlook through the mid-1980s—and probably beyond—is for an expected expansion of printing volume, but a decline in the number of employees because of the trend to high speed phototypesetting and typesetting computers which require fewer operators.

Likewise, jobs for electrotypers and stereotypers, whose ranks numbered 4000 in 1976, were expected to be scarce in the future, due to automatic plate casting, plastic plates, and offset. Press operators, 145,000 in number in 1976, will expand their ranks more slowly than the average for all occupations, the growth in the amount of printed material being somewhat absorbed by higher press speeds.

On the other hand, the 29,000 people in lithographic occupations, which include camera operators, artists, and strippers, will benefit by the expansion of cold type and offset printing. Employment of skilled workers in this field is forecast to grow faster than the demand for the average of all occupations.

On the editorial side, opportunities for budding young newspaper reporters are not encouraging, according to U.S. Department of Labor projections. In 1976 there were 40,000 reporters, 40 percent of them women. However there is "strong competition for jobs, especially on the large city dailies." But because newspapers are "not expected to share equally in this growth" of mass communication industry expansion, "employment of reporters should increase more slowly than the average for all occupations." *

Wages

Newspaper production workers had average wages in 1977 of $6.67 per hour, making them among the highest paid of all such workers in nonagricultural industries. Unionized newspaper employees, however, had still higher wages, seen in Table 8.2 at $8.17 per hour in 1976. Although building trades workers were the only higher group of those listed in Table 8.2, newspaper employee wages have experienced the slowest growth, about equal to the all-industry composite. In part this may stem from their being well ahead of the others in 1960. But the lack of demand for skilled workers and the diminished need for certain production skills (see Chapter 6), may have lowered the overall wage level and lessened union bargaining leverage.

Actual wages vary considerably from city to city. Tables 8.3 and 8.4 sample some of these differences. As of January 1, 1979, a typographer in New York earned $11.06 per hour on the day shift, while one in Birmingham made only $7.92. The mean wage in this nonprobability sample is very similar for all three crafts. Among Guild-represented employees, reporters and display ad salespersons tended to be given equal pay. The *Washington Post* paid the highest salaries to reporters, classified solicitors, and display ad salespersons, but *The New York Times,* which was second to the *Post* in these categories, led in wages for circulation managers.

Guild contracts should not be taken as necessarily typical for the industry. Since they are heavily concentrated in the larger and more urban newspapers, it should be expected that the median Guild salaries are somewhat above the median for the industry.

---

*U.S. Dept. of Labor, Bureau of Labor Statistics, *Occupational Outlook Handbook, 1978/79* (Washington, D.C.: U.S. Government Printing Office, 1978), p. 595.

Table 8.2 Minimum Hourly Union Wages in Selected Trades, Selected Years 1960-1976

Year July	All Industry Union & Nonunion	Bldg. Trades Journeymen	Motor Truck Drivers & Helpers	Local Transit Operators	Book & Job Printers	Newspaper Printing
1960	$2.09	$3.86	$2.65	$2.37	$3.08	$3.48
1965	2.45	4.64	3.22	2.88	3.58	3.94
1970	3.22	6.54	4.36	4.03	4.65	5.13
1973	3.92	8.02	5.85	5.04	5.91	6.43
1974	4.22	8.55	6.34	5.62	6.34	7.01
1975	4.54	9.32	6.81	6.25	6.86	7.36
1976	4.87	9.92	7.36	6.63	7.41	8.17
Compounded Annual Rate of Increase						
1960-1976	5.4%	6.1%	6.6%	6.6%	5.6%	5.5%

Sources: U.S. Bureau of Labor Statistics, *Employment and Earnings*; U.S. Bureau of Labor Statistics, *Union Wages and Hours*, annual.

Table 8.3   Mechanical Union Hourly Wages in Selected Cities, January 1, 1979

	Mailers	Typographers	Pressmen
Anchorage, Alaska	—	$10.50	$10.70
Birmingham, Ala.	$ 7.19	7.92	—
Boise, Idaho	—	6.99	7.98
Chicago, Ill. (*Tribune* only)	8.10	9.57	9.77
Memphis, Tenn.	8.00	8.11	—
Minneapolis, Minn.	9.76	9.76	11.30
New York, N.Y. (*News* & *Times* only)	8.54	11.06	9.88
Philadelphia, Pa.	7.95	9.36	8.16
Phoenix, Ariz.	9.51	9.54	9.59
Seattle, Wash.	9.18	10.50	10.60
Washington, D.C.	10.19[a]	11.60[a]	9.66[b]
Wichita, Kan.	8.03	8.03	8.61
Mean	8.64	9.41	9.62

[a]*Post.*   [b]*Star.*

N.B.   Figures for Day Rates. Night Rates are about 15¢/hour higher. Work week varies from 34.50 hours to 40.00.

Source: *Editor & Publisher International Year Book*, 1979.

THE ITU AND NEW TECHNOLOGY

The ITU has felt the brunt of the new technology. In 1968, before the electronic composing room was available, there were 123,000 ITU members, although not all worked for daily newspapers. By 1976, their ranks had thinned to 100,000. In a series of arbitration decisions over control of the electronic equipment, neither the union nor management had gained any clear advantages, but contract settlements have finally seen ITU acceptance of technological displacement.

The ITU has generally taken the position that its jurisdiction includes the setting of type, which covers any input for phototypesetters, as well as page make-up. Management, on the other hand, would lose much of the benefit of high speed, automated equipment if anything which is typed or scanned into the system was covered by "bogus clauses" with ITU locals. These contractual provisions gave the union the right to reset copy which had been set by punch-paper tapes transmitted, for example, by the wire services; the re-set type was called bogus, as it was never used.

A similar situation had developed with the United Telegraph Workers (UTW) at the wire services. The AP and UPI installed VDT-based systems in their bureaus before many

Table 8.4 Top Minimums Under Labor Contracts*

Classification	Highest	Lowest	Median
Reporters and Photographers (in effect Dec. 31, 1978)	$503 after 5 years *Washington (D.C.) Post*	$175 after 6 years *Parkersburg (W.Va.) Sentinel News*	$355 after 7 years *Santa Barbara (Calif.) News-Press*
Classified Inside Phone Solicitors (in effect Oct., 1975)	$301 after 4 years (*Washington Post*)	$129 after 4 years *Salem (Ore.) Statesman & Capital Journal*	$188 after 3 years (min. guarantee plus commission) *Denver (Colo.) Rocky Mountain News*
Display Ad Salespeople (in effect Oct., 1975)	$475 after 4 years *Washington Post*	$185 after 5 years *Monessen (Pa.) Valley Independent*	$290 after 5 years *Erie (Pa.) News*
Circulation District Managers (in effect Oct., 1975)	$405 after 4 years (plus car allowance) *New York Times*	$121 after 6 months (plus mileage) *Coos Bay (Ore.) World*	$271 flat (plus car allowance) *Long Beach (Calif.) Independent & Press Telegram*

*Includes Canadian newspapers.

Source: Reporters and photographers: *Editor & Publisher International Year Book*, 1979.
Others: *Editor & Publisher International Yearbook*, 1976.

newspapers had gone electronic. Previously, after an editor was finished with a reporter's typewritten story, it was put on the wire by a teletype or teletypesetter operator—in effect rekeyboarding. Under the new system, stories were written and edited on the VDT. When the editor was finished, he or she sent it to a central computer which in turn sent it to member papers, thus eliminating the job of the UTW operator. At separate arbitration hearings, in which the UTW charged that it had clear jurisdiction for all transmission of clean copy functions, the arbitrators recognized that technically the editors were now performing these transmission functions. However, in the Associated Press case, the arbitrator found that, "It is apparent that where comingling [of editorial and transmission functions] is necessarily involved, the dominant feature of the operation will ordinarily be editorial."[2] In the United Press International case, the arbitrator substantially agreed, saying:

> . . . there is much to be said for the [U.P.I.'s] argument that the newsman does not really transmit the news through the use of VDT, but merely uses the VDT to send stories back to the computer which itself does the transmission.[3]

In the cases which went to arbitration involving the ITU, the results were less clearcut. In cases at the *Detroit News* and *Oakland Tribune*, compromises gave management only limited freedom to eliminate rekeyboarding. A 1973 contract settlement in Atlanta struck a similar middle ground, with the publisher winning the right to use machine-readable copy except when "the foreman or his assistants determine (re)keyboarding is necessary."

Another contract settlement, this one with the San Francisco newspapers, provided that only material which was not of scannable quality had to be rekeyboarded by composing room personnel, but this was to be handled by ITU members in a typing pool, with pay at 75 percent of a regular journeyman's rate. Still, printers would still set all advertising copy and operate VDT editing terminals to make corrections requested by the news department.

Although the barriers against reduction of ITU members' role were slowly coming down, the final breakthrough was in New York, where New York Typographical Union No. 6 had long resisted the desire of the remaining daily papers to automate their composing rooms. However, in March 1974, after more than a year of negotiations, the *Times* and *Daily News* settled on a pact with the printers giving the newspapers full freedom to automate, in exchange for guaranteeing "lifetime" positions for union members then on the payroll.

The *Times* was thereby able to reduce through attrition the number of printers from 816 to 630 by mid-1977, a yearly savings of about $4.1 million. At about the same time, pacts with the *Washington Post* and Long Island's *Newsday* were concluded, along similar lines. Labor mediator Theodore W. Kheel called the New York agreement an "occurrence of tremendous importance" in the history of collective bargaining because of the pattern it set for others.

The jobs which remain in the post-electronic composing room—primarily page paste-up (until the advent of full pagination by the phototypesetter), some corrections, feeding scanners—are relatively unskilled or low skilled jobs which would ordinarily justify lower pay scales than those provided for in ITU-organized plants. A tour of the composing room in Atlanta, for example, finds the broad, burly men who had formerly been needed to operate the Linotypes and haul around heavy lead forms now gently operating IBM Selectric typewriters and carefully glueing cold type galleys on page forms. Some papers, therefore, would rather not have an ITU contract at all, but be free to hire lower paid people who can handle the new jobs.

The ability of a management to take a strike by the printers varies with the local labor situation. The key, however, is frequently delivery. If truck drivers will cross a picket line during a strike, management can expect to continue to turn out the newspaper, even if clerical and executive personnel have to write and produce the newspaper using the new technology. Thus, in Richmond, Va., when the *News-Leader* and *Times Dispatch*, both owned by Media General Co., demanded the right to introduce OCR and photocomposition equipment in 1971, the ITU local would not come to contract terms and struck. The Teamsters, however, continued making deliveries and the papers eventually hired non-union workers at lower wages to work in the new composing room. The papers continued publishing and the ITU has never settled. As a byproduct, Media General management can also point out the number of women working in the composing room, previously a virtually exclusive male domain.

A similar situation developed at the *Omaha* (Neb.) *World-Herald*. When the ITU local walked out in a jurisdictional dispute over OCR devices in May 1973, six other unions stayed on the job and the paper continued to be printed at full volume with half the number of workers in the composing room. In December, the strikers "unconditionally" offered to return to their jobs, but permanent replacements had already been hired, leaving the printers at least temporarily without work.

OTHER UNION ISSUES

Stereotypers, an endangered species because of the movement to thin metal and plastic letterpress and offset plates, have merged into the pressmen's union, which itself has changed its name from the International Printing Pressmen and Assistants' Union to the International Printing and Graphic Communications Union.

The Lithographers & Photoengravers—now called the Graphic Arts International Union—are also facing pressures due to automation. Currently, pictures and half tones still must be processed and negatives made from page paste-ups. But a computer make-up to engraved plate technology, with digital storage and production of graphics, would eliminate this function as well. In at least one case, the photoengravers lost a jurisdictional dispute with the printers' union. At the *Fresno* (Calif.) *Bee*, plates were being made by a Laser Graphic System unit in the composing room. The publisher allowed the ITU workers to have responsibility for its operation and the award was accepted by a National Labor Relations Board hearing officer. Even when the *Bee* changed to a NAPP plastic plate process, the NLRB upheld the award, based in part, on "area practice, job impact, and the fact that the typographers [sic] jurisdiction would result in greater efficiency and economy of operation."

The Pressmen

In many ways the pressmen would seem to be in the most secure position. They are well paid and even with changes to new plates or offset presses, there is no challenging their jurisdiction. "Plateless" presses or other electronically transmitted papers are still far in the future. They should be, says one publishing executive, the "safest unions."

But there has been serious pressure at many papers organized by Pressmen's locals to reduce the manning levels in the pressroom. Many papers have had "unit" manning levels, with contracts spelling out the minimum number of pressmen required per press unit. Evidence of a rapidly growing trend toward ridding newspapers of restrictive manning clauses is apparent from settlements in Atlanta, Knoxville, Fort Worth, and other cities that have eliminated unit manning and given publishers complete control over crew sizes in the pressroom. In Memphis, this new flexibility resulted in a 20 percent reduction in work crew size.

As in the ITU changes, some newspapers were faced with pressmen strikes in order to achieve favorable pacts. Gannett was negotiating for new manning levels at its unionized papers. At the *Bridgewater* (NJ) *Courier-News* the pressmen struck, but other workers, including ITU printers, crossed the picket lines and inexperienced hands ran the presses to produce papers as large as 80 pages.

One of the most publicized strikes by the pressmen was against the *Washington Post*, beginning in October 1975. Before they walked out, however, the pressmen damaged some of the presses and allegedly beat up an assistant foreman. The *Post* did not publish on October 1, but then resumed publication by having the paper printed at other plants outside of Washington, until gradually its presses were repaired and clerical and executive personnel took over the presses. At the height of the crisis, the presses were being run by only 35 people, compared to the normal complement of 205 pressmen. "The state of the art is such that a handful of people can now put out the paper," observed *Post* executive editor Benjamin Bradlee. The *Post* had also prepared for the strike by sending 55 non-union white collar workers to a special Oklahoma City school for a three-week press course.

As in other cases, the *Post* was able to continue operations because most Guild members refused to honor the picket lines, the electronic composition equipment allowed unskilled clerical people to perform typesetting and layout when the printers refused to report to work, and because truck drivers continued to deliver the papers to vendors. By the end of February 1976, the Mailers' Union, also on strike, settled for a contract they admitted was "pretty bad" but was approved by the membership because the mailers feared that the *Post* would give their jobs away to nonunion workers as they had done with the pressmen. Only 37 striking pressmen returned to the *Post,* but the union itself did not. This fact saved the newspaper an estimated $2 million in 1976 alone, not only because there were 25 percent fewer workers, but because of elimination of what management spokesmen categorized as "featherbedding" work rules.

The three month newspaper shutdown in 1978 of *The New York Times* and *New York News* (the *Post* settled after two months) centered on the press manning issue. But here the other unions agreed to honor the pressmen's picket line. The negotiated contract did provide some manning relief for the publishers.

Implications

The strikes at the *Post* and the virtual capitulation of the mailers, photoengravers, and stereotypers and the destruction of the pressmen has been termed "a monumental labor-management dispute that has major implications for the newspaper industry."[4] Unlike the ITU, which finally recognized that the days of their craft were numbered, the pressmen seem to "have had a sense that conditions would never really change, and, as a result, they refused to look squarely at the technological change that was occurring."[5] The success of the *Post* in weakening the position of the craft unions may make bolder other large city newspapers with what they perceive to be similar contractual constraints to insist on increased flexibility for manning and other work rules.

The position of the Guild is also made more perilous because members must face decisions on whether or not to honor picket lines of fellow unionists who may be resisting change, or cross them and thus weaken their own position should they strike. In a three-week strike by the Guild local at the *Philadelphia Inquirer* and *Daily News* in February 1977, other locals at the papers, including the Teamsters, honored the Guild picket lines, completely shutting down the two Knight-Ridder newspapers. The Guild thus owes these others similar respect should their contracts expire without a settlement.

The Newspaper Guild

The Guild has been generally unaffected by technological innovations. As a result, its continuing goals include job security and money settlements which will advance salaries "beyond increases in living costs and productivity. . . ."[6] Locals do express some concern for the VDT and electric typewriters they are now using by seeking inspection of new equipment (there was some unsubstantiated concern about radiation leakage from VDTs), and guarding against establishment of speed and accuracy standards in the use of the new devices.

The Guild did lose a case in 1976 before the National Labor Relations Board (NLRB) which ruled, against the wishes of the Guild, that codes of ethics for reporters were not bargaining issues and therefore could be instituted unilaterally by publishers. The Guild had argued in several separate cases that such codes were "unilateral changes in terms and conditions of employment"[7] and thus an unfair labor practice. Although this point was upheld by administrative law judges, the board itself ruled that such codes were management prerogatives, although any penalties which would be associated with violations of the code are subject to bargaining.

In another NLRB decision, the board upheld in 1976 a 1948 ruling that journalists were not professionals, as NLRB defined it. Since most newroom employees are reporters and editors, publishers would just as soon have them declared to be professionals, which would make it more difficult to include them in a bargaining unit with non-professional news department personnel, such as typists, clerks, and photographers. The National Labor Relations Act defines a professional as "an employee doing work that requires advanced knowledge of a type 'customarily acquired' by specialized study." The majority concluded that this was not necessary for a journalist. The ruling in this case came as the result of the International Typographers Union seeking a representation election among *news* department employees at the *San Antonio* (Tex.) *Express* and *News.*

Possible ITU-Guild Merger

Technological innovations have resulted in the elimination of some processes and changes in the nature of other jobs. As implied in the wire service arbitration rulings, reporters and editors working at VDTs are, in effect, becoming the transmitters or typesetters, with the aid of the computer. In effect, this gives overlapping jurisdiction to Guild members and ITU printers. Moreover, with complete pagination further threatening the duties of printers, the ITU locals face further attrition losses. As a result, there is increasing acceptance of a need for a merger between the Guild and ITU, a concept which both unions openly accept.

Both the ITU and the Guild have been actively exploring avenues for ultimate consolidation. At the *Washington Star*, a task force of the two unions helped put together a ten-union settlement to aid the struggling daily. In Cincinnati and St. Louis, the two unions also cooperated in efforts to save jobs and improve the labor situation at those papers. The two unions are expected to engage first in more joint bargaining and cooperative organizing to break down barriers between the two organizations at the local level, with the ultimate goal of institutional unity. The process has not proceeded, however, without conflicts.

SUMMARY

Big city newspapers must deal with as many as 11 separate unions, four of them specifically part of the newspaper industry.

Newspapers are labor intensive, but the new production process has helped reduce the number of total employees in the industry, especially in production jobs.

Wages are still among the highest of unionized trades, but increases have come more slowly than in other trades since 1960. There are considerable differences in pay scales among newspapers for similar jobs, but top minimum pay for reporters was $503 at the *Washington Post* in 1978, with display ad sales personnel receiving similar compensation.

The International Typographers Union has been especially hard hit by the developments in technology. But after a period of obstruction and jurisdictional disputes, the ITU and management have reached general accommodation providing for lifetime security for current workers and basic jurisdiction over what remains of the composing process.

Other newspaper unions have already merged to counter declining membership and decreasingly distinct jurisdictions. The Newspaper Guild, representing business and edi-

**Table 8.5   Summary of Major Arbitration Awards and Contract
Settlements in Labor/Management Disputes**

Participants and Date	Issue	Resolution
Associated Press and United Telegraph Workers, 1971	Jurisdiction of VDT. Is it primarily an editorial or transmission device?	Arbitrator ruled that it is basically editorial, the transmission function being minimal, thus reducing UTW role.
United Press International and UTW, 1972	Same as above.	Same as above.
San Francisco News Printing Co. and ITU, 1973	Jurisdiction rights over VDT and OCR.	ITU retains jurisdiction over operating OCR and rekeyboarding any non-scannable input, all display ads, and corrections using VDTs. Input that is OCR ready does not have to be retyped. Arbitration with no dissent.
Atlanta newspapers and ITU, 1973	Jurisdiction of OCR.	Settlement gives ITU full control over input and output of OCR and computer devices. OCR-ready copy is acceptable, but any retyped material done by ITU typist pool at 75% regular pay scale.
Oakland, Calif. Tribune and ITU, 1973	Jurisdiction of OCR.	Interim arbitration ruling gives paper right to use OCR, with copy prepared outside composing room. No ITU members can be laid off.
Detroit News and ITU, 1974	Jurisdiction of VDT.	VDT & OCR entry and editing for all *News* entered copy allowed, but hard copy from any source requiring minimal editing keyboarded by composing room employees.

torial employees at some papers, has been exploring a merger with the ITU. The pressmen have been under pressure to accept reduced manning levels and a particularly ugly altercation at the *Washington Post* ended in the elimination of the union's role there and sent a message to other locals that such reductions may be inevitable.

The prevailing trends apparently confirm the assertions of the hypothesis that the unions are bending to meet the realities of new working conditions and have begun seeking ways of coordinating efforts, perhaps leading to merged organizations of The Guild and ITU.

A summary of major arbitration awards and contract settlements in labor/management disputes is given in Table 8.5.

Table 8.5, continued

Participants and Date	Issue	Resolution
New York Times/ Daily News and N.Y. Typographical Union No. 6, ITU, 1974	Use of new technology in composing process and "bogus" requirements.	Contract agreement gives newspapers unrestricted right to use automated typesetting equipment. Typographers given lifetime employment guarantees, with bonuses for early retirement.
St. Louis Post-Dispatch and the Pressmen, 1975	Pressroom manning levels.	Contract agreement permitted reduction in union workforce through attrition. Financial incentives offered for early retirement.
Washington Post and Pressmen, Local 6 of IP& GCU; 1975-76	Pressroom manning levels.	Pressmen struck, but Post ran presses without them, hired replacements. Reduced manning from 204 to 150. Reduced strength of pressmen, mailers, guild.
New York Times, New York News and Pressmen, 1978 (Post returned to operations, offering to give union whatever was agreed on at other two papers.)	Pressroom manning levels.	Pressmen struck in August and other unions followed. Both papers shut down for three months. No clear victor, but concessions made by pressmen on manning in exchange for job guarantees for current situation holders.

Source: Compiled by author.

FOOTNOTES

1. Ben H. Bagdikian, "Maximizing Profits at The Washington Post," *Washington Monthly,* January 1976, p. 32.

2. *The Associated Press and United Telegraph Workers, A. P. System, Division No. 14 of United Telegraph Workers, AFL-CIO,* Arbitration Award, March 29, 1971, p. 25.

3. *United Press International, Inc. and United Press International System, Division No. 47 of United Telegraph Workers, AFL-CIO,* Arbitration Award, November 15, 1972, p. 13.

4. Ben A. Franklin, "Chastened Unions Lick Their Wounds as Last Holdouts in 20-Week Washington Post Strike Return to Work," *The New York Times,* February 29, 1976, p. 39.

5. "The Post Breaks a Union's Iron Grip," *Business Week,* December 29, 1975, p. 30.

6. Darnell Leo, " 'Meat and Potato' Issues Occupy Guild Convention," *Editor and Publisher*, July 19, 1975, p. 12.

7. I. William Hill, "Guild Wins Another Round in Code of Ethics Dispute," *Editor and Publisher,* September 27, 1975, p. 61.

9

The Newsprint Industry

The newsprint industry is largely a stephchild of the newspaper industry. About 85 percent of the total production of newsprint is consumed by daily newspapers. Another 5 percent is used by weekly newspapers, Sunday supplements, comics, and inserts. The remainder is used for telephone directories, periodicals, and commercial printing.

Chapter 9 looks briefly at the nature of this close ancillary to newspaper publishing, with a particular emphasis on the price of newsprint, which, along with supply, is of major import to publishers.

TRENDS

Consumption

Trends in newsprint consumption are traced from 1960 to 1978 in Table 9.1. Newsprint consumption is highly sensitive to the fortunes of the daily newspaper. Thus, despite stagnant circulation, newsprint usage climbed steadily, if slowly, as newspapers became fatter. This can be seen in the declining number of newspaper copies per ton of newsprint compared to the increased ad revenue per ton. At its present weight, newspapers get about 80 pages per pound. The cost of paper alone for a six-pound Sunday *New York Times* was $1.19 at 1979 prices. As calculated in Table 9.2, however, the consumption of newsprint has grown at a considerably slower rate than GNP in constant dollars.

Sources

Most newprint used by United States newspapers comes from Canada, although as seen in Table 9.3, U.S. mills have made strong gains in the years since 1959, when only 25.7 percent of newsprint tonnage was domestically manufactured. The South is the country's major newprint producing region, followed by the West, primarily Oregon and Washington. The most substantial reason for the growth of U.S. newsprint was the 106 percent boost in Southern mill output.

Profitability for Manufacturers

The newsprint business has traditionally been one plagued by boom and bust cycles of excess capacity and then too much demand. Profitability as a percentage of invested

Table 9.1   Newsprint Consumption in the United States, 1960-1978

Year	Consumption (Million Tons)[a]	Ave. Annual Percent Change	Advertising Revenue/Ton	1,000 Circulation/Ton
1960	7.0	—	529	8,412
1965	8.0	2.9%	557	7,545
1970	9.1	2.7	631	7,764
1973	10.2	4.0	745	6,191
1974	10.1	− 1.0	792	6,126
1975	9.2	− 8.9	918	6,593
1976	9.6	4.3	1,032	6,352
1977	10.2	6.3	1,091	6,050
1978	10.8	5.9	1,175	5,726
Compound Annual Rate of Growth 2.4%			4.5%	− 2.1%

[a]Pre-1974 tonnage converted to 30 pound weight equivalent.

Sources: Newsprint: American Newspaper Publishers Association, Reston, Va. Advertising and Circulation calculated from Tables. 2.2 and 3.2.

Table 9.2   Newsprint Consumption Compared to Constant Gross National Product, 1950-1978
(Index: 1960 = 100)

Year	Newsprint Consumption Index	Constant 1972 Dollars GNP Index
1950	81	72
1955	89	89
1960	100	100
1965	115	126
1970	134	146
1971	141	150
1972	145	159
1973	147	168
1974	141	165
1975	129	162
1976	132	170
1977	150	181
1978	154	190

Sources: GNP: Calculated from constant dollar GNP, U.S. Bureau of Economic Analysis; newsprint: calculated from Table 9.1.

Table 9.3   Sources of Newsprint Supply for U.S. Daily Newspapers, 1959-1975

Location of Suppliers	Tons Supplied (000) 1959	1975	Percent Change	Share of Supply 1959	1975
UNITED STATES	1,466	2,865	95.4%	25.8%	38.9%
Northeast	342	445	30.1	6.0	6.0
North Central	8	108	1250.0	0.1	1.5
South	751	1,648	109.4	13.2	22.4
West	365	663	81.6	6.4	9.0
CANADA	4,114	4,467	8.8	72.3	60.7
East	3,557	3,791	6.6	62.5	51.4
West	556	685	23.2	9.8	9.3
OVERSEAS	111	29	− 73.9	2.0	0.4
TOTAL SUPPLY TO U.S.	5,692	7,369	29.5	100.0	100.0

N.B.   Subtotal may not add to total due to rounding.

Based on daily newspapers reporting to ANPA. Does not include foreign language, college, or special service dailies, *The Christian Science Monitor, The Wall Street Journal, The Journal of Commerce,* or the *Daily Racing Form.* Adjusted for temporary losses due to major strikes. 1959 figures adjusted to average basis weight of 1975.

Source: American Newspaper Publishers Association, *Newsprint & Traffic Bulletin, January 5,1977.*

capital is low by manufacturing standards. In 1965, five leading Canadian newsprint manufacturers had a return on capital rate in the range of six to ten percent. In 1971, the best of the group had a four percent return, while two were under two percent. In 1974, with plants running at full capacity to keep up with a demand heightened by expectations of a strike in the mills in 1975, return to capital ranged from nine to 17 percent.

Plagued by lengthy strikes that shut mills in Canada for months, combined with strong demand in 1977 and 1978, prices rose rapidly, as did profitability.

For the entire paper, fiber, and wood products industry, the median return on stockholder's equity for major firms in 1978 was 15.5 percent, compared to 15.1 percent for the all-industries median.[1]

The rapidity of the price escalation (Table 9.3) left industry spokesmen in some embarrassing situations. In September 1973, the consensus in Canada was that $205 a ton would be a "fair price" for newsprint. By late 1973, industry sources claimed that price increases would not come "as quickly as had been expected." At the time, the price per ton was about $170 in New York and one company president announced that a price of "between $235 and $245 a ton" was needed before a producer could justify investing $150 million to build a new mill.[2] Nine months later, many firms had reached that price, but revised their figures upward, speculating that a price of "around $300 a ton" was needed for new capacity. That price was arrived at by early 1977, and a few announcements of new mills and added capacity followed.

NEWSPAPERS' STRATEGIES

Several of the larger newspaper companies have acquired interests in newsprint companies as a hedge against price increases and to help insure supply during shortages. In 1978, The Washington Post Co. bought almost 50 percent of the 175,000 ton capacity of the Bowater Mersey Paper Co., a Canadian mill in which it owns a 49 percent interest. As a result, $1.8 million of the $26.6 million the firm spent with Bowater came back to the Post as its share in the newsprint company's profits. The Post also became a 30 percent owner in a newsprint mill that was under construction in 1978-1980.

Times Mirror Co. owns Publishers Paper Co. and bought most of its output for about $83 million in 1978. The New York Times Co. has substantial minority interests in three Canadian mills and Dow Jones has a 40 percent interest in a Canadian producer. Media General Co. owns a manufacturer in New Jersey which produces recycled newsprint and Knight-Ridder and Cox newspaper chains have joined with Media General in building a new mill using two-thirds recycled paper.

Newsprint Prices and Conservation Measures

Although newspaper executives have been very concerned about the seemingly skyrocketing cost of newsprint in the 1970s, the fact is that newsprint prices have increased at a compounded annual rate of 4.6 percent between 1955 and 1979, not much more than the rise in the wholesale price index of all commodities, as seen in Table 9.4. What makes the increase seem so dramatic is that prices were nearly stagnant during much of the 1950s and 1960s, increasing only 1.3 percent annually from 1955 to 1970. But since 1970, they jumped at a yearly compounded average of 10.6 percent, several percentage points above that for all commodities. The cost of energy, near $80 per ton, plus expensive wage settlements, has contributed to increased expense at the mills. The price of newsprint is of far more concern to large papers than to the smaller ones. In fact, newsprint expense as a percentage of revenue is directly correlated to circulation. For newspapers of varying size, the norms are provided in Table 9.5 for 1975 and 1979.

This increased percentage for larger newspapers relates to the greater amount of advertising linage (hence the higher proportion of revenue from advertising, as shown in Chapter 2) and therefore a greater number of pages per issue.

The rapid price escalation did move the newspaper industry to institute strict conservation measures beginning in 1973. Moreover, strikes in the paper mills during periods of tight supply in 1974 and 1975 worried publishers, who built up inventories from the usual 30 days to twice that and cut back on usage in response. The steep decline in consumption

Table 9.4   Newsprint Price Per Ton Compared to Wholesale Price of Commodities Index, 1955-1979
(Index: 1967 = 100)

Year	Newsprint[a] Cost/Ton	Newsprint Index	Producer Price Index
1955	$126.00	90	88
1960	134.00	96	95
1965	134.00	96	97
1970	152.00	109	110
1971	157.33	112	114
1972	164.58	118	119
1973	175.00	125	135
1974	210.00	150	160
1975	260.00	186	175
1976	285.00	204	183
1977	305.00	218	194
1978	325.00	243	217
1979	375.00	280	235[b]

[a]Annual average contract price/ton delivered in New York. Prices through 1973 for 32 lb. paper and since then for 30 lb. Measured in short tons (2000 pounds).

[b]Estimate.

Sources: Newsprint prices: 1955-1977: Canadian Pulp Paper Association; 1977-1978: published prices of leading suppliers. Producer prices: U.S. Bureau of Labor Statistics, *Producer* (formerly *Wholesale*) *Prices and Price Indexes*, monthly and annual.

Table 9.5   Newsprint, Ink and Handling as a Percent of Revenue for Newspapers with Varying Circulation, 1975 and 1979

Circulation	Paper, Ink Handling Expense 1975 (000)	1979 (000)	Percent of Total Revenue 1975	1979
5,000	$ 39	$ 53	9.2%	9.4%
10,000	106	142	11.0	11.2
20,000	284	381	13.1	13.4
40,000	765	1,020	15.6	16.0
75,000	1,880	2,500	18.3	19.8
200,000	7,639	10,600	23.4	28.3

Sources: 1975: Inland Daily Press Association, Chicago, Illinois from 355 midwestern newspapers; 1979: Knowledge Industry Publications, Inc., estimate.

in 1975 reflects such conservation, as well as economic conditions. Among the major steps taken by newspapers especially since 1974 are:

1.   A change from 32-pound to 30-pound newsprint at most newspapers. This alone has the impact of reducing tonnage figures 6.25 percent from an equivalent amount of the heavier weight paper. Moreover, since a roll of 30-pound paper contains more newsprint than a 32-pound roll of equal weight, newspapers would save on fewer rolls being transported and handled and fewer changes on the press—reducing the opportunity for time-consuming web breaks, and enabling them to store 6.25 percent more paper in the same space as previously. For a paper which used 100,000 tons (*The New York Times* uses about 300,000 tons annually), 7800 fewer rolls would be handled.

2.   Reduction in trim size from the standard 60-inch rolls to 58-inch web width or even down to 55-inch. This can save another 3.3 percent to 8.3 percent in paper weight.

3.   Movement to a six-column news, nine-column display ad, and ten-column classified ad format. Wider width of the editorial columns results in greater editorial copy in the same amount of space because of fewer alleys between columns compared to the traditional eight-column layout. The *Houston Chronicle* figured that by changing to the six-column format and a nine point slug (from 9½) it could get almost ten percent more copy in the space. Some papers switched to other formats designed to reduce newsprint. Table 9.6 shows potential savings at the *Chronicle,* which was using 82,000 tons of newsprint, from some of these changes.

4.   Paradoxically, some papers and the ANPA have found that increasing the web width to 62 inches or even 68 inches may be even more beneficial, since the wider columns permit more news and ads on a page. It also requires using fewer press units and press manning requirements. Fewer pages mean less composing room time and fewer plates—a real savings for offset or direct printing plates. One midwest paper found that it would save $464.000 by going to a 55-inch width, and an additional $63,484 on a 62-inch roll.

5.   As noted in Chapter 3, newspapers began cutting down on fringe area circulation and newsstand distribution (to minimize waste in returns), thus contributing somewhat to the drop in circulation in 1974 and 1975. The rapid newsprint cost escalation also helped quicken the rise in the number of 15 cent and then 20 cent newspapers to help recover this variable cost.

Despite these and other measures, newsprint bills continued upward. *The New York Times,* which changed to the 6/9 column format in 1976, calculated that the increased efficiency would mean that an 88-page paper in the previous format would become 84 pages "without any reduction in content." Other conservation steps (and declining circulation) helped the *Times* reduce its newsprint usage 31 percent between 1969 and 1975. Nonetheless, its newsprint bill was up over 16 percent in that period.

Table 9.6   Estimated Projection of Newsprint Savings Possible from Selected Format Changes (Reported in Percent of Total Newsprint Saved)

IF Format Changed To:	Editorial Usage Reduction	Display Ad Usage Reduction	Classified Ad Usage Reduction	Potential Annual Savings/Tons
"Los Angeles Times" 55-inch 9-column classified 8-column display 6-column news		2.4%	0	1,968
"Miami Herald" 55-inch 9-column classified 6-column news & display	1.3%	2.4%	0	3,034
58-inch width 10-column classified 9-column display (photo comp.) 6-column news (hot metal)	2.45%	5.4%	0	6,437
58-inch width* 10-column classified 9-column news & display (all photo comp.)	3.1%	5.4%	0	6,970
58-inch width 10-column classified 9-column display (photo comp.) 9-column news (hot metal)		5.4%	0	4,428
56-inch width* 10-column classified 8-column news & display (all photo comp.)	0.9%	1.5%	1.1%	2,788
60-inch width 11-inch column classified 9-column display (photo comp.) 9-column news (hot metal)		3.5%	1.9%	4,428

*These formats call for optical shrinking of editorial type faces.

N.B.   All savings based on usage of 82,000 tons of newsprint annually under the existing format.

Source: Gene McDavid, *The Houston Chronicle*, 1976.

By reducing waste, newspapers appear to have kept their increased newsprint expenditures in line with all other expenses. For the 260,000 circulation composite newspapers shown in Table 2.9, newsprint and ink accounted for 36.5 percent of total expense in 1978, compared to 37.5 percent in 1969. Between these years, total expenses increased 74 percent while newsprint and ink rose 69 percent. (Ink, rising in price due to increased petroleum prices, accounted for 1.8 percent of the combined newsprint and ink figure in 1978, the same as in 1969 and lower than the 2.5 percent it accounted for in 1975.)

OUTLOOK FOR NEWSPRINT

Making predictions beyond a year or two can be hazardous in the newsprint area. For years newsprint prices and consumption did seem to change quite predictably, leading official ANPA analyst Jon Udell to use several variables (real GNP, adult population, number of households, newspaper advertising) to construct a regression model which in 1970 predicted a range of newsprint usage in 1980 "conservatively projected" to reach 13.1 million tons of 32 pound paper which would be adjusted to 12.3 million tons under the lighter weight. Actual usage for 1980 was projected in late 1979 to reach almost 11 tons (about equal to 1979).

The newsprint situation grew increasingly critical in 1979, with many newspapers having to import foreign newsprint, at reported prices of $600 or more per ton. Some papers were forced to temporarily omit some material (*The Boston Globe* cut out engagement and wedding announcements). With inventories exceedingly low, even the addition of new capacity would not provide substantial price relief. With continued labor unrest in Canada, U.S. publishers can be expected to build up their inventories in preparation for future disruptions in supply.

Between 1979 and 1984, Canada is expected to increase its newsprint production capacity by 1.4 million tons, while U.S. increases will total about 1.2 million tons. But at the same time, there is growing foreign demand for North American newsprint. In addition, demand is expected to increase from non-daily newspaper and "shoppers," as well as from advertisers using pre-prints and others, such as directory publishers.

The investment in new plant construction is a major consideration. The cost of building a pulp mill to turn out 70 tons per day of newsprint was estimated to be $250 million in 1976. This is exclusive of the cost of forest lands. The joint venture Cox/Media General/ Knight-Ridder recycling mill in Georgia cost $110 to $120 million, which was 50 percent higher than an estimate only a year before construction started. The president of Bowater, Inc., complained in 1974 that the cost of new mills was rising at the rate of between 1.0 percent and 1.5 percent a month, while the lead time from a commitment to first production had extended from 24 months in early 1974 to 28 or 30 months by the end of the year, making planning that much riskier. Investment in mandated pollution controls was expected to absorb $410 million to $1 billion by 1986.[3]

Technological Developments

One hope for eventual stabilization of newsprint prices is the still experimental thermo-mechanical pulp (TMP) process being tested by several Canadian mills and newspapers. The TMP process produces a pulp of greater strength than the conventional mechanical pulping process, enabling the production of lighter weight newsprint without sacrifice in strength. It has the potential to increase yield 20 percent from the same amount of wood needed in the present process. The implication of this is that poorer grades of wood may be used for newsprint and existing mills would be able to increase capacity without adding equipment or increasing acreage. On the other hand, TMP would require a high initial capital investment, higher labor and transportation costs, and increased energy expense, so that at best the process would only help stabilize, not reduce, newsprint prices.

Potentially an even more promising development involves making newsprint from kenaf, a prolific plant related to cotton. Several newsprint manufacturers as well as the U.S. Agriculture Department are interested in using kenaf to replace all or most of the wood in newsprint. On a test basis it has been used on conventional presses. Tests indicate that its strength is nearly the same as wood-pulp newsprint and it is of similar brightness, though it has a yellow tinge.

Under any set of assumptions, the price of newsprint must be expected to continue to increase with regularity, even if supply does catch up with demand. This is due in part to the energy intensive nature of paper manufacturing: it is the fourth largest consumer of energy among all manufacturers. It also depends for the time being on wood, a resource that is being used faster than forests are being grown. And the major source of supply continues to be Canada, where long strikes and large wage settlements have become a regular feature of the industry.

SUMMARY

The newsprint industry is closely tied to the fortunes of daily newspapers, which consume 85 percent of its output. Most newsprint used in the United States is produced in Canada, but U.S. production has been steadily increasing in proportion.

After decades of remarkably steady prices and oversupply, newsprint prices jumped almost 147 percent between 1970 and the beginning of 1980.

As a result, newspaper management took a number of steps to keep the impact of these sudden hikes under control. Among them: reducing web widths from the standard 60-inch width; switching from 32-pound to 30-pound weights; making editorial columns wider and fewer, reducing wasted white space, and eliminating some fringe area circulation.

The expectation is that newsprint production capacity and demand will continue to produce a tight market in the early 1980s. The cost of constructing new facilities has escalated along with the price of the commodity. One technological development, thermo-mechanical pulping, may further help stretch existing capacity and stabilize prices, while another, newsprint from kenaf, may help reduce dependence on expensive and possibly increasingly scarce wood pulp.

Newsprint cost will continue to be a major expense item for all but the smallest newspapers, so consumption will be closely monitored. Overall consumption is expected to grow only along with real economic growth, even under the most optimistic scenario. But price increases will continue, due to the large amounts of energy involved in the manufacturing process, as well as continued labor unrest in Canada.

FOOTNOTES

1. "How 1,200 Companies Performed in 1978," *Business Week,* March 19, 1979, pp. 69-104.

2. Nick Thomas, "Newsprint Price Rise May be Spread Out, But Not Enough to Justify Increased Capacity," *The Wall Street Journal,* November 8, 1973, p. 20.

3. Ibid, p. 44.

10

Newspapers
as Part of the Mass Media Milieu

For the better part of man's history, the printed word was the primary documentary form of mass communication: first books, then newspapers and magazines. The print media had this field entirely to themselves in the United States until the end of the 19th century, when the technological breakthroughs of Edison and the commercial venturesomeness of others gave birth to new forms of mass communication.

However, movies served a different function from the print media and their initial impact was slight. But a new challenge soon appeared in radio, and by 1925 every portion of the frequency band was occupied, some by several stations. Radio had the capability of reaching the listener even more instantaneously than a newspaper "extra," but its biggest immediate threat was its decision, after exploration of some other alternatives, to finance itself through sales of advertising. Its effect on newspaper share of advertising was swift; as the new electronic medium's share of the total advertising pie rose, that of newspapers slipped from 45.1 percent in 1935 to 32 percent ten years later. Radio grew from 6.7 percent to 14.7 percent in the same period (see Table 4.2).

This period coincided with the strong years of the general interest consumer magazine: *Life,* begun in 1936, *Saturday Evening Post, Colliers, Look,* the newsweeklies, among others. If magazines could not usurp the timeliness of the newspaper, they could compete for the reader's time and the advertiser's dollar, increasing by 50 percent their share of advertising in the 1935 to 1945 period.

Finally, there came television, adding yet another medium seeking support from advertisers and offering users a sight and sound package of entertainment and some news. Perhaps more than any previous medium, TV has threatened the health of the daily newspaper, not so much by siphoning off advertising dollars, but by distracting the reading public from newspapers—and to some extent from general interest magazines.

Within this increasingly cluttered media mix, newspapers appear to have preserved their premier place by performing strongly on several indices. As has been seen, despite the addition of two major competing media and the continued health of magazines, newspapers have maintained a strong hold on the local advertiser, presumably because the daily newspaper performs a function which other media can only partially replace. Television has seemingly eroded little of the newspaper's share of the advertising dollar and newspapers have maintained a steady 30 percent of the market since 1960.

On the consumer side, Maxwell McCombs has lent credibility to Scripps' Constancy Hypothesis, which essentially states that, "The amount of money spent on mass communication is relatively constant" and the amount of economic support provided for mass communication media follows the ebb and flow of the general economy.[1] This means that there is a fixed proportion of expenditures that the population budgets for media purchases and although the total fluctuates with the state of the economy, the proportion itself remains constant. The implication of this is that the addition of successful new media must result in a relative reduction in expenditures on existing media.

The evidence supporting this hypothesis can be seen in Table 10.1 as well as in Table 4.1. In Table 10.1 media expenditures as a percentage of personal consumption expenditures are seen to be generally stable at slightly over 3 percent, with the exception of the Depression year of 1935 and the war year of 1945. During this period personal consumption expenditures increased from $77.2 billion to $1,094.0 billion, or 1315 percent. Thus, the amount spent by consumers on media increased immensely in absolute terms. But in 1929, this money went to newspapers, magazines, books, movie admissions, radio receivers—none, of course, to television. Yet the percentage of the total sum spent on newspapers and magazines in 1976 was actually greater than the proportion spent in 1929, although it was lower than the peak year of 1945, when such expenditures were their lowest and the availability of radio receivers was limited because of the war effort.

Overall, relative expenditures on print media stayed generally stable through the entire period. Although total audiovisual media expenditure therefore remained stable, within this category movie admissions suffered the most dramatically, falling with the post-war increase in expenditures on television sets.

Table 4.1 showed that advertising expenditures have remained constant as a percentage of Gross National Product, especially since 1940. Thus, as with consumer expenditures, a constancy hypothesis would also seem to apply to advertising levels.

The implications of this consistency on both the consumer and advertising side of revenues for media—and newspapers in particular—is twofold. First, it means that, at least up to the mid-1970s, newspapers have been strongly supported by both constituencies, even in the face of added competition. Secondly, it portends a warning for the future, for although newspapers have held up well, each new medium is bound to bring some erosion from current levels. Video cassettes, cable television, and pay and subscription-TV are becoming more widely available, while consumer video disk machines have been developed by at least three firms as of early 1980.

Television screen facsimile in the form of viewdata, CEEFAX, and ORACLE type systems are now being tested. On-demand information displayed on home terminals from central computers, such as Britain's Prestel, are among the various media forms which may be contending for the mass media consumer and advertising dollar, as well as the limited time of mass media users. These will likely be expensive goods and services.

The video cassette machines are selling for about $1000, and even with impending competition, one will still cost more than a good color television console. The blank cassettes themselves sell for $16 for a two-hour tape. Unlike the video disk, the cassette machines can tape television programs for later viewing, thereby reducing time spent

Table 10.1 Percentage of Consumer Spending on Print and Audio-Visual Media, Selected Years, 1929-1976

	Media Expend. as % of Per. Consump. Exp.	Newspapers, Magazines, Sheet Music	Books & Maps	Total Print	Radio, TV Recv'rs, Records, Instruments	Radio & TV Repairs	Movie Admis.	Total AV Media[a]
1929	3.37%	20.65%	11.86%	32.51%	38.85%	1.00%	27.64%	67.49%
1933	2.76	33.20	12.04	45.24	15.45	1.11	38.19	54.75
1940	2.94	28.26	11.23	39.43	23.70	1.53	35.27	60.50
1945	2.82	28.66	15.44	44.10	10.22	2.61	43.07	55.90
1950	3.25	23.92	10.78	34.70	38.74	4.53	22.02	65.29
1955	2.94	25.10	11.64	36.74	38.53	6.97	17.81	63.31
1960	2.67	25.32	15.06	40.38	39.39	9.25	10.98	59.62
1965	3.00	22.23	15.98	38.21	46.61	8.00	7.19	61.80
1970	2.97	22.33	18.75	41.08	45.38	7.20	6.33	58.91
1974	3.04	26.01	11.20	37.21	48.99	4.58	9.21	62.78
1975	3.00	25.49	11.54	37.03	49.53	4.80	8.62	62.95
1976	2.94	25.12	11.15	36.27	49.88	4.58	9.27	63.73

[a]Total may not add to 100.00% due to rounding.

Source: U.S. Bureau of Economic Analysis.

watching original programming. The initial investment in the video disk machines is expected to be $500 to $800 in 1980 dollars, with preprogrammed disks at $6 to $20 each. Cable systems charge $8 to $10 per month, with special programming such as that provided by Time Inc.'s Home Box Office, another $8 or $9 monthly. It is still too early for good estimates on costs for facsimile or on-demand video news systems, but they too will absorb much of the media budget, if the Constancy Hypothesis continues to hold.

FOOTNOTES

1. Maxwell E. McCombs, "Mass Media in the Marketplace," *Journalism Monographs* 24:5-6, August 1972.

11

Summary and Findings

This study set out to do more than answer a few questions about the daily newspaper industry. Its objective: to bring together a wealth of scattered information, trends, characteristics, and events which together might help to put the discrete elements of one of the country's oldest industries into a contemporary perspective. This is particularly important in the 1980s because of the dynamism affecting the newspaper business, from both the technology within it as well as the increasingly competitive communications technologies developing around it.

At the most general level of analysis, this study shows two major themes which will affect the mid- to long-term future of the newspaper as it exists today. On the one hand, there are the economic and sociocultural trends, such as smaller families, more households, the population decline in the Northeast and the commensurate rise in the Sunbelt states, increased leisure time, and a standard of living which permits greater choice in the use of this time.

At the same time, this study has noted the changing technology in the mass communications industries, from radio and television, toward video games, cassettes, and disks. Other possibilities include the technology which will combine telecommunications or cable with computers for some form of interactive system between the home and information storing computers. Technology, however, has also improved the productivity, physical quality, and profitability of newspapers.

In evaluating the possible results of these themes as they pertain to the future of the ink-on-newsprint newspaper of the eighties, it is useful to summarize the current status and directions of specific areas of circulation, advertising, labor, technology, newsprint, and concentration and consolidation patterns of the industry.

CIRCULATION

There can be little doubt that newspapers must take the initiative if they wish to reverse the stagnation in circulation since the mid-1960s. The rising cost of paper, a change in lifestyle, the general disinterest on the part of the young and minority group audiences, distribution problems in high rises, and the impact of television all contribute to the leveling off. There are no simplistic answers.

203

Strategic Considerations

Following from Theodore Levitt's concept of "marketing myopia," we can question whether the newspaper industry has been too concerned with the functions of production and immediate sales, rather than focusing attention on the marketing of its products and services. In the last years of the 1970s some newspaper publishers have developed a "marketing concept." This does not necessarily mean abandoning the newspaper to packaged goods executives who will segment and differentiate. Nor does it mean the same as selling. Selling focuses on ways of convincing readers and advertisers to exchange their cash for the publisher's product. Marketing, on the other hand, does mean understanding the needs of the consumer, then anticipating those needs and satisfying them with a combination of programs which may include editorial content, layout, advertising, and distribution of the newspaper. This assumes that editors, circulation directors, and advertising managers must work together—a practice which runs counter to many of the traditions in the daily newspaper field.

Adopting the marketing concept means solving problems before they occur, and thus relies heavily on a commitment to market research and interdepartment communication. It also means each newspaper must have its own plan: The needs of a small-town afternoon paper may be very different from a large city afternoon daily which faces direct morning competition.

And implementing the market concept means looking beyond the statistics to their implications. For example, market research finds that one reason people are not reading newspapers is that they claim they do not have the time. But what they really may mean is that there are other things they would rather spend their money or time on that return a higher utility. Newspapers must therefore be made more valuable to people, so they will find the time and money.

Thus, if newspapers no longer have a monopoly in the presentation of breaking news—or even a particular strength in this—they do have the ability to provide other types of information which concern people: What does the news mean to their lives? What is happening around them that they should know about, but which may not have the immediate time peg that newspaper editors have usually looked for? Features as well as advertisements also play crucial roles in creating a newspaper that is needed each day.

Editors in central cities that are faced with declining white populations and rising black and/or Spanish-speaking populations might also begin looking for ways to meet the needs of these groups as an alternative to reaching further out into the suburbs and competing directly with the outlying dailies and weeklies. Not only might they fill a niche waiting to be satisfied, but there may well be sources of untapped advertising wanting to reach this constituency.

Yet understanding the product is only part of the solution. Getting it to the reader is another part. In cities where there have been problems, publishers must be willing to consider new ideas: paid-in-advance subscriptions and computerized subscription lists; newspaper boxes that are activated by coded cards which can serve subscribers in apartment buildings; greater professionalism in the circulation department which may require the separation of selling, servicing, distribution, and collection functions.

Extensive zoning may be part of the answer but it should not be the automatic response. Some newspapers have taken the strategy that rather than promote hard news coverage of each suburban area, they would rather concentrate on covering items that are the concerns of suburban readers in general, e.g., rising property taxes, crime in high-priced residential areas, drugs in good schools. It may well be that the metropolitan paper cannot scoop the local suburban daily or weekly newspaper in each community on school board meetings and local charity drives.

For example, *The Philadelphia Bulletin,* which has made a serious effort at zoned editions and local emphasis, has felt far greater losses in circulation than has the competing *Inquirer,* which eschews zoning for regional and strong national and international coverage, in apparent contradiction with the recommended "trend" for big city papers. The *Inquirer* also has been outdistancing the *Bulletin* in advertising linage with this strategy. Although one example does not make the case, the point is that universal solutions may obscure other needs.

It may be reasonably proposed that many of the reasons for the lack of growth and the drop in household readership have had their maximum impact. Broadcast television has matured and is well established. But new cable programming, pay TV, video disk, and other technological changes may fragment the traditional television audience and have a greater impact there than on newspapers. The move of the population to the suburbs has slowed.

Another trend that may favor newspapers is the natural aging of the population. The over-20 year old population, which increased 26.3 million between 1960 and 1975, should grow by 33.0 million in the following 15 years. The number of households, which increased 18.3 million during the 1960-1975 period, may increase another 19.1 to 23.1 million by 1990. Although this group is the television-oriented group of the 1960s, a substantial number should find a greater interest in newspapers, especially if newspapers develop features consistent with their needs.

Newspapers are also finding it more economically attractive to add Sunday or weekend editions to their schedule. Whereas in 1950 31 percent of newspapers had such an edition, by 1979 40 percent were publishing on Sunday. And during the no-growth era of daily circulation since 1960, Sunday circulation has risen over 13 percent.

Finally, we could look at circulation figures from a "half-filled" glass rather than "half-empty" glass perspective. After all, one may reason that despite intense competition from other media and other activities, the mature, staid newspaper is still purchased by an average 82 percent of all households, by 44 percent of all adults. And if the total readership concept is adopted rather than circulation, then the indications are that perhaps as many as 85 percent of adults see a daily newspaper on a regular basis. Many people still view the newspaper as an important communications medium.

ADVERTISING

Newspaper advertising has more than held its position within the media mix over the years. It has withstood the addition of radio and then television and still accounts for 30 percent of all advertising dollars spent in the United States. In both retail and classified advertising, it has a near monopoly. National advertisers alone have looked to newspapers less over the years, preferring instead the mass market that television is able to creatively reach, or the segmented market offered by special interest magazines.

There are several factors which indicate that newspapers may be able to get back some of the national advertisers, including better quality reproduction through offset printing, more flexible formats, and total—or more selective—distribution. Greater fragmentation of the broadcast television audience from cable and UHF competition, as well as video disks or cassettes may help restore newspapers as an economical mass market medium. High-speed inserting equipment and escalating postal rates may make newspaper distribution more attractive to those who use direct mail.

Barriers to further national advertising remain. Chief among them is the high rate differential above the local retail rate. Another is the existence of 300 different page formats. The ADS System provides guidelines for effective standardization, but newspapers must apply and adhere to them. Small newspapers still have a hard time getting on the national media schedule, but sales through consortia and distribution of the ad mechanical by facsimile means could improve the logistics for national advertisers.

At the same time, newspapers cannot overlook the challenge to their retail clientele. Television is one source of erosion, but there appears only a limited amount of dollars it can take away—advertisers do need the newspaper format. But even two or three percent of the total switched to local television can mean hundreds of millions of dollars to the industry. The other threats are the "shoppers" and weekly papers, some of which are totally devoid of editorial material. These cater to the small shops and chain stores in an area that wish to reach a highly localized audience. Some of them might be potential customers for zoned editions, others too small even for this. But as many publishers have discovered, it is ill-advised to look only at television as an alternative for current users of their services. As a countermove, many owners are starting or purchasing "shoppers" in their territories.

Computer technology can bring the advertising department closer to the circulation department. The circulation lists the newspapers have—or can get easily enough—provide the basis for a goldmine of knowledge for potential advertisers, local as well as national. The newspaper can use this information either to sell directly, or to attract new advertisers. Smaller papers which are part of chains will have many of the same service features a large paper could afford.

FUTURE DIRECTIONS FOR NEWSPAPER UNIONS

The trends of organized labor in the newspaper industry crafts are already clear. High on the list of union priorities is simple recognition—as seen in the willingness of the printers in Omaha and the mailers in Washington to return to work under management's terms. At least they wish to salvage their jurisdiction. Equally important to the mechanical unions is security. Settlements in many locals—New York, Long Island, St. Louis, Atlanta, etc.—have stressed lifetime job guarantees for current printers, pressmen, or whatever, in exchange for reduction in staffing by attrition, early retirement incentives, and the like. Wage increases have at times been substantial, but in other cases have been quite secondary to these other priorities.

Besides recognition and security, labor has accepted the necessity of consolidation. Several mergers have already occurred, and the ITU-Guild combination is a strong possibility in the early 80s. The move is a natural one, given the graying of the jurisdictions between these two unions, and the others as well. Merger also means the possibility of somewhat greater labor clout, since newspapers with a union-organized composing room but an unorganized news department (or vice versa) will then have a larger segment of the work force covered by a collective bargaining agreement.

Both unions and management will also welcome combined expiration dates for contracts with all unions. With as many as 11 unions to contend with, scattered expiration dates mean management is faced with frequent negotiations and the possibility of any single union causing a complete shutdown. In St. Louis now, all 11 contracts expire on a common date. For the unions, this means more concentrated strike threats and bargaining, without the risk of some locals continuing to work and thus enabling the newspaper to continue publishing.

As newspaper organization becomes further integrated, with the eventual elimination of the composing, camera, and engraving departments, surviving workers may well find it in their interests to integrate vertically into a single union on the industrial model, a National Newspaper Workers Union.

COMPETITION AND OWNERSHIP

Mergers and acquisitions are gradually consolidating the newspaper business into fewer hands and into conditions of isolate or local monopoly situations. This process is the fulfillment of the waste that Munsey wrote of in 1908. Although there are those who are critical of this consolidation on philosophical grounds, there has been little empirical evidence that either readers or advertisers have been ill-served by this process. In fact, the changes in the ownership pattern in the industry reflect changes in the basic structure and needs of the industry and its clients.

The fact is, the largest 25 percent of newspapers in 1978 actually accounted for a smaller percentage of total circulation than the same proportion accounted for in 1923 or 1963. A similar pattern holds for the largest one percent of the firms, which would include the largest 18 chains.

Although group ownership may continue, there can be little further consolidation of ownership within cities, as only 35 cities still had competing newspapers in 1979. Moreover, there are signs that entrepreneurs have not given up trying to promote new papers in one-ownership cities. A twice-weekly paper, the *Austin* (Tex.) *Citizen*, went daily in 1976, in competition with the Cox-owned *American-Statesman* morning/evening combination.

But most activity has been in the small cities surrounding the central cities. Instead of buying the metropolitan dailies, residents of these areas are increasingly being given the opportunity to buy a local paper with advertisements and news coverage more indigenous to their communities.

But getting started is not easy, especially in a large city. The well-financed *Suffolk Sun* fought with *Newsday* for three years on Long Island before giving up. The well-financed *Trib* lasted four months in New York. The *Philadelphia Journal,* started by Quebecor, a Canadian chain, survived as that city's fourth daily at an estimated cost of $8 million in its first two years. Thus, newspaper owners who wish to expand tend to buy from the existing, finite pool of newspapers and chains.

As long as there are newspapers, however, there will be a large number of them, because the function of the newspaper is to report and pursue local news. In the last analysis, however, the usual entrepreneurial motivation that can spot a consumer need, e.g., an alternative to a single newspaper in a community, is not operable in newspaper economics. This is because the primary source of revenue for the newspaper producer is not the purchaser/reader, but the advertiser. And it appears that this constituency finds it in their interest to reach their audience most cheaply by supporting only a single newspaper firm in a given community.

Moreover, there is at least a suggestion of evidence from Table 4.8, that even having a monopoly position does not really give the newspaper a *carte blanche* in setting linage rates. Rosse points to the umbrella effect of overlapping newspapers. Moreover, dailies have competition from other media, as well as weekly and shopper newspapers. Finally, retailers require ad rates which are compatible with their own economic structure. If forced to spend too high a percentage of their sales to maintain current linage, retailers could wind up budgeting a fixed percentage of sales to buy decreasing amounts of space. The general economic health of a community may be an additional factor in determining a given newspaper's ability to set rates.

DIRECTIONS FOR TECHNOLOGY

The production of the newspaper changed radically in the last decade. Just how much was summarized by Table 6.2, which indicated the magnitude of the change in the 179 percent increase in photo- or CRT-typesetters between 1971 and 1978 (with a good number of the earlier ones used exclusively for headlines and display advertising), and the drop in the number of hot metal linecasters to an eighth of the 1971 level.

But the machinery tells only part of the story. The new technology has breathed new life into this oldest of news media. Its speed, accuracy, and flexibility have helped newspapers hold down costs, brighten the product, and, in some cases, improve the editorial package. The technology has brought newspapers into the electronic age, if not with the same immediacy as television or radio, then with many of their techniques for instantaneous and remote transmission of the news back to the waiting pressroom.

Nor is the revolution restricted to the big newspapers. Much of the cold type innovation was on the part of the smaller dailies and it is this group which has been first to take advantage of the added quality offered by offset printing. Newsroom systems have been developed to allow all size papers to economically justify OCR or VDT input, digital storage, and VDT editing. Classified and display advertising production likewise has been enhanced by the new systems.

Moreover, this rapid change appears to have been implemented without major displacement of people or a weakening in the newspaper. The tools may have changed, but the input from reporters remains the same, and the early indications are that editors have not only adapted well to their new hardware, but are just learning about the advantages that the systems can provide.

With the widespread acceptance and use of the front-end systems and the cold type production, change over the next 10 to 20 years will be mostly a matter of further refinements: gradual elimination of paste-up for full pagination and then bypassing the page to negative stage altogether for a direct computer-to-plate output. Although presses may become offset or direct lithography, the age of plateless printing still appears to be remote.

NEWSPRINT

The primary raw material for the finished newspaper product is newsprint. If there was any industry which saw less innovation in production than did newspapers before 1970, it was the manufacture of newsprint. After years of plentiful supply and almost constant price, newsprint demand exceeded supply and higher costs for pulp and energy forced a rapid escalation in newsprint price between 1973 and 1979, reaching $375 as the published price per ton.

As a result, daily newspapers devoted added attention to ways of holding down their expenses on this item. Supplies were extended by switching from a 32-pound basis weight to 30-pound. Newsprint executives are readying their newspaper clients for eventual production of even lighter weight papers. Many publishers reduced their web width from 60 inches to 58 or 55 inches and modified their editorial and advertising column formats to reduce wasted space. Greater concern was given to reducing printed waste.

New processes, such as thermo-mechanical pulping and paper from kenaf, are now being explored by newsprint manufacturers to help stretch supplies and reduce reliance on expensive chemicals. Some money is being expended for new plants or added capacity, including new recycling plants in the United States. A greater proportion of newsprint consumption is being domestically produced.

The outlook is for an adequate supply into the 1980s, but prices will continue to escalate, fueled in part by the great energy demands of paper production.

FINDINGS

Chapter 1 presented several hypotheses concerning trends in the newspaper industry.

Three hypotheses related to the new production technology:

(1)   The rapid introduction of new technology into many phases of newspaper operations qualifies this print medium for inclusion as an electronic medium.

(2)   Although newspaper production may change, the final product as received by the subscriber will remain physically quite similar to the present form.

(3)   New technology will provide newspaper publishers with opportunities for new roles and formats for information distribution in the coming decades.

Certainly there has been a rapid and pervasive introduction of electronics into the newspaper production process. The state of the art includes optical character recognition and video display terminal input and editing devices. Photomechanical and CRT-equipped machines produce type at speeds 50 to 100 times faster than even the fastest Linotypes could. Reporters at remote locations can send copy via telephone lines directly into a computer and advertisements are composed at video terminals. Classified ads are sorted, merged, checked, and billed in a single entry. Laser beams have been used to burn a printing plate, and computer-to-plate technology is more than a dream. All this is made possible through the speed and accuracy of computers and computer-like electronic instrumentation.

While electronics has transformed the production of copy, it has barely touched the actual printing of the paper and has barely changed its physical distribution. Computers may help in keeping track of customers or providing total marketing coverage, but it still takes this mechanical giant of a press to deposit a fraction of an ounce of ink onto 18 cents worth of newsprint, and the finished product is still manually distributed door-to-door. Investments in present plant and equipment are considerable, and a radically new process must promise returns on a scale similar to those now seen in the cold type process before newspaper owners will be encouraged to develop and implement newer methods.

Certainly newspapers must carefully select those innovations which are useful and desired by consumers, for if they take too narrow a view of their function as newspaper publishers, they may default to other entrepreneurs the opportunity to market the information which computer and cable technology will make possible. A newspaper firm by its very existence is a repository of great amounts of information. Though much of this information never finds its way into print, it may now be spending some time stored in the computer or on a disk. The New York Times Information Bank and the Dow Jones and *Boston Globe* data banks are examples of newspaper companies creating operational systems for capturing and repackaging much of the information that those organizations collect as part of their daily routine. Knight-Ridder is in the forefront of testing a residential-oriented viewdata system, while Mead Data Central's Nexis is an example of how a non-newspaper publisher can provide "electronic newspaper" functions.

Although such systems are today quite expensive to assemble and maintain, the cost of computer storage has declined constantly since the first generation of these machines.

Newer and even cheaper bubble memory may mean that before the end of the 1980s even small newspapers may be able to provide some variety of electronic transmission or on-demand information. Just as front-end production systems have been made financially feasible for newspapers of all sizes, so may vast (in capacity, not size) computer-controlled storage and retrieval packages be developed for this market.

Even so, newspaper owners may find further advantages to being part of a group as such alternative delivery systems evolve, as they could share much of their information and hardware.

Thus, if an electronic medium is taken in the same sense as radio or television, with its almost instantaneous quality, the daily newspaper does not yet qualify. The new technology may have shortened deadlines and provided for a somewhat more timely paper, but not much. Not until—if ever—plateless printing becomes feasible, will a newspaper in its present format qualify. With plateless presses, either electrostatic, ink jet, or a presently unknown process, content can go directly from the computer to the page, with changes in copy possible during the press run. At best this possibility is not likely in other than prototype fashion in this century.

Moreover, the very notion of an ink-on-newsprint medium is antithetical to an electronic process. The newspaper will truly qualify for the electronic rubric when it overcomes the current distribution system and moves directly from plant to home, which means a facsimile transmission of some sort. A page-by-page hard copy facsimile transmission to each subscriber has been largely ruled out on economic grounds. A video form of output does not appear to meet the real and psychological needs for hard copy.

Therefore, some halfway point may be the eventual solution, with the daily paper still home delivered on newsprint, containing advertisements and news. But certain specialized features and advertisements may be sent, as requested, to individual households from the newspaper's central storage computer to TV screens, via cable or telephone lines. Newspaper publishers could charge an additional fee for each request, or make a certain number of transmissions available to bona fide subscribers.

But this approach is far in the future for the typical household. At least through the 1980s and perhaps through the end of the century, technology specialists surveyed for this study do not see a widespread adaptation of alternative means of distribution of the primary information content of the newspaper.

Specifically, then, the first hypothesis cannot be accepted, since final production and delivery are still mechanical processes.

The second hypothesis, however, has been largely substantiated. Talk of home facsimile eliminating the ink-on-newsprint newspaper goes back to the 1930s. The prospect of a different form of newspaper is still in the realm of what is technically feasible. At the cost of even 20 cents or 25 cents, it is unlikely that any other hard copy form can replace the current mass production techniques used to print and distribute the newspaper. Some video forms may supplement some information, just as television news viewing supplements the newspaper's function for many. But studies have shown that newspaper readership is higher among those who do watch TV news; so might these supplemental cable or similar news services act as an additional source, not a replacement for the newspaper.

Electronic Newspaper

Someone must pay for the information that would be delivered by a video displayed electronic newspaper. In Great Britain's Prestel, the user pays a varying charge per "page" (screenful) of material. Even at a fraction of a cent a page, "browsing" through the electronic newspaper could get quite expensive—especially when considering the extremely limited number of words that appear on the screen (100-130). The editorial content alone of the newspaper would take hundreds of video pages.

There is also the initial cost of the equipment, either in the form of an adapter to the present television set or an added video display tube. In fact, if the electronic newspaper does become widespread, most households will likely need at least one additional VDT, since the family color television will presumably be kept quite busy with its many cable and broadcast channels, not to mention playing back video cassettes or disks.

Finally, most tests to date, including Britain's Prestel and Telidon in Canada, are using telephone lines to provide the link between the home and the information computer. Many residences will have to incur the expense of an additional telephone line, unless they are willing to tie up their current line for extended periods while using the interactive system for accessing the news, shopping, information gathering, playing games, etc.

Thus, even if advertising finds a way to subsidize some of the costs of an electronic newspaper, the cost to consumers may be substantially above what they are now paying to acquire much the same information. While businesses are more likely to pay for readily accessible, timely information, it is doubtful that consumers will feel the same way in large enough numbers to make such a medium widely enough available to serve as a replacement for the newspaper in print form.*

As for the third hypothesis, newspaper publishers would be the logical distributors of the supplemental news and information service noted above. But this is only one possible future opportunity for newspapers. By improving the information they hold about subscribers in their circulation systems, publishers are only a short step away from providing the most complete data base about their locality. They can have ready access to data on numbers of residents, housing units, land use, and combine that with census tract information on income, age, and education, etc., to offer advertisers and land developers great quantities of useful information. This information can be sold—hence an additional source of revenue—or used to attract new advertising through convincing sales presentations. The same technology has already helped newspapers offer 100 percent marketing saturation with inserts and direct mail or delivery to nonsubscribers. Once these various data bases are assembled, imagination may become the limiting factor on new opportunities.

One hypothesis addresses the role of the newspaper as an advertising medium:

(4)   The daily newspaper has no replacement in the foreseeable future as a major vehicle for local advertisers.

---

*For a more thorough examination of Prestel and other videotext systems, see Efrem Sigel, ed. *Videotext: The Coming Revolution in Home/Office Information Retrieval* (White Plains, N.Y.: Knowledge Industry Publications, Inc., 1980).

From the display advertiser's perspective, there is still no medium which can replace the local daily newspaper in reaching the market. This can be seen in the strength of newspaper's share of the advertising dollar in the face of intense competition from new as well as existing media. There has been some erosion, to be sure, but the constant proportion which newspapers have maintained at the local level, especially classified, is explicit acknowledgement by those who use this medium that television and radio are not substitutes for the hard copy of the paper. The national advertiser does have alternatives, but not the retailer.

Nor do the possible alternative delivery modes for newspapers in the more distant future provide a substitute outlet for these advertisers. Would users of a video displayed newspaper merely "flip" pages on the screen in much the same way as the actual page is turned with a hard copy paper? Will there be printers to enable readers to get a hard copy of a cents off coupon? It is hard to picture the advertising world without a hard copy alternative.

Classified advertising, on the other hand, does lend itself more to these futuristic delivery modes. Since these ads are specifically sought out, they would be likely candidates for early omission from the printed newspaper. Subscribers who wish to find out what used cars are for sale or the availability of new homes at a given price range in a specific location could readily get this information displayed on their home screens.

This would appear to be one area in which newspapers may well have to take the lead, before existing cable TV companies or others usurp this function. But this, too, is still at the far edge of the planning horizon, because like other technological possibilities, it really depends on the widespread placement of interactive systems in most households.

To be sure, as the cost of newsprint escalates and that of electronic computer handling decreases, certain types of information, including some advertising, may become logical candidates for transfer from hard copy to electronic distribution.

The final response, then, to this hypothesis may depend on the time frame one puts on "foreseeable future." But even considering the various technologies discussed, there does not appear to be a medium which can perform the broad advertising function of the daily newspaper at a similar cost and with comparable effectiveness. If anything, the importance of this function of the newspaper may actually override technological developments which might otherwise alter the delivery of the editorial content of the paper.

The fifth hypotheses considered the issue of circulation:

(5)   Current trends notwithstanding, aggregate newspaper circulation will stabilize and enjoy modest increases through the remainder of the century.

The advertiser may need the newspaper, but does the present reader need it? Although circulation revenue accounted for only a fourth of revenues, the stagnant circulation levels are of considerable concern to publishers because without readers, advertisers would find no need to spend their dollars which make up the bulk of newspaper income. The answer must be that newspaper circulation will grow in the long run.

All the demographic and economic trends point to this assessment. It is true that many signs have augured well for substantial circulation growth for years—consider

Nixon's well reasoned analysis in 1955 predicting over 100 million circulation by 1975 and Udell's seemingly convincing conclusion in 1970 that the ensuing decade would be one of the greatest decades of circulation growth. With this track record, it may be most prudent merely to predict that newspaper circulation will continue to rise in the growing cities and small towns and continue to fall in the older, declining cities, as a continuation of the trend cited in Chapter 3.

Much of the lack of growth of the 1960s and 1970s may be attributed to competition for leisure time and the increased use Americans are making of television news, among other explanations discussed in Chapter 3. But some unmeasurable portion may stem from the relatively rapid increase in cost, from five cents to 15 or 20 cents per day, resulting in fewer multi-newspaper households and greater passalong or sharing between households.

Moreover, the birth of a few suburban newspapers with 15,000 circulation does not take up the slack resulting from the suspension of a large city daily. For example, the 265,000 circulation lost in the 1977 closing of the *Long Island Press* was not made up by a corresponding jump in the circulation of *Newsday* and other New York papers. Many of these subscribers no doubt were already reading another paper besides the *Press* and will now just do without the *Press*. Similarly, the merger of separate morning and evening papers into a single paper often results in a lower combined net circulation. (A notable exception was *The Boston Globe* in 1979.)

Finally, a small number of subscribers have been cut off in fringe areas, due to the higher cost of newsprint and the inability to pass along such faraway readership in charges to local advertisers.

The extent to which newspapers increase their circulation may in part depend on the conscious efforts of editors to respond to the content and style which market research efforts recommend. If the intrusion of other media has changed the needs readers have for the newspaper, then editors must not be so myopic as to insist on their traditional forms. There is every indication that these changes are underway, as new types of coverage and packaging at the *Chicago Tribune, The New York Times,* and many smaller papers make clear.

Against the factors which have been holding down circulation are those which act to promote growth: increased numbers of households, continued interest as an advertising conveyance, the fundamental benefits of print media, and a widespread effort to reposition the newspaper in the mass media mix. The outcome should be the modest gains predicted in the hypothesis.

A final hypothesis concerned the effects of newspaper concentration and monopoly:

(6) Direct newspaper competition within cities continues to diminish, but the impact of this on readers and advertisers is not yet clear.

Although the number of cities or communities with their own daily newspaper is at its highest level in history, there can be no doubt that the number of cities with truly competing newspapers has been diminishing, from 502 in 1923 to 35 in 1980. Nonetheless, researchers have not been able to come up with convincing evidence that monopoly or isolate newspapers have resulted in a generally weakened editorial product or service to the advertisers. Studies have shown that local news content did not decline when competition ended in a community, nor that competing dailies automatically guarantee a marketplace of ideas.

Although one study found that consumers pay more under monopoly conditions with no added quality, another could find no statistically significant evidence that local advertisers pay higher rates.

In fact, these results may be the outcome of a media environment in which even local monopoly dailies compete with regional and big city newspapers, television and radio, weekly newspapers, and free shoppers. Direct competition between newspapers in the same city or town has been replaced by a broader, subtler form of competition.

12

Conclusions: The Daily Newspaper in the Eighties and Beyond

THE MEANING OF TECHNOLOGY

A key point made in the discussion of future technology was that "futurists" must be sensitive to those improvements which can be proven to be economically feasible in addition to being technically available.

An example of this dichotomy is the development in 1976 and 1977 of page make-up VDT terminals. Although several manufacturers had shown them in operation, publishers realized that these expensive units would not save them money so long as their output was still in the form of a full-page positive which still must go through the conventional plate-making stages. In the 1980s or thereafter, when digital storage of pictures and graphics becomes feasible and laser plate-making is perfected, then a VDT page make-up combined with computer-to-plate capability will save several steps. Only then will it become a cost effective process.

Meanwhile, for all the improvements in front-end and production systems, the newspaper is still printed on a monster press which is little changed from the design of over 100 years earlier. The presses were built to handle heavy lead type. With stereotype plates weighing about 40 pounds each, appropriate gearing and engineering was designed into the letterpress. The offset press apparently is largely a modification of this old design.

Without waiting for the breakthrough in plateless printing, it would seem to be time now to devise new presses which are simpler and lighter, constructed for the printing needs of the lightweight plates. The ANPA Research Institute and some private efforts have begun working on prototypes for such a press. Its adoption will be one of the major advances in printing of the decade.

The implications for a simpler press go beyond a mere desire for change. The press is today the single most expensive piece of capital equipment needed by a newspaper. Prices have escalated for all categories of presses. By making the press a less complex piece of equipment, press prices should at least level off in real dollars. Together with the modest cost of photocomposition machines and newsroom input devices, the reduced cost of entry into the daily newspaper field may make it economically feasible for additional newspapers to enter some markets which analysis shows could support a competing daily.

The Product Is the Message

The introduction of the technology of the 1970s has made the newspaper industry an exciting one to follow in these years. It is rare to see a well-established production process change so dramatically in such a short time. Nonetheless, it must be kept in mind that the mechanics of production are only a means to an end. The production flow is only an intermediary between the input and the final product. The technology is not the newspaper.

Thus, as enticing as technology may be, editors and publishers must exploit it not just to add to profits in the short run, but to make the product better. This includes funneling some of the production savings into the editorial budget. It also encompasses exploring the resources of the systems in ways that enhance formats and layouts, reduce errors, and maximize the timeliness of the daily newspaper.

CHAIN OWNERSHIP

In Chapter 5, it was noted that there is as yet no substantial body of research which shows that chain ownership or one-ownership newspaper towns reduce quality or service, although there is no evidence that these forms of ownership regularly improve newspapers either. Nonetheless, there is an air of uneasiness loitering around gatherings of newspaper people—a sense that sooner or later these trends to larger groups and less competition are going to trigger some government action. It is a highly sensitive area, because of the Constitutional guarantees that the news media alone of all industries can look to for shelter.

Government action

On the other hand, perceptions are often as important as objective reality. There is a prevailing ethic in the United States that bigness connotes badness and although such institutions as IBM or General Motors dominate their respective industries far more than even the largest newspaper groups, they are no buffer to moves against newspaper bigness. Newspapers by their nature are highly visible, and in the process of going about their business they may anger the same policy makers and law makers who can then initiate actions against newspaper ownership forms. Certainly the media as a whole aroused the ire of the Nixon Administration and drew the wrath for a time of former Vice President Spiro Agnew.

Rep. Morris Udall (D., Ariz.) included the newspaper industry in his Congressional study of business concentration. There was considerable anxiety among some newspaper executives when, within the space of several weeks, the Booth and Speidel chains were bought by larger chains and Australian Rupert Murdoch added to his international holdings by buying the *New York Post, New York Magazine,* and the weekly *Village Voice.* In 1978-1979, the Federal Trade Commission devoted a special task force to studying concentration of ownership of the media.

For the most part, group owners have exercised restraint in determining editorial policies at each property, but it is purely voluntary. An example of the potential for abuse was reported by *The New York Times* of June 25, 1977. John P. McGoff, president of the Panax chain of eight dailies and 40 weekly papers, fired two respected editors who refused to print two articles the chain's headquarters urged for front page display. One article said that President Carter condoned promiscuity among his staff and the other claimed that the President was grooming his wife to be Vice President. One of the fired editors considered the material to contain "half truths" and "innuendos," while the other was quoted as saying, "That type of journalism I can't stomach. I wouldn't be able to shave in the morning." McGoff acknowledged the two were dismissed because they ignored his orders.

It is this type of domination which can undo the positive roles of many of the chains and may even outweigh the lack of overall empirical evidence of systematic malevolence by chain owners.

The government can do little about one-ownership communities and so long as there are competing media, interest in the effects of this phenomenon is largely academic. But chain ownership is a more sensitive issue and one which newspaper owners must not be too greedy to ignore.

TELECOMMUNICATIONS POLICY

The newspaper industry should also be paying more attention to federal telecommunications policy. For a time, for example, the major impediment to wire service transmission of editorial copy and photographs to newspapers via earth satellite were FCC regulations regarding the building of ground receiving stations. Even though these were changed to make it easier for every newspaper to install its own receiving dish, communications costs in 1980 were still determined largely by telephone company tariffs over which neither the wire services nor newspapers have much control.

The newspaper industry also has a stake in regulations affecting cable television. Since a truly useful television screen facsimile service demands two-way communication between the home and the controlling computer, newspapers that see a facsimile operation as a natural adjunct to their conventional operations must follow closely FCC regulations encouraging or delaying the installation of this interactive capability. Newspapers may also wish to prepare for this service by building up their data bases, acquiring cable companies, or at the very least exploring cable technology.

OTHER MEDIA

The daily newspaper has demonstrated its inherent worth in its ability to maintain its pre-eminent position among the mass media despite the advent of other media which share some of its functions. Its most recent challenge has come from television, with which it competes in local markets as a news medium, and advertising medium, and as alternative use for leisure time. Television has the advantage of requiring less effort on the part of users and providing greater action and color.

Nonetheless, newspaper publishers and editors should be less concerned about television *per se* than about other print media, primarily local weekly newspapers, free "shoppers," and special all-classified advertising newspapers. These publications serve many of the same functions as the daily newspaper. Although they tend to cater to small advertisers who may not be able to afford to advertise in metropolitan dailies, they do compete more directly with daily papers in small towns.

Moreover, the developing media conduits such as video disks and cassettes do not appear to lend themselves to any newspaper functions, but rather should fragment the market for television broadcasts. Between these devices and the numerous channels which cable provides, television users will have a greater choice than ever, but it may also mean that a single network buy from an advertiser will reach fewer households at one time than at present. Thus, these advertisers may look to national magazines as well as to newspapers for the coverage which they now have on television. At present, daily newspapers obtain an average of only eight percent of the $27 billion in national advertising expenditures; even a small increment would yield tens of millions more revenue for newspaper publishers.

NEWSPAPERS AS AN INDUSTRY

One tends to speak of an industry in the singular, although it is made up of hundreds of separate ownerships. When it is suggested that the industry should do something, this is really asking many individuals to make a decision to do the same thing. To the extent that it is clearly in the self interest of each, they may in fact all do so. Such has been the case as the industry adopted the new technological processes. Cold type, electronic newsrooms, and plastic plates are so plainly agreed to as being both efficient and profitable that in an amazingly short period hundreds of newspapers have bought the new equipment.

Although the newspaper industry could be historically characterized as being composed of many individualistic entrepreneurs, frequently imbued with the calling of journalism, today it is far more corporately oriented—for better or worse. It does have, however, a strong intra-industry organization. The American Newspaper Publishers Association is an active coordinator for industry concerns and its associated Research Institute has provided much of the dissemination of technical information which has helped individual publishers understand and convert to the modern production methods.

There are also active groups such as the International Circulation Managers Association and the Newspaper Advertising Bureau on the business side and the Associated Press Managing Editors Association and the American Society of Newspaper Editors on the editorial end. Since few newspapers are directly competing with each other, meetings of these and other similar groups often result in far greater sharing of useful information than in industries in which the participants may be direct competitors. To this extent, the lack of extensive competition may in fact promote improved products and methods that would otherwise come at greater expense or delay to each newspaper or group.

MARKETING THE NEWSPAPER

If the newspaper did not exist, but someone felt the need for a publication which contained news and other editorial material, took advertisements from retailers and manufacturers, ran classified notices from individuals and business, and came out each day, how would the product be developed?

One early step would probably be some market research. Potential consumers would be asked what they would expect to find in this product. They would be shown several proposed packages or formats to rate. They would be asked where they would buy the product and how much they would be willing to pay for it.

Unfortunately, the newspaper is a very old product and is steeped in many traditions. In most cases it is the editor or top editors who decide what material readers will see and in what form. Distribution is largely through newsboys and newsstands. In fact, the newspaper is very much taken for granted. It is a mature product, with high primary demand and declining market penetration. When other consumer goods reach this point, manufacturers know it is time to introduce a new version of the product and therefore we get "new, improved" laundry powders or toothpastes.

A purist may bristle at the idea that newspapers can be marketed like packaged goods. In many respects, they must be. For many years, newspapers were sheltered from this need because they had a near-monopoly in respect to other newspapers and even other media, at least until radio and television. But as some newspaper executives have finally realized, a newspaper which is not purchased does no one any good, no matter how fine the editors think the paper may be. An important step was undertaken by the industry with its readership project, a large scale field study to help determine why people read—or do not read—the daily paper. Hundreds of individual dailies started their own surveys in 1978.

It should not be anathema to editors, therefore, to work with the business managers to find out what items people are reading most in their papers and what they would like to read. Research may also find those items which editors would like to eliminate but are important to a small number of people. It may well be that a small but hard core group buys the newspaper just for the crossword puzzle.[2]

This is not a call to make the newspaper a print version of the local television "happy talk" news format. A daily newspaper must provide the depth and analysis of the hard news which television news handles so poorly. But beyond this, it must provide a broad-based mixture of features and services which in many respects will vary with each community. There may well be no single formula, other than to provide information which readers may come to view as being unique and somewhat indispensable.

In addition to the basic content, the newspaper must be made into an attractive package, with a well thought-out format that remains consistent each day. This newly designed format is perhaps the most common first step a publisher takes when he learns about marketing, but it should be used as part of a total reconsideration of the newspaper package.

Consumers must then be made aware of this product. Made aware of the newspaper? Everyone, of course, knows that there is a newspaper available, but once a person gets out of the newspaper buying habit (or in many cases never learns the habit), he or she must be convinced to make a trial purchase, just as if it were a new brand of soft drink or cigarette. This may mean billboard advertisements, frequent radio spots, or television commercials. *The Philadelphia Inquirer,* for example, has run one-minute radio ads during morning "drive time" slots on the city's all-news radio station. These spots reached an audience interested in news, weather, sports, and features. The commercials have mentioned several items which are in that day's issue, including the promise of greater details for the same stories the radio announcer may have just passed over in a 25-word account while presenting "the news."

Finally, the newspaper must be readily available to potential readers where and when they want the paper. A good, efficient home delivery is basic. But this can be made more attractive to many by offering monthly or quarterly billing, credit card payment, or other such conveniences. For many newspapers, especially in the cities, newsstand locations or boxes must be plentiful. In New York City it is possible to walk blocks through mid-town, including through Times Square, without finding a newspaper outlet. In Southern California, on the other hand, one cannot go very far without seeing a row of dispensing machines with a large assortment of metropolitan, regional, and local newspapers.

In sum, there should be nothing wrong with the concept of marketing as applied to newspapers. It means nothing more than putting out a quality product in an attractive form, making it readily and conveniently available, and letting nonreaders know about it.

* * * * * *

During much of the 1970s, cost per thousand in newspaper rates increased faster than equivalent rates for other media. The pace cannot continue. Newspaper executives must concentrate on boosting circulation and advertising linage. They can also offer new services, such as total market coverage and data base related information services. The newspapers of the 80's may be financially strong, but it will take sound strategic planning to secure a similar position for the daily newspaper at the end of the 20th century.

The newspaper industry is economically healthy and appears to hold a firm place in the media mix of advertisers and consumers. But it does face strong competition for the consumer's money and time. Television has taken over its function as a dispenser of hot news. As a result, newspapers are using market research, both formal and informal, to try to realign their content to include that information which the newspaper form is strongest in conveying: in-depth analysis, features, and personal improvement copy. Advertising is a strength, because it is needed by the local retailers and useful to the readers.

Thus the function of the newspaper has been changing, slowly. Those papers which have been most successful, the somewhat atypical *Wall Street Journal,* for example, have done so by becoming indispensable to their readers. In part, this is indigenous to newspapers because of their hard copy, short lead time, and daily appearance. Superior editorial product can reinforce this usefulness and help justify the circulation price.

The form of the newspaper by the year 2000 should be remarkably similar to the newspaper of 1980. There may be more color and better quality reproduction, but printing will still be the production mode. The paper may be thinner as certain sections may be replaced by electronic distribution. Thus, parts of the "newspaper" may be printed and distributed much as it was in 1980, while other parts such as classified ads or stock pages will be left in a computer for electronic transmission to the user's video screen.

It does not seem likely that the United States needs a national newspaper, although the use of earth satellites for transmission at low cost to numerous printing facilities makes this financially feasible, should there be an advertising need. *The Wall Street Journal* comes closest to this and is making increasing use of satellite transmission. This technology may spawn some new special interest daily newspapers. Most such newspapers today are printed in a single plant and mailed to subscribers from that location. But just as the *Journal* is aimed at business readers, other markets may exist for a daily sports newspaper or perhaps one for international affairs. As in the case of other technically feasible options, the implementation of this type of publication depends more on the identification of a need than the development of additional technology.

Firms that own newspapers have been increasing profits not only through acquisitions, but in recent years they have benefited from an extraordinary breakthrough in technology which significantly improved their back-shop productivity. For most newspapers, this surge has now been realized. That means that future internal growth must come from real expansion in circulation and advertising linage. Higher ad rates have often covered up reduced linage and circulation revenue. But even in non-competitive towns and cities, the newspaper cannot charge more than the local merchants can afford, nor can they get too far out of line from prevailing costs in other media, such as the local radio station and spot television, as well as direct or weekly shopper newspapers.

There is no simple key to the successful future of the daily newspaper industry. It cannot look to the technology of 2000 because unless the current newspapers maintain their usefulness to their constituencies, they may be replaced by other forms by then. The newspaper must constantly justify its existence, especially in light of the newer and developing media. But the newspaper does have a unique function and an unduplicated form. Neither form nor function can be well served by a product which is very much different from the ink-on-newsprint vehicle that is so commonplace today.

FOOTNOTES

1. "How The Public Gets The News," (Newspaper Advertising Bureau, New York, 1978).

2. The complexity of determining what may be dropped from the paper with the least consequence is described in Philip Meyer, "The Comic Strip Problem," *ANPA News Research Report,* No. 24, November 21, 1979, pp. 2-6.

13

Profiles of Major Newspaper Publishers and Groups

AFFILIATED PUBLICATIONS, INC.
Boston, Mass.

Properties

The Boston Globe
WFAS-AM and WWYD-FM, White Plains, N. Y.
WSAI-AM and WSAI-FM, Cincinnati, O.
KRAK-AM and KEWT-FM, Sacramento, Calif.
KMTS-AM and FM, Seattle, Wash.
WHYN-AM and FM, Springfield, Mass.)
Research Analysis Corporation, (Boston, Mass.)
Three distribution firms

Total newspaper circulation, A.B.C., March 31, 1979:   493,709 daily
                                                               693,679 Sunday

Affiliated is primarily the *Boston Globe*. The North Adams (Mass.) *Transcript* paper, a 13,000 circulation daily in the western end of the state, and the White Plains and Cincinnati radio stations were purchased in 1976 in separate transactions for $8.6 million plus 200,000 shares of common stock. In late 1979, Affiliated sold the *Transcript* for $5 million, in part to reduce possible conflict with the purchase of the Springfield radio stations.

Boston is still one of a dwindling number of cities with head-on newspaper competition, although the demise of the *Herald Traveler* in June 1972 left only Hearst's weak combined *Herald American* as a rival. As a result, the *Globe*'s circulation, which was 416,123 for the 12 months preceding the *Herald-Traveler*'s suspension, climbed to 462,916 immediately afterwards and to 480,691 in 1978 after switching to "all-day" editions. Advertising linage, which had been stuck at about 43 million lines in the four years before the *Herald-Traveler*'s end, shot up to 50 million lines in 1972 and hit 58 million in 1978.

Although it seems intent on expanding through acquisition, the firm still has much room for profit improvement through introducing the composing room and editorial technology which most other papers have already implemented. It apparently faces little competition from the *Herald American*, which was busy redesigning its format and recruiting new writers. Circulation of the *Herald American*, which had fallen from 424,654 as an all-day paper in 1972 to 309,381 as a morning paper in 1973 continued its slide in 1978 to 286,941. The *Globe* is strongest in the close-in suburbs, but faces its greatest challenge from the many strong local newspapers in the nearby cities surrounding Boston.

As a big city paper, the *Globe* is subject to all the exigencies of this environment: union demands, traffic, greater dependence on the cycles of the economy for classified and national advertising. Thus, Affiliated has two avenues for improvement: increased use of technology internally, and diversification on the outside. Management, however, has not really changed from the days of a family run company and has not proven its ability to master either channel.

CAPITAL CITIES COMMUNICATIONS, INC.
New York, N.Y.

Properties

Daily Newspapers

Kansas City Star/Times
Oakland Press (Pontiac, Mich.)
Belleville (Ill.) *News-Democrat*
Fort Worth (Tex.) *Star-Telegram*
Wilkes-Barre, (Pa.) *Times-Leader*

Total newspaper circulation, A.B.C., March 31, 1979: 1,022,138 daily
1,390,058 Sunday

Other Publications:

Arlington (Tex.) *Citizen Journal*
Fairchild Publications, including
    Women's Wear Daily
    W
    Daily News Record
    Supermarket News
International Medical News Group Magazines

Broadcasting

WPVI-TV, Philadelphia, Pa.	WPAT-AM-FM, Paterson, N.J.
WKBW-TV, Buffalo, N.Y.	KPOL-AM, Los Angeles, Calif.
KTRK-TV, Houston, Tex.	WJR-AM-FM, Detroit, Mich.
WTNH-TV, New Haven, Conn.	WBAP-AM, KSCS-FM, Fort
WTVD-TV, Durham-Raleigh, N.C.	Worth, Tex.
KFSN-TV, Fresno (UHF), Calif.	WKBW-AM, Buffalo, N.Y.
KZLA-FM, Los Angeles, Calif.	WPRO-AM-FM, Providence, R.I.
	WROW-AM-FM, Albany, N.Y.

Capital Cities looks for communications properties which are primarily advertising supported. About 80 percent of its revenues are derived from advertising. Originally involved strictly in broadcasting, Capital Cities entered publishing in 1968. In 1976, publishing revenue accounted for over half of total sales for the first time. By 1978, publishing accounted for 64 percent of the firm's $367.5 million in revenue, but only 41 percent of pretax operating income.

Until 1977, Capital Cities' publishing operations were split virtually equally between trade and consumer publications. The former consists of Fairchild Publications, best known for *Women's Wear Daily* and the trendy *W*, but it is also the publisher of *American Metal Market, Electronic News, Men's Wear*, the new *Energy Users News,* and other publications. In December 1976, it also added a group of six controlled-circulation medical magazines, including *Clinical Psychiatry News* and *Pediatric News.*

The company's involvement in general interest newspapers has been an outgrowth of the statutory limit on the number of broadcast facilities available to a single ownership. The *Oakland Press* was purchased in 1969 and the Belleville daily in 1972. The first big city daily was not acquired until the acquisition of Forth Worth in late 1974.

With the purchase of the two Kansas City newspapers from its employee/ owners for $125 million in February 1977, Capital Cities has more than doubled the size of its publishing division, since the Kansas City operation produced over $180 million in revenue in 1976—an amount almost equal to Capital Cities' total revenue. But the new acquisition has a slim net income margin of only 3.2 percent of sales, well below the margin of the company's publishing division. In 1978 Capital Cities purchased the Wilkes-Barre newspaper and several months later a long an acrimonious, violence-laced strike began. The impasse continued through 1979, with the paper published by non-union workers. A rival daily was published by the striking union members.

Of Capital Cities' six television stations, four are ranked first in their respective markets and four are also affiliated with the ABC network. Radio stations in Detroit, Fort Worth, and Providence rank first in each of their markets.

Under the cross-media ownership divestiture rulings Capital Cities would have exposure with the AM and television combination in Buffalo, its newspaper in Oakland (a Detroit suburb) and its radio stations there, and with the newspaper and radio properties in Fort Worth. Thus, Capital Cities would not be able to sell these properties as a unit, but they do not have to divest themselves of these combinations.

In purchasing the Kansas City papers, Capital Cities has deepened its commitment to print media. As an alternative, it could have spent its investment capital on another UHF television station or on acquiring some cable systems. In this latter regard, however, the firm has stayed true to its policy of seeking out communications properties which are primarily advertising supported, so newspapers are more compatible with this goal than are subscriber-supported cable systems.

Kansas City has not been easy to digest. The purchase required a $72 million bank loan and creation of $10.2 million in notes payable. Before the purchase the firm had existing debt of only $43.1 million and stockholders' equity of $208.5 million.

Meanwhile, both circulation and advertising have been suffering in Kansas City. The 1978 audited circulation of 601,891 for the combined papers compares to 647,016 in 1972. Advertising linage hit almost 67 million lines in 1973, then plummeted to 51 million lines in 1975, but rebounded to 62 million lines by 1978. They have also invested heavily in conversion to DiLitho printing, accompanied, according to some reports, by continued problems and high newsprint wastage.

DOW JONES & CO., INC.
New York, N.Y.

Properties

Newspapers

> *The Wall Street Journal*
> *Barron's*
> *Asian Wall Street Journal Weekly*
> Ottaway Newspapers:
> > *Middletown* (N.Y.) *Times Herald-Record*
> > *New Bedford* (Mass.) *Standard-Times*
> > *Joplin* (Mo.) *Globe*
> > *Danbury* (Conn.) *News-Times*
> > *Cape Cod Times* (Hyannis, Mass.)
> > *Sharon* (Pa.) *Herald*
> > *Medford* Ore.) *Mail Tribune*
> > *Sunbury* (Pa.) *Daily Item*
> > *Traverse City* (Mich.) *Record-Eagle*
> > *Plattsbrugh* (N.Y.) *Press-Republican*
> > *Oneonta* (N.Y.) *Star*
> > *Stroudsburg* (Pa.) *Pocono Record*
> > *Port Jervis* (N.Y.) *Union-Gazette*
> > *Beverly* (Mass.) *Times*
> > *Glocester* (Mass.) *Times*
> > *Newburyport* (Mass.) *News*
> > *Peabody* (Mass.) *Times*
> > *Mankato* (Minn.) *Free Press*
> > *Owatonna* (Minn.) *People's Press*

Other
> Book Digest
> Richard D. Irwin Books
> Dow Jones News Service
> AP-Dow Jones News Service
> Affiliates (minority interest)
>> Riviere du Loup, Quebec newsprint mill (39.9%)
>> Far Eastern Economic Review, Hong Kong (49%)
>> South China Morning Post, Hong Kong (22%)

Total newspaper circulation, A.B.C., March 31, 1979:   2,082,187 daily
                                                            291,510 Sunday

Dow Jones has been working to reduce its reliance on income from its major publication, *The Wall Street Journal,* since this publication's fortunes follow those of the business cycle. In 1970 the company acquired the Ottaway chain of small daily newspapers and in 1975 added Richard D. Irwin, in which it had previously acquired a minority interest. Irwin is one of the three largest publishers of college level business and economics textbooks.

The company suffered a setback in 1977 when it finally decided to terminate the *National Observer,* a weekly magazine in a newspaper format which never had a profitable year since its start-up in 1962. At its demise, it had a circulation of 434,000, down from its peak of 559,000 in 1974. This was particularly serious, because unlike the usual structure of newspapers and magazines in which advertising revenue predominates over circulation income, the latter accounted for 56 percent of the *Observer's* gross income.

Barron's, Dow Jones' highly respected financial weekly, was also significantly below its peak circulation level of 244,000 in 1968. Advertising linage, however, continued to show healthy gains.

The Wall Street Journal accounted for 58 percent of Dow Jones' revenue in 1976, compared to 65 percent in 1972, so progress toward broadening the base has come slowly. This is partly due to the continued success of the *Journal.* Circulation reached an all-time high in 1979 of over 1.6 million, reflecting a 28 percent growth since 1972. Advertising linage and revenue has shown similar strength.

The Ottaway newspapers are all in small cities and towns and none of them has direct, local daily newspaper competiton. Most of them are in cities in the Northeast. Nonetheless, circulation of the group has outperformed national circulation growth by a substantial margin. Total daily circulation for the group was 445,933. Ottaway papers are well-run and are among the leaders in converting to cold type and offset or direct printing.

Prior to Dow Jones' purchase (via stock) of Richard D. Irwin, it had owned a 21 percent interest in the book publisher. The addition of Irwin was a logical one for Dow Jones, because of the publisher's predominance in the field of business textbooks. Irwin was in the business textbook business long before the current boom in enrollments in business courses at colleges and universities. Thus, it was in an excellent position to ride the expansion of the market while others had to play catch-up. Irwin's sales approached $28 million in 1976, but contributed a proportionately larger share to corporate earnings than to revenue.

Besides its interests in newsprint production and minority ownership of two Hong Kong-based business and financial publications, Dow Jones has invested heavily in the start-up of the *Asian Wall Street Journal,* which began publication on September 1, 1976. Approximately 60 percent of subscribers are Asian nationals in executive positions. Initial results "exceeded [DJ's] best expectations." Dow Jones ventured into this area because it saw that American trade with East Asia exceeded U.S. trade with Common Market countries in Europe and was growing at 30 percent annually.

The New York Printing and Publishing Analysts rated Dow Jones the best managed company in the newspaper industry—a designation which shows up in the strong price to earnings ratio of the company's common stock. One of Dow Jones' primary strengths must be in its clear understanding of its own identity and goals. Management's stated objectives include: 1) to bolster existing publications; 2) to diversify, thus reducing exposure to the business cycle; and 3) to re-use existing resources for incremental revenue.

As an example of the first goal, Dow Jones has invested heavily in the technological revolution. As noted in Chapter 6, it has reduced facsimile transmission costs substantially by using satellite rather than microwave transmission for *Wall Street Journal* pages. Mailrooms at the *Journal* have been converted to computer-controlled equipment that addresses newspapers at the rate of 60,000 per hour. Editorially, it has consciously worked to provide the reader of *The Wall Street Journal* increased value—to make the paper indispensable—a necessity if it is going to have to ask for higher subscription rates.

The second objective is clearly seen in the Irwin, Ottaway, and newsprint manufacturing investments. Unlike most newspaper publishers, Dow Jones had a long-standing policy of *not* expanding into broadcasting, since television and radio stations are licensed by the federal government and Dow Jones is philosophically opposed to getting involved in businesses which are so regulated. However, in 1978 it reversed its position and acquistions in this arena became a possibility.

The third objective is also partially responsible for the *Asian Journal,* since it is able to use much of the material produced for the domestic edition, while stories written and information collected by the Asian staff often find their way into the U.S. edition. The work of both sales staffs also overlaps. Dow Jones can also recycle information it gathers for its newspaper through its news services as well as the on-demand Dow Jones-Bunker Ramo computerized news retrieval service. This latter is a major data base of Dow Jones-gathered information and currently is operating at a profit.

Dow Jones gets high grades for integrity in its publications and its name is almost synonymous with business. It can also be a hardnosed operation, as its sudden suspension of the *National Observer* makes clear (although some may argue that the move was overdue).

There are problems the company must face, however. Perhaps foremost among them is the continued escalation in second class postage rates. With 8.0 million deliveries per week, the stiff increases in the postage rate saw the Dow Jones postage bill soar from $6 million in 1971 to $18 million five years later. It will be an estimated $89 million by 1983, despite increased printing locations and more efficient sorting procedures.

As one response, Dow Jones has been increasing the number of *Journals* delivered by its own carrier. By 1979, about 20% of its daily circulation was delivered privately, including those to the offices of the Postal Service in Washington.

Richard D. Irwin, although a leader in its field, faces increasingly stiff competition from other well-established college textbook publishers who see strong enrollments in college business programs as an area to take up the slack from depressed sales in their traditional social science or other publishing disciplines.

Ottaway, although strong in its present markets, has found expansion through additional acquisitions difficult because of the intense competition for properties by many other newspaper groups. So far, Ottaway has held off being sucked into the bidding wars which have brought record prices for newspapers. Without additional purchases, further internal development must be realized for growth.

On balance, however, Dow Jones must be rated one of the premier newspaper publishing companies. It made an early and firm commitment to quality products, introduced technological innovations which are economically justified, and adopted a marketing strategy which provides the potential for substantial growth, especially in the Far East.

GANNETT CO., INC.
Rochester, N.Y.

Properties

Daily Newspapers

Arizona
  Tucson Citizen
California
  Oakland Tribune
  Salinas Californian
  San Bernardino, The Sun
  Stockton Record
  Visalia Times-Delta
Colorado
  Fort Collins Coloradoan
Delaware
  Wilmington, The Morning News
    and *Evening Journal*
Florida
  Cocoa, TODAY
  Fort Myers News-Press
  The Pensacola Journal and *News*
Guam
  Pacific Daily News
Hawaii
  Honolulu Star-Bulletin
Idaho
  Boise, The Idaho Statesman
Illinois
  Danville, The Commercial-News
  Rockford, Morning Star and
    Register-Republic
Indiana
  Lafayette, Journal and Courier
  Marion, Chronicle-Tribune
  Richmond, The Palladium-Item

Iowa
  Iowa City Press-Citizen
Kansas
  The Coffeyville Journal
Louisiana
  Monroe Morning World and
    News-Star
  The Shreveport Times
Michigan
  Battle Creek, Enquirer and News
  Lansing, The State Journal
  Port Huron, The Times Herald
Minnesota
  Little Falls Daily Transcript
  The St. Cloud Daily Times
Missouri
  Springfield Daily News
  Springfield Leader and Press
Nebraska
  Fremont Tribune
Nevada
  Reno, Nevada State Journal and
    Evening Gazette
New Jersey
  Bridgewater, The Courier-News
  Camden Courier-Post
New Mexico
  Santa Fe, The New Mexican
New York
  Binghamton, The Sun-Bulletin
    and *Evening Press*

Elmira Star-Gazette
The Ithaca Journal
Niagara Gazette
Poughkeepsie Journal
Rochester Democrat and
  Chronicle and *The Times-Union*
Saratoga Springs, The Saratogian
Utica, The Daily Press and
  The Observer-Dispatch
Westchester Rockland News-
  papers:
Mamaroneck, The Daily Times
Mount Vernon, The Daily Argus
New Rochelle, The Standard-
  Star
Nyack-Rockland, The Journal-
  News
Ossining, The Citizen Register
Port Chester, The Daily Item
Tarrytown, The Daily News
Westchester County, TODAY
White Plains, The Reporter
  Dispatch
Yonkers, The Herald Statesman
Ohio
  Chillicothe Gazette
  Cincinnati Enquirer
  Fremont, The News-Messenger
  The Marietta Times
  Port Clinton, News-Herald
Oklahoma
  Muskogee Daily Phoenix and
    Times-Democrat
Oregon
  Salem, The Oregon Statesman and
    Capital Journal
Pennsylvania
  Chambersburg, Public Opinion
  New Kensington-Tarentum,
    Valley News Dispatch
South Dakota
  Sioux Falls Argus-Leader

Tennessee
  Nashville Banner
Texas
  The El Paso Times
Vermont
  The Burlington Free Press
Virgin Islands
  St. Thomas, The Daily News
Washington
  The Bellingham Herald
  Olympia, The Daily Olympian
West Virginia
  Huntington, The Herald-Dispatch
    and *Advertiser*

Weekly Newspapers:

  Connecticut
    Westport Fairpress
  Florida
    Melbourne Times
    Titusville Star-Advocate
  Minnesota
    Pierz, Royalton, Royalton Banner
    and Pierz Journal
  New Jersey
    Cherry Hill, Suburban Newspaper
      Group (10 weeklies)
  New York
    Bronxville Review Press-Reporter
    Saratoga Springs, Commercial
      News
  Pennsylvania
    New Kensington, Butler County
      News, North Hills News Record
      (semi-weekly)
    New Kensington, The Herald

Total newspaper circulation, A.B.C.,
March 31, 1979:   3,429,620 daily
                       3,268,505 Sunday

18 Non-daily newspapers

Broadcasting

Radio
    KIIS-AM & FM, Los Angels, Calif.
    KSDO-AM, San Diego, Calif.
    KEZL-FM, San Diego, Calif.
    WVON-AM, Chicago, Ill.
    WGCI-FM, Chicago, Ill.
    WWWE-AM, Cleveland, O.
    WDOK-FM, Cleveland, O.
    WDEE-AM, Detroit, Mich.
    WCZY-FM, Detroit, Mich.
    KSDO-AM, St. Louis, Mo.
    KCFM-FM, St. Louis, Mo.
Television
    KARK, Little Rock, Ark.
    KTAR, Phoenix, Ariz.
    KBTV, Denver, Colo.
    WXIA, Atlanta, Ga.
    WPTA, Fort Wayne, Ind.
    WLKY, Louisville, Ky.
    KOCO, Oklahoma City, Okla.

With the addition of the 13 Speidel group in May 1977, Gannett increased its position as the largest newspaper publishing group in the United States. In 1979 it completed a merger with Combined Communications, bringing in not only two large newspapers (Oakland and Cincinnati), but a full complement of broadcast properties.

Gannett papers are mostly in small and medium size cities and are virtually free of direct competition. The company sold the *Hartford Times* in 1973, an operation which did sufffer from strong competition and which had been a poor performer. Gannett does own several newspapers which publish under joint leading operating agreements with editorial competitors in Nashville, Shreveport, Tucson, and Honolulu. (In Nashville, it bought the dominant *Tennessean*, at the same time selling the *Banner.*)

In making its acquisitions, Gannett looks for family type operations which can add substantial profit to Gannett through its management expertise. The crucial factor in the analysis is not what the most recent earnings have been, but what the realistic potential may be.

Its financial figures appear to vindicate this approach of small and medium size papers in growth areas with little or no competition. Even through the recession of 1974-1975, Gannett maintained its growth, not just by acquiring more papers to boost revenues and total profit, since profit margins actually increased in this period, as did earnings per share. Revenue and profits have grown over the years without a decline. Revenue in 1978 was $690 million, reflecting a 12.9 percent compound growth since 1970. Profit after tax grew 18.3 percent. Combined Communications earned $79 million $189 million in sales, so that entering the 1980s, Gannett is a $1 billion in sales company.

Gannett is a large, apparently well-managed organization which knows what it is about. Its strong financial performance and balance sheet have made it a perennial favorite of Wall Street investors.

Gannett did get burnt in a non-newspaper related venture. Between 1972 and 1975, Gannett invested $11.6 million in Laser Graphic Systems Corporation, in an attempt to develop a relief printing plate made directly from the paste-up copy, eliminating the negative stage. The system was tested at the Elmira, NY newspaper, but in 1975 the company took a $9.8 million write-off on the investment, having deemed the profitability of the system "too uncertain and too far off" to warrant continuation of the project. In fact, it would seem that the technology had been by-passed by increased use of offset plates and printing.

In 1976, the company added the Gannett Newspaper Advertising Sales force to act as the agent for all the Gannett newspapers. This replaced an arrangement in which the papers had contracted with independent agents for $20 million in national advertising at a commission cost of $1 million in 1975. GNAS, along with the Gannett News Service and corporate marketing teams, provides some of the synergy necessary to justify chain ownership of newspapers.

As editorial products, Gannett papers get mixed reviews. Its small city papers are no worse—and many perhaps better—than they would be under independent ownership. But none of its larger papers—where journalistic excellence might be more prominently displayed—is known for consistently noteworthy performance.

Gannett has not set the pace for innovation in technology, but it has been proceeding to switch to photocomposition, offset, or plastic plate printing, and front-end systems. By the end of 1977, 90 percent of the Gannett papers had complete electronic printing systems.

Gannett has been one of the leaders in promoting higher circulation prices. It has also been expanding internally by adding Sunday editions in more cities. In 1976, the eight Westchester-Rockland newspapers in suburban New York added Sunday papers, at a start-up cost of $900,000. Penetration appeared slow, however, as many Westchester residents still bought the *Times* or *News* on Sunday, and the *Times* has counter-attacked with a Sunday Westchester section. But the long New York strike in 1978 helped establish the Sunday edition, as well as a new morning paper, *Today*, which sold for 10 cents. There are still some papers without Sunday editions, many of which may be future prospects.

Gannett appears to be rolling merrily along, acquiring properties on a regular basis, occasionally disposing of a newspaper which is a chronic drag on earnings. It makes some mistakes—the Laser Graphic Systems investment being an obvious one. But on the whole it must be rated a well managed organization which has a clear sense of its business and its mission. Management does appear to be concerned about the limited future growth through newspapers alone, given the finite number of newspapers and the fierce competition for acquisition. The merger with Combined Communications represents Gannett's first major move to diversify and it will likely expand into magazine, cable TV and book publishing in the 1980s.

HARTE-HANKS COMMUNICATIONS, INC.
San Antonio, Tex.

Properties

Daily Newspapers

Texas
> *Abilene Reporter-News*
> *Corpus Christi Caller* and *Times*
> *San Angelo Standard* and *Times*
> *Big Spring Herald*
> *The Eagle*, Bryan-College Station
> *Corsicana Daily Sun*
> *The Denison Herald*
> *The Herald Banner*, Greenville
> *The Huntsville Item*
> *Marshall News Messenger*
> *The Paris News*
> *Wichita Falls Record News* and *Times*

Other states
> *Anderson* (SC) *Independent* and *Daily Mail*
> *Yakima* (Wash.) *Herald-Republic*
> *South Middlesex Daily News* (Framingham, Mass.)
> *Hamilton* (O.) *Journal-News*
> *Gloucester County Times* (Woodbury, N.J.)
> *Ypsilanti* (Mich.) *Press*
> *Russellville* (Ariz.) *Daily Courier-Democrat*
> *Malvern* (Ark.) *Daily Record*
> *Searcy* (Ark.) *Daily Citizen*
> *Stuttgart* (Ark.) *Daily Leader*

Total newspaper circulation, A.B.C., March 31, 1979:   540,621 daily
                                                               535,532 Sunday

62 nondaily newspapers and "shoppers"

Broadcasting

Television

    KENS-TV, San Antonio Tex.
    WFMY-TV, Greensboro, N.C.
    WTLV-TV, Jacksonville, Fla.
    KYTV-TV, Springfield, Mo.

Radio

    WSGN-AM, Birmingham, Ala.
    KUY-AM, Phoenix, Ariz.
    KQYT-FM, Phoenix, Ariz.
    WLEY-AM, Tampa, Fla.
    WRBQ-FM, Tampa, Fla.
    KMJK-FM, Lake Oswego, Ore.
    WEZI-FM, Memphis, Tenn.
    KULF-AM, Houston, Tex.
    KYND-FM, Houston, Tex.
    WRVQ-FM, Richmond, Va.

All of the Harte-Hanks daily newspapers are the only ones of general circulation in their respective markets and all are in small and medium size cities. The largest newspaper, since the 1973 sale of the San Antonio flagship paper to Rupert Murdoch, is in Corpus Christi, a city with approximately 210,000 population and a combined daily circulation of 90,000. Many of the non-daily papers are in markets congruent with the daily papers, while several are in markets which could not yet support a daily paper. The largest of the free shoppers is the Van/De *Pennysaver*, with 792,780 copies sent to Orange County, CA residents each Thursday. The chain of San Diego bi-weekly papers are predominately free, but include some paid subscribers. In several markets, such as Greenville, Tex., Corpus Christi, Hamilton, O., and Woodbury, N.J., shoppers are published in addition to paid-for dailies, consistent with the firm's strategy that each publication provides a distinct service to its readers and advertisers and hence increases overall market penetration in these areas.

There is no local television station in at least 12 of Harte-Hanks' daily newspaper markets. In 1978, its own broadcasting operations accounted for 19 percent of total revenue, but a larger proportion of operating income. None of its broadcast operations is in markets which directly overlap its own daily newspapers.

Harte-Hanks has followed a long-run strategy which is consistent with its definition of its business: publications composed of ink-on-newsprint. Thus, more than any other publicly owned newspaper group, it has sought out acquisitions of not only less-than-daily newspapers, but shoppers as well. These latter publications are frequently devoid of all news and consequently enjoy low prestige in the newspaper business. However, they may be quite profitable. They rely on much the same marketing and production expertise involved in producing a daily newspaper. Some analysts of the newspaper business see the shopper publications as more of a long-term threat to the health of the daily than television. Thus, co-opting this vehicle may be a sound strategy for the newspaper publisher—and Harte-Hanks has accepted this reasoning.

The Harte-Hanks management is very marketing oriented, having formed its own in-house research outfit, RMH Research, Inc., whose efforts have aided in surveying local markets, developing new formats, and revamping distribution systems. It was among the first groups to adopt the "total marketing approach" to selling newspapers.

Basically consisting of small newspapers, the group's dailies do not have a particular reputation for quality journalism. They have upgraded their commitment to editorial product, however, and have raised the proportion of operating expenses devoted to news operations.

Overall, in 1978 84 percent of the firm's publishing revenues came from advertising. As with most small papers, almost all of its advertising revenues were from local display and classified sources.

With only 6 percent of its work force represented by unions, Harte-Hanks did not face labor obstacles in converting its operations to photocomposition. Between 1972 and 1977, the company spent $21 million on capital improvements primarily in the composing room and pressroom. However, only then did the company begin the front end conversion to text editing systems. The addition of such systems will aid in further increasing productivity.

In 1976, the company resumed its acquistions, following a year in which only one television station was purchased. Additions included a chain of seven daily and weekly newspapers around Russellville, Ark. for $4.3 million, a daily paper in Wichita Falls, Tex. for $15 million (or almost $290 per subscriber), and a weekly shopper in Southern California for $1 million.

In 1977, Harte-Hanks acquired the WFMY-TV franchise for $1.9 million and two twice-weekly newspapers and a weekly tourist guide in Gatlinburg, Tenn. for 75,000 shares of common stock. Since then, it has concentrated in adding to its broadcast holdings.

The free *Pennysaver* publications are sent by third class mail or delivered by private carrier and with 1.4 million distributed weekly, it faces some exposure from escalating postal rates and related delivery services.

Harte-Hanks is in a relatively strong financial position and can be expected to make further acquisitions. Its management is also among the most farsighted and understanding of the news media environment, and this finds its way into the firm's strategic planning.

HEARST CORPORATION
New York, N.Y.

Properties

Newspapers

> *Albany* (NY) *Times-Union* and *Knickerbocker News*
> *Boston Herald-American*
> *Los Angeles Herald-Examiner*
> *San Antonio* (Tex.) *Light*
> *Baltimore News American*
> *San Francisco Examiner*
> *Seattle Post-Intelligencer*
> *Edwardsville* (Ill.) *Intelligencer*
> *Huron* (Mich.) *Daily Tribune*
> *Midland* (Mich.) *Daily News*
> Midland (Tex.) *Reporter-Telegram*
> *Plainview* (Tex.) *Herald*

> Total newspaper circulation, A.B.C., March 31, 1979:   1,402,311 daily
> 2,166,260 Sunday

Magazines

> *Cosmopolitan*
> *Good Housekeeping*
> *Harper's Bazaar*
> *House Beautiful*
> *Motor Boating & Sailing*
> *Popular Mechanics*
> *Science Digest*
> *Sports Afield*
> *Town & Country*
> *American Druggist*

Broadcasting

Television:
> WBAL-TV, Baltimore, Md.
> WISN-TV, Milwaukee, Wis.
> WTAE-TV, Pittsburgh, Pa.

Radio
> WAPA-AM, San Juan, P.R.
> WBAL-AM, Baltimore, Md.

WIYY-FM, Baltimore, Md.
WTAE-AM, Pittsburgh, Pa.
WXKX-FM, Pittsburgh, Pa.
WISN-AM, Milwaukee, Wis.
WLPX-FM, Milwaukee, Wis.

Other

Arbor House Books
Avon Books
King Features Syndicate
Periodical Publishers Service Bureau
International Circulation Distributors
Hearst Metrotone News
Real estate, mining, paper products, livestock

William Randolph Hearst got his start in the newspaper business when his father, George, made him publisher of the family-owned *San Francisco Evening Examiner* in 1888. "W.R." brought on some extraordinary writers and editors and tripled the *Examiner*'s circulation to 60,000 in five years.

The Hearst empire really didn't begin to form until 1904. He had come to New York in 1896 to start the *Journal* in direct confrontation with Joseph Pulitzer's *World*. But in 1904 he started another *Examiner* in Los Angeles and bought a paper in Boston. In 1912 he bought the Atlanta *Daily Georgian* and a year later added the *Morning Call* in San Francisco. Over the next ten years, he expanded with 16 more papers, including the *Detroit Times, Seattle Post-Intelligencer*, the *Washington Herald*, the *Syracuse Journal*, and the *Los Angeles Herald*. For good measure, he included the *San Antonio Light*, the *Milwaukee Sentinel*, and founded the *New York Mirror*.

At the peak of his empire, the papers had perhaps six million daily readers—almost twice the size of the largest chain today. Expansion continued into the Depression. In all, Hearst either bought or started 42 daily newspapers. But by 1940, only 17 remained as 14 were merged with others, seven were sold, and four abandoned.

Hearst died in 1951, but in 1960 the chain still had 13 daily papers and lead all other chains with four million in circulation. However, with further attrition, the newspaper operation of the Hearst Corp. was reduced to seven daily newspapers and 1.4 million daily circulation before another acquisition binge at the end of the 1970s brought on board several small dailies, whose circulation barely compensated for the continued losses of its big city papers.

Moreover, several of the remaining newspapers are in trouble. The *Herald-Examiner*, at one time the predominate daily in Los Angeles, has been weakened by a massive strike in 1967 and low employee morale. Circulation peaked in the early 1960s at 775,000 making the paper the largest afternoon daily in the United States. By the time of the strike, circulation had dropped to 725,000. But by 1978, circulation stood at an embarrassing 316,000. Advertising linage decreased as well. In 1967 the *Herald-Examiner* ran 23.6 million lines. In 1978, linage was only 15.5 million, including Sunday and part-run.

In Baltimore, the evening *News American* dropped almost 15 percent in circulation while the rival *Sun*'s evening paper fell 12 percent. In advertising linage, the *Sun*'s evening/Sunday total was the same in 1976 as in 1972, but the *News American*'s linage was nine percent lower.

Similarly, in Boston, the *Herald American,* which incorporated the defunct *Herald Traveler* in 1972, lost 27 percent in circulation from 1972, although that was partly due to conversion from an all-day to a morning edition. The *Globe,* meanwhile, held its 1972 circulation level in 1976, with evening losses balanced by morning gains. Advertising linage for both papers was aided by the elimination of the third daily, with the Hearst paper gaining 6.6 percent over its 1972 level, but stiil running only about one third the linage of the *Globe.*

Again, in San Francisco, where the competing morning *Chronicle* and Hearst's *Examiner* operate under a common advertising, distribution, and production agreement, circulation has suffered for Hearst. The *Chronicle,* with three times the circulation of the *Examiner,* maintained its circulation during the 1972 to 1976 period; the *Examiner* dropped 17.5 percent. In Seattle, the *Times,* although an evening paper, lost less circulation than Hearst's morning *Post-Intelligencer* over the same four years. And in San Antonio, where Rupert Murdoch acquired the *Express* and *News,* the *Light,* although still leading in the evening field, edged up four percent to a 16 percent gain for the *News.*

Hearst was for many years unique among the group owners in that all of its newspapers were in large cities and all except the Albany properties faced direct competition. For the most part, however, the Hearst papers are coming out second best in a field of two. In recent years Hearst management has been in a state of flux, with numerous changes in the newspaper division. Some year-to-year gains have been made, but generally, the newspaper operations are still likely to undergo further consolidation in existing properties. Hearst was a late-comer into the competition to buy up small, independent dailies with no direct competition, so they are forced to pay top dollar.

The Magazine Division is reported to be making money and it has some strong properties in *Cosmopolitan, Good Housekeeping,* and several of the smaller special interest publications. It is not likely, however, that Hearst is as profitable as the Newhouse group.

KNIGHT-RIDDER
Miami, Fla.

Properties

Daily Newspapers

> *Miami Herald*
> *Philadelphia Daily News* and *The Philadelphia Inquirer*
> *Detroit Free Press*
> *San Jose Mercury* and *News*
> *Akron Beacon Journal*
> *St. Paul Pioneer Press* and *Dispatch*
> *The Charlotte Observer* and *News*
> *Long Beach* (Calif.) *Independent* and *Press-Telegram*
> *Wichita Beacon* and *Eagle*
> *Lexington* (Ky.) *Herald* and *Leader*
> *Gary* (Ind.) *Post-Tribune*
> *Macon* (Ga.) *News* and *Telegraph*
> *Columbus* (Ga.) *Ledger* and *Enquirer*
> *The Journal of Commerce* (New York)
> *Duluth* (Minn.) *News-Tribune* and *Herald*
> *Tallahassee* (Fla.) *Democrat*
> *Centre Daily News* (State College, Pa.)
> *Pasadena* (Calif.) *Star-News*
> *Daily Camera* (Boulder, Colo.)
> *The Bradenton* (Fla.) *Herald*
> *Grand Forks* (N.D.) *Herald*
> *Boca Raton* (Fla.) *News*
> *Aberdeen* (S.D.) *American News*
> *Seattle* (Wash.) *Times**
> *Walla Walla* (Wash.) *Union-Bulletin**

Total circulation, A.B.C. March 31, 1979:   3,746,591 daily
                                                        4,546,328 Sunday

Other

> 12 non-daily newspapers
> Comodity News Service
> Knight News Service
> HP Books
> ADAMS (Alternative Distribution and Marketing Systems) Corp.

*Owns 49.5 percent of voting common stock and 65 percent of non-voting common.

Broadcasting

> WJRT, Flint, Mich.
> WPRI, Providence
> WTEN, Albany

With the exception of newspapers in Miami, Philadelphia, and Detroit, the Knight-Ridder properties are in communities with no direct daily newspaper competition. Papers in those three cities, however, account for over one-third of the company's revenue, although a smaller percentage of income. Other Knight-Ridder papers do circulate in cities that have extensive competition from nearby papers.

Knight-Ridder had been one of the purest newspaper owning chains, in that its business was almost completely newspapers. But in mid-1977 the company announced an agreement to buy a group of broadcast properties for $70 million.

The firm's flagship paper in Miami clearly dominates that market. The *Herald* is the largest circulation newspaper in the southeastern United States and includes distribution to Latin America. A section is printed in Spanish for the large Cuban population in the Dade County area. The *Herald* competes as part of a joint operating agreement with the evening *Miami News,* a Cox-owned newspaper. But the *Herald* runs all operating and business functions for both newspapers.

In Philadelphia, the *Inquirer* has been winning Pulitzer Prizes and other signs of recognition of journalistic excellence, marking a true turn-around from its pre-Knight days. Thanks to large-scale promotion efforts, the journalistic reputation is finally being translated into profits, with the two papers finally reporting a modest operating profit in 1976. The circulation of the morning *Inquirer* is stable after years of decline, while the rival evening *Bulletin* has continued losing readers. The long-time Sunday lead of the *Inquirer* has gotten larger. The *Daily News*, sold primarily within the city limits and 88 percent from the newsstand, has been relatively stable.

However, the Philadelphia papers are still beset by labor problems, with a Guild walkout effectively shutting down operations at both papers for 24 days in 1977.

The *Detroit Free Press* has almost achieved circulation parity with the afternoon *News*, but as the only morning paper in Michigan, the *Free Press* has a much larger state-wide circulation. Still, the *News* maintains a substantial lead in ad linage, since it has the higher household penetration in the Detroit SMSA—the territory which many local retailers would want to reach. Nonetheless, linage increased almost 17 percent in 1976 for the *Free Press*, about twice the rate of increase of the *News*, and the Knight-Ridder paper has been increasing its share of total linage.

The San Jose papers are within an SMSA which grew 15 percent in population between 1970 and 1975. Although they are the only daily papers in San Jose itself, they do face some competition from other San Francisco Bay area papers, which reach about 18 percent of area households. Similarly, the Long Beach dailies have relatively low household penetration, as they lie well within the sphere of influence of the powerful *Los Angeles Times;* and the St. Paul papers vie with the virtually congruent trading area of the Minneapolis newspapers. Elsewhere, the Knight-Ridder properties face less rigorous competitors. Eleven of its 22 markets are in Sunbelt communities which are projected to have a growth rate at well over twice the national average through the early 1980s.

Other than the broadcasting acquisition, the company's major non-newspaper investment in recent years has been its commitment to be a one third partner (with Cox and Media General) in a 155,000 ton capacity newsprint mill in Georgia. Knight-Ridder's 50,000 ton annual share represents about 10 percent of its needs outside of its western newspapers. The company has also established a subsidiary, Viewdata Corporation of America, which is engaged in experiments with a viewdata-type delivery system. Its partner is American Telephone & Telegraph Co.

The Knight organization is generally rated as one of the best of the group owners in terms of commitment to editorial quality. Its willingness to buy the Philadelphia properties and pump a substantial sum of money into physical plant and editorial product is a sign of this commitment. The Ridder newspapers, on the other hand, were considered to be mediocre at best. One of the Ridder family reportedly told a bright young assistant that there was no future for him in the business because, "What we need is a constant supply of mediocrity."

In 1973, its last full year before their merger, Knight had an after-tax profit margin of 6.4 percent, compared to 8.7 percent for Ridder. With the digestion period over and the effects of the recession behind, the margin in 1976 was, significantly, in between these two points. At first, former Knight management had been in the top policy and operating positions. Brothers John and James Knight, who own over 40 percent of the common stock, have resigned all active management roles. But with several Ridder descendants who are young and still working their way up in the organization assuming major policy roles, the nature of the combined organization may start to shift away from the commitments of the Knights.

In the meantime, Knight-Ridder appears set on a path that eschews the small town newspapers for medium and large size units. The company sold its smallest paper, the *Niles* (Mich.) *Daily Star* because management judged its size (8103 daily) too small when compared with its potential. Although the Boca Raton paper was about the same size in 1972, it is published in a community which increased by 61 percent in population between 1970 and 1976 and grew to 12,000 circulation, while Niles stayed level. Management has expressed a willingness to make acquisitions of new papers as large as 200,000 daily circulation, so long as the market is growing faster than the U.S. average.

The company has reduced its labor expense to 35 percent of total revenue in 1976, from 37.1 percent in 1975, largely as a result of gains in new technology. Only the Philadelphia papers had not been converted to total photocomposition by mid-1977, a goal reached in early 1978. In 1976, it spent $7.1 million on new equipment, after $5.3 million in 1975. Moreover, having completed the installation of new presses in Philadelphia, Knight-Ridder announced a $37 million commitment for a new plant in Detroit featuring 36 Goss offset presses. However, much of the money saved in production from these investments is being fed back into circulation and promotion expenses in the more competitive markets.

LEE ENTERPRISES, INC.
Davenport, Iowa

Properties

Newspapers

> *Decatur* (Ill.) *Herald* and *Review*
> *Wisconsin State-Journal* (Madison)
> *Quad-City Times* (Davenport, Ia.)
> *Racine* (Wis.) *Journal-Times*
> *Lincoln* (Neb.) *Star* (49% owned)
> *LaCrosse* (Wis.) *Tribune*
> *Mason City* (Ia.) *Globe-Gazette*
> *Ottumwa* (Ia.) *Courier*
> *Kewanee* (Ill.) *Star-Courier*
> *Muscatine* (Ia.) *Journal*
> *Billings* (Mont.) *Gazette*
> *Kansas City* (Kans.) *Kansan*
> *Butte* (Mont.) *Standard*
> *Missoula* (Mont.) *Missoulian*
> *Helena* (Mont.) *Independent Record*
> *Corvallis* (Ore.) *Gazette-Times*
> *Southern Illinoisan* (Carbondale)
> *Bismarck* (N.D.) *Tribune* (50% owned)

Total circulation, A.B.C., March 31, 1979:   590,486 daily
                                                          604,366 Sunday

Broadcasting

Television
  KOIN-TV, Portland, Ore.
  KGMB-TV, Honolulu, Hi.
  WSAZ-TV, Huntington-Charleston, W. Va.
  KHQA-TV, Hannibal, Mo./Quincy, Ill.
  KIMT-TV, Mason City, Ia.
Radio
  WTAD-AM, Mason City, Ia.
  WQCY-FM, Quincy, Ill.
  KFAB-AM, Omaha, Neb.*
  KOUR-FM, Omaha, Neb.*

Other

  NAPP Systems, Inc. (50% ownership)—plastic printing plates
  Equine Events magazine
  Wisconsin magazine

*Partially owned through Lincoln Newspapers.

Lee's papers are all relatively small operations, with the *Wisconsin State Journal*, at 73,000 daily circulation, the largest of the group. The closest the Lee papers come to competitive situations are those publications in Madison and Lincoln which work under joint operating agreements with another daily.

In 1979, Lee purchased five papers from the Lindsay-Schaub chain for $60.4 million, its largest single acquisition, but immediately sold three of the papers for $16.0 million to the Hearst Corporation in order to reduce debt during a period of high interest rates and economic uncertainty.

Much of Lee's efforts since 1972 have been in the development of NAPP Systems, the plastic plate-making operations in which it shares ownership with Nippon Paint Co. of Japan. This company registered almost a 344 percent increase in sales between 1974 and 1978, to $33.6 million. NAPP's net profit in 1978 was $2.8 million, up 84 percent from net income in 1975. NAPP has over 250 customers for its precoated plastic plate and its volume makes it the largest such manufacturer worldwide. It has well over 50 percent of the U.S. and Canadian plastic plate market, as well as a growing number of European customers.

Lee's income statement belies its size. The revenues from its three unconsolidated 50 percent owned holdings (49.75 percent in the case of the Lincoln Journal-Star Printing Co.) totaled $40 million in 1978, yielding a net profit of $4.7 million. Accounting procedures, however, result in only Lee's equity in this net income showing up under total corporate revenue.

The company's management sophistication also outstrips its size. It is a forward-looking company which has devoted considerable energy not only to normal short-range operating plans, but to strategic planning as well. Lee executives view themselves as being in the "information transfer business," which opens up opportunities for development beyond newspapers and broadcasting. Notes one Lee manager, "We're looking for more newspapers and TV properties, but so is everyone else." Thus, Lee has evolved a long run concept as an information company, utilizing digital storage and retrieval technology to its fullest extent.

As one small step in this regard, Lee has been working to get greater use from its high speed typesetting equipment. For purely newspaper applications, it is used at only 20 percent to 30 percent of capacity. So, Lee is offering to put video input devices in the plants of non-newspaper customers who need typesetting. They can feed their material directly to the typesetter and pay by the meter for work done.

Lee has been a leader in adopting new technology. It installed the first photocomposition machine in 1954. All the Lee newspapers are set in cold type and printed either on offset or NAPP plates. All but two papers have VDT input. Man-hours per page for composition and make-up have been reduced at the flagship Davenport paper from a common four to seven hours to under 54 minutes. As a result of this complete commitment to new technology, Lee reduced its total number of printers from 300 in 1973 to 134 in 1976. Adding back in the number of new positions which had to be created as part of the change, there was a net reduction of 128.5 positions in the three years, resulting in a real 15.1 percent reduction in average monthly production labor cost, despite a 32 percent inflation rate. Payroll costs, although up, dropped from 45 percent of revenue in 1973 to 40 percent in 1976 and to 34 percent in 1978.

More than coincidentally, the number of union bargaining units has decreased as technology has been improved. From 46 bargaining units in 1968, there were only 12 in 1976. Management attributes this reduction to increased benefits, training, and the opportunity offered those displaced by technology to learn new skills.

The NAPP operation has been an outstanding success. The NAPP plate is generally rated as yielding the best results of the plastic plates. Its widespread use has come despite its being priced substantially higher than the competition. Many of the larger newspapers using it have taken advantage of the greater relief by using it as a pattern plate. In late 1976, NAPP introduced a new product, the Waterplate™. The market for the photo-polymer plastic plate, however, is likely to be of finite duration, since the use of these plates is only an intermediate step prior to a plant's replacing its old letterpress with the generally accepted offset presses. *Newsday,* for example, a NAPP customer, has ordered new offset presses which will end its need for the plastic pattern plate. NAPP is thus expanding its line with the Waterplate, while at the same time increasing its position in the plastic plate market.

Lee has been mentioned as a candidate for a take-over, much as Speidel and Booth were bought up in 1976. Management, however, has expressed a firm desire to remain independent and has changed the corporation's by-laws to make unfriendly buy-outs very difficult. Lee also views its strong position in FCC regulated broadcast properties as a further buffer in any take-over move.

Overall, Lee is a solid communications company, with superior management. Its newspaper markets are not glamorous, but they are stable. The newspapers have been improved by channeling some of the production savings into editorial operations. Lee is not likely to get into bidding wars for additional properties, but should be expected to make acquisitions in information businesses.

MEDIA GENERAL, INC.
Richmond, Va.

Properties

Newspapers

> *Richmond* (Va.) *Times-Dispatch* and *News Leader*
> *Tampa* (Fla.) *Tribune* and *Times*
> *Winston-Salem* (N.C.) *Journal* and *Sentinel*

Total circulation, A.B.C., March 31, 1979:   581,088 daily
                                                            539,412 Sunday

Newsprint

> Garden State Paper Co., (Garfield, N.J., Pomona, Calif.) 20% ownership
> Southeast Paper Manufacturing Co. (Dublin, Ga.) 33.3% ownership
> Pronapade Newsprint (Mexico) 49% ownership

Broadcasting

> WFLA-TV-AM-FM (Tampa, Fla.)
> Cablevision of Fredericksburg (Fredericksburg, Va.)

Other

> M/G Financial Services (Richmond, Va.)
> Beacon Press (Richmond, Va.)
> Golden Triangle Printing Co. (Greensboro, N.C.)
> Cliggot Publishing Co. (Greenwich, Conn.)

Media General's newsprint recycling business has grown to the point where this part of the company's operations is almost as large as newspaper publishing. In fact, all of Media General's expansion between 1973 and 1979 was in the non-media areas of newsprint and printing. Its newspapers, all in growing, medium size cities in the South, have nonetheless suffered a decrease in circulation during this period. Advertising revenue, although up substantially, owes more to rate increases than added volume.

However, the Media General papers have no direct newspaper competition in any of their markets. The Tampa stations are extremely profitable, but new cross-media ownership rulings may force the divestiture of either the newspapers or the stations in that city.

Newsprint manufacturing has had outstanding performance due to strong demand for newsprint along with low prices for wastepaper—the raw material for recycling. Although demand for newsprint has been cyclical, high demand years such as 1979 can be very profitable.

Media General's early lead in adopting technological change in the Richmond operation—a model for others in 1973—has long since dissipated. Richmond finally added VDTs for classified ad takers in 1976, and Tampa did not enter the VDT text-editing world until the end of 1976. In 1976, less than 25 percent of Media General's $12.9 million capital expenditure went to newspaper operations, while half went to the newsprint division. Media General is also part of the three newspaper consortium (with Cox and Knight-Ridder) which built a 155,000 ton recycling mill in Georgia at a cost of $130 million. MG has responsibility for operating the facility.

Media General newspapers get little national recognition for journalistic achievement, despite their relative size. The lack of emphasis on editorial may help explain their circulation slide, despite being in growing markets. MG has also hesitated to push too hard on advertising and circulation rates, having among the lowest of the major newspaper chains. Circulation income which accounted for a consistent 20 percent of total newspaper revenue for several years, slipped slightly to 18 percent by 1978, which is on the low side for newspapers of their size.

Media General may not be a major factor in the rush to buy newspapers, but it has been creating its own blend of vertical integration which has proven to be financially successful.

MULTIMEDIA, INC.
Greenville, S.C.

Properties

Newspapers

Gallipolis (Ohio) *Daily Tribune*
Moultrie (Ga.) *Observer*
Greenville (S.C.) *News* and *Piedmont*
Asheville (N.C.) *Citizen* and *Times*
Montgomery (Ala.) *Advertiser* and *Alabama Journal*
Clarksville (Tenn.) *Leaf-Chronicle*
Point Pleasant (W. Va.) *Register*
Pomeroy-Middleport (Ohio) *Daily Sentinel*
Winter Haven (Fla.) *Daily News Chief*
21 less than daily and "shopper" newspapers

Average circulation, A.B.C. Sept. 30, 1978:   300,562 daily
296,979 Sunday

Broadcasting

WFBC-TV, AM, FM, Greenville, S.C.
WBIR-TV, Knoxville, Tenn.
WMAZ-TV, AM, FM, Macon, Ga.
WXII-TV, Winston-Salem, N.C.
WLWT-TV, Cincinnati, O.
WZTV-TV, Nashville, Tenn.
WAKY-AM, Louisville, Ky.
KAAY-AM and KEZQ-FM, Little Rock, Ark.
KEEL-AM and KMBQ-FM, Shreveport, La.
WEZW-FM, Milwaukee, Wisc.
WVEZ-FM, Louisville, Ky.
Syndication: The Phil Donahue Show

Multimedia is a Southern-based broadcasting and newspaper publishing firm with about half its revenues derived from each medium. Its newspapers are all in small or medium size cities in which there is no direct competition.

Although the newspapers are located in Sunbelt communities, most had lower circulation levels in 1978 than in 1976. Advertising linage were also mediocre. In both cases, however, rate increases resulted in significantly higher revenues.

The purchase of the Cincinnati television stations in 1976 for $16.3 million gives the company its maximum allowance of five VHF properties. WLWT, the

NBC affiliate operating in the country's 22nd largest market, is also the group's largest operation. The other broadcasting operations are all in growing communities and the division yielded a 32 percent pre-tax operating profit in 1978, down from its 34 percent level in 1972.

The Cincinnati deal also brought with it the national syndication rights to the Phil Donahue Show. In buying into a major midwestern city, Multimedia also bought some labor troubles, as it found out when the International Brotherhood of Electrical Workers struck in early 1977. The station continued to operate with supervisory personnel.

Multimedia has been focusing on the broadcast end of its business, perhaps a reasonable strategy given the fierce competition for newspaper properties and the higher profits obtainable in broadcasting. To make its 1976 acquisitions of a major television station and radio stations in three cities, the company had to assume considerable debt.

The company spent $7.1 million for newspaper equipment to complete the conversion of all its newspapers to photocomposition. Greenville, the largest paper with 107,000 daily circulation, has an all-VDT news and classified system. The paper is still printed on a letterpress with relief plates, but Montgomery and Clarksville have new offset presses and Asheville has converted to DiLitho.

Over the years, Multimedia has been one of the industry leaders in profitability. It has strengthened its position in broadcasting and eliminated investments in non-mass communication businesses. Ownership of broadcasting properties make an unwanted take-over attempt less likely. After a period to assimilate the new TV and radio stations and reduce its debt a bit, Multimedia became active in 1978 in seeking additional newspaper properties. Quite likely the company will continue to buy weeklies and shoppers, as well as the hotly fought-for daily papers, with concentration on Sunbelt growth markets. Meanwhile, approaching the limit of television station ownership (five VHF, two UHF), Multimedia is looking increasingly to cable systems. Its first step was the purchase in 1979 of Kansas State Television Network, Inc., a cable television network.

NEWHOUSE NEWSPAPERS
Newark, N.J.

Properties

Newspapers

Staten Island (N.Y.) *Advance*
Syracuse (N.Y.) *Post-Standard* and *Herald-Journal*
St. Louis (Mo.) *Globe-Democrat*
Portland Oregonian and *Oregon Journal*
Newark (N.J.) *Star-Ledger*
Jersey City (N.J.) *Journal*
New Orleans (La.) *Times-Picayune* and *States-Item*
Birmingham (Ala.) *News*
Huntsville (Ala.) *News* and *Times*
Mobile (Ala.) *Register* and *Press*
Mississippi Press (Pascagoula)
Springfield (Mass.) *Union* and *News*
Harrisburg (Pa.) *Patriot* and *News*
Cleveland (O.) *Plain Dealer*

Booth Newspapers (Michigan):

Grand Rapids Press
Flint Journal
Kalamazoo Gazette
Saginaw News
Ann Arbor News
Bay City Times
Jackson Citizen Patriot
Muskegon Chronicle

Average circulation, A.B.C., March 31, 1979:   3,214,306 daily
                                                    3,488,932 Sunday

Magazines

Parade
Condé Nast Publications:
  Vogue
  House & Garden
  Mademoiselle
  Glamour
  Bride's
  Self
  Gentlemen's Quarterly
  Condé Nast England/France/Italy/West Germany

Broadcasting and other

>   WSYR-TV-AM-FM, Syracuse, N.Y.[1]
>   WSYE-TV, Elmira-Corning, N.Y.[1]
>   WAPI-TV-AM-FM, Birmingham, Ala.[1]
>   WTPA-TV-FM, Harrisburg, Pa.[1]
>   KTVI-TV, St. Louis, Mo.
>   20 cable TV systems
>   Catawaba Newsprint Co. (49% interest)
>   Random House, Inc.[2]

[1]Sales to Times Mirror Co. pending FCC approval in 1980.
[2]Agreement for purchase reached with RCA Corp., 1980.

Newhouse is now the third largest newspaper-owning chain in total daily circulation and is probably the largest in revenue and net income. Its newspapers are almost all in medium and large size cities. Several, such as the *Cleveland Plain Dealer,* the *St. Louis Globe-Democrat,* and the *Birmingham News* are in two-newspaper towns, but Birmingham has a joint operating agreement with its morning competitor under the Newspaper Preservation Act and the *Globe-Democrat* is printed by the *St. Louis Post-Dispatch.*

The Booth Newspapers were acquired in late 1976, after Newhouse bought a 25 percent interest in the company earlier in the year. The final $47 per share price put a $300 million value on the acquisition and outbid a $40 per share offer from Times Mirror Co. Booth was an extremely attractive take-over target because of its strong cash position (a three to one current ratio) and its freedom from any long-term debt. In 1975, generally a bad year for newspapers, Booth earned $13.2 million on sales of $158.7 million, both figures setting company records.

S.I. Newhouse, who died in 1979 at the age of 84, built his empire slowly, starting with the *Staten Island* (N.Y.) *Advance* in 1922. This property still serves as the major holding company through which all other operations are controlled. Ten years later he bought the *Long Island Press,* which was finally shut down in 1977 after years of declining circulation and losses. The pace picked up with the purchase of the Newark paper in 1935 and the Syracuse papers in 1939. By 1955 he had added papers in St. Louis, Birmingham, Harrisburg, Jersey City, Huntsville, and Portland. Papers in these last three cities are now among the least profitable properties.

In the 1960s, the chain expanded quietly but explosively. Nine dailies were added at a reported cost of $128.4 million, including the *Plain Dealer* in 1967 at a then-record $54.3 million. With no outside stockholders to report to and with a strong cash flow, Newhouse can offer top dollar to acquire a property.

Occasionally some sought-after properties do get away, such as the *Philadelphia Inquirer* and the *Cincinnati Enquirer,* snapped up by Knight and Combined Communications, respectively.

The Conde Nast group of women's magazines was acquired in 1957. Like many of Newhouse's purchases, it was a money-losing company which provided a turn-around opportunity. In this case, he got out of the printing business and subscription fulfillment service, while also dumping a few marginally profitable magazines. The result is a profitable operation with publications earmarked for distinctively segmented audiences. In early 1980, the Newhouse organization agreed to pay RCA Corp. between $65 and $70 million for Random House, Inc., a group of publishing houses that includes Random House, Alfred A. Knopf, and Ballantine.

Unlike many other chain owners, S.I. Newhouse was never a journalist. His interest in newspapers, magazines, and broadcast facilities was purely financial. As a result, once he bought control of a publication, he did little if anything to meddle in its editorial affairs. Local editors and publishers have considerable leeway in how they run their operation. Controls, such as they are in the loosely-run Newhouse organization, are primarily in the form of profitability standards. Much as Frank Munsey and E.W. Scripps before him, Newhouse assumed control of an ailing paper and resuscitated it by cost cutting and vigorous promotion or circulation and advertising.

Thus, Newhouse-owned newspapers are uniformly mediocre by most standards of journalistic excellence. The *Plain Dealer* has perhaps the best reputation.

Newhouse management and organization are contrary to everything the business schools teach. There is no corporate staff and most in top management are Newhouse relatives. Each has operating responsibility for at least one specific property and generally oversees others through on-site visits. Notes Thomas Vail, publisher and former owner of the *Plain Dealer,* "No one has ever asked me to meet a budget. . . . There is no participation editorially. There is no place where we sit down and say we want a given profit." Operating responsibility has been divided between S.I. Newhouse's two sons and the management style is not expected to change radically.

Newhouse had been reported to court heirs of newspaper properties owners who needed to get cash for their paper to pay taxes, as well as elder publishers who may have wanted to enjoy the fruits of their labor. He also knew how to spot a situation with dissident stockholders, such as the Booth deal which came about because of disagreements of controlling stockholders about how best to use their profitable assets. He then came in and offered cash, rather than the stock which publicly owned acquiring firms prefer to use. Newhouse was patient: One newspaper broker with many irons in the fire for Newhouse claimed that some may take three to five years to emerge as deals.

Thus, with little fanfare and with a low profile, Newhouse has surpassed the long established Hearst and Scripps-Howard chains and emerged in the 1970s as a major factor in the newspaper industry in the United States. With revenues in excess of $1 billion annually, the organization Newhouse built is now likely to move into cable television and other newer media using a proven formula for growth.

THE NEW YORK TIMES CO.
New York, N.Y.

Properties

Daily Newspapers

> *The New York Times*
> *Lexington* (N.C.) *Dispatch*
> *Hendersonville* (N.C.) *Times-News*
> *Wilmington* (N.C.) *Star-News*
> *Lake City* (Fla.) *Reporter*
> *Palatka* (Fla.) *Daily News*
> *Leesburg* (Fla.) *Daily Commercial*
> *Lakeland* (Fla.) *Ledger*
> *Ocala* (Fla.) *Star-Banner*
> *Gainesville* (Fla.) *Sun*
> Four weekly papers (Fla.)

Average circulation, A.B.C., March 31, 1979:   1,058,808 daily
                                                    1,608,260 Sunday

Magazines

> *Family Circle*
> *Golf Digest*
> *Tennis*
> *Us*
> *Australian Family Circle*
> *Better Homes & Gardens* (Australia)

Other

> KFSM-TV, Fort Smith, Ark. (pending FCC approval)
> WREG-TV, Memphis, Tenn.
> WQXR-AM and FM, New York
> Arno Press

Cambridge Book Co.
Quadrangle/New York Times Book Co.
New York Times Information Bank
New York Times News Service
Microfilming Corporation of America
Teaching Resources Corp.
Teaching Resources Films

The nucleus of the diversification program on which The New York Times Co. planned to embark after going public in 1968 remains the 1970 acquisition of the Cowles properties which brought *Family Circle* and the Florida and North Carolina newspapers. *The New York Times* itself has only recently begun making up ground from the years of erosion of its circulation and advertising base. As New Yorkers moved to the suburbs and began buying the local papers, advertisers followed them, both in opening up branches and placing their advertising in *Newsday, The Bergen* (N.J.) *Record* and Gannett's Westchester-Rockland Newspaper group. Daily circulation, at 908,000 in 1971, had fallen continuously to an average 821,000 in the September 30, 1978 ABC audit, although this represented an improvement from barely 800,000 in 1976. Sunday circulation was also up slightly to 1.41 million.

In 1976, the *Times* finally began to fight back, first with some real market research on its suburban markets and then with some new editorial products, including true Sunday supplements with local advertising. In early 1977 two more suburbs were added, so that Long Island, New Jersey, Westchester Co., and southern Connecticut were all covered.

Also in 1976, the first special weekday section, "Weekend," began appearing in the Friday edition. Within five months of its appearance, Friday circulation was up five percent and linage increased 20 percent. Subsequently, a "Living Section" was added to the Wednesday paper and "Home" on Thursday. Total circulation picked up considerably, averaging 846,000 daily for the first half of 1977. In 1978, an expanded sports section was added on Mondays and a science section on Tuesdays. Finally, a separate and strengthened business section was added daily.

Even so, the *Times* faces an uphill battle to win back lost advertisers. Both *Newsday* and the *Daily News* moved quickly to pick up the bones left by the demise of the *Long Island Press*. As it was, *Newsday* had a household penetration of 62 percent in the growing Long Island market and the *Daily News* 31 percent compared to the 11 percent of the *Times*.

On the other hand, the company's affiliated newspapers have been thriving. Circulation of the group jumped 6 percent in 1978, advertising linage 12 percent. Operating profit was 27 percent of revenue in 1978. Households in Florida were expected to expand almost 24 percent between 1975 and 1980, along with a 73 percent growth in effective buying power.

The magazine group has also continued strongly, despite competition in each field. The weak link, the *Modern Medicine* group of magazines, was sold to Harcourt Brace Jovanovich, Inc. in 1976, the immediate catalyst being a series of articles in the *Times* outlining alleged incompetence in the medical community. The series prompted some drug companies to pull their advertising from *Modern Medicine* and the magazine itself bought an ad in the *Times* to disassociate itself from the series. The business publications group was sold for $6.1 million.

The company also sold its floundering music publishing venture in 1976 for an undisclosed sum. The basis of the publishing operation was a music catalogue acquired from Metromedia, Inc. in 1973.

Perhaps the firm's most ambitious venture has been the 1977 inaugural of *Us*, a blatant imitation of Time, Inc.'s high successful *People*. In many ways, *Us* is a natural addition for the Times Co. since, like *People*, it is designed to be sold on newsstands and supermarket checkout counters, thus using the already strong distribution network in place for the 8.3 million circulation *Family Circle*. Issued initially as a biweekly, *Us* was approaching 1 million per issue circulation in 1979, but was still not covering its full costs. Rumors circulated in early 1980 that *Us* was for sale.

The heart of The New York Times Co. is still *The New York Times*. So long as the *Times* has a mandate to be the paper of record, it is unlikely that it can approach the profitability of other city papers. Nonetheless, in its attempt to penetrate the suburbs, the *Times* has to be careful that it does not commit too much of its resources to the soft news that goes into those special sections, at the risk of diluting its basic strengths in national and international reporting. There has already been reported grumbling on the news staff that the suburban desks are pulling needed staffers from their more traditional beats. The *Times* must tread a fine line between adding features that are the popular trend in newspaper publishing, while still appealing to the affluent suburban readers who want the *Times* because it is providing material different than their local daily.

On the cost-saving side, automation at the *Times* has been making itself felt. In mid 1978, the last of the hot metal Linotypes was shut down. The entire paper is now photocomposed and a sophisticated Harris editing and composition system is in operation. In the three years following the implementation of the *Times* contract with Local No. 6 of the ITU (in 1974), the number of guaranteed situation holders for printers was reduced through attrition by 186, at a saving conservatively estimated to be $4.1 million annually. Positions are being vacated at the rate of almost 30 per year. The long 88-day pressmen's strike in 1978 resulted in a contract permitting further savings by reducing pressroom manning levels.

Meanwhile, a new, highly automated printing plant in nearby New Jersey has begun printing and inserting most of the advance sections of the Sunday paper, making plates from facsimiles pages transmitted from New York. A third of the main news section on weekdays as well as Sunday is printed in this plant. The new facility uses 28-unit Goss Metroliner offset presses, which is a strong indication that the gray *Times* may some day offer color ads.

Management of the company finally appears to have been firmed up, with much of the dead wood from the old family days having retired or been otherwise moved out.

The Information Bank, although a marvel of technology, continues to be a drain on the company. The potential market for its use was broadened through the addition of access channels which allow customers to utilize existing telecommunications networks and hardware. Additional sales offices are being opened across the country. By 1978 it had nearly 1000 customers.

One of the brightest spots of the organization continues to be the small weekly and daily newspapers in the South. These are all produced by cold type and several have installed computerized total systems. Their pre-tax profit margin far exceeds that of the rest of the company. They are in areas of strong growth and should continue to outperform the other divisions of the company, with the exception of broadcasting.

SCRIPPS-HOWARD NEWSPAPERS
(Subsidiary of E.W. Scripps Co.)
Cincinnati, Ohio

Properties

Newspapers

> *Birmingham* (Ala.) *Post-Herald*
> *Fullerton* (Calif.) *News Tribune*
> *Denver* (Colo.) *Rocky Mountain News*
> *Evansville* (Ind.) *Press*
> *Covington* (Ky.) *Post*
>   (separate edition of *Cincinnati Post*)
> *Albuquerque* (N.M.) *Tribune*
> *Cincinnati Post*
> *Cleveland Press*
> *Columbus* (O.) *Citizen-Journal*
> *Pittsburgh* (Pa.) *Press*
> *Knoxville* (Tenn.) *News-Sentinel*
> *Memphis* (Tenn.) *Press Scimitar* and *Commercial Appeal*
> *El Paso* (Tex.) *Herald-Post*
> *Hollywood* (Fla.) *Sun-Tattler*
> *Stuart* (Fla.) *News*
> *San Juan* (P.R.) *Star*

Average circulation, A.B.C. March 31, 1979:

1,848,092 daily
1,580,798 Sunday

Other

21 nondaily newspapers
United Feature Syndicate
Newspaper Enterprise Association
United Press International

E.W. Scripps was the first of the newspaper chain owners. The chain itself was born when Scripps borrowed $10,000 to buy the *Penny Press* in Cleveland in 1878. He added the *Cincinnati Post* in 1883.

Scripps handled most of his expansion from his home in Miramar, Ga. His method of acquisition was to find promising young editors and publishers for a new enterprise and give them the opportunity to buy ten percent of its stock, lending them the money to do so. The papers were generally run as low-cost operations and were noted for their shabby facilities. Although the papers were autonomous, Scripps did try to instill in his subordinates his own philosophy and methods.

Roy Howard began his career as a reporter and became the president of the United Press before taking over the chain after Scripps died. It was Howard who bought the *New York Telegram.*

E.W. Scripps actually was responsible for several chains. His oldest son, James, had an unreconcilable difference with his father and in the break, James got control of five West Coast papers which became the Scripps League. Grandson John P. Scripps established a chain which bears his name in California. E.W. Scripps' brother, James, started and ran the *Detroit News* independently of "E.W." James' son-in-law, George Booth, left his job at the *News* to buy the *Grand Rapids Press* and began the chain which became Booth Newspapers, now part of the Newhouse empire.

The Scripps-Howard newspapers have been known for crusading, community-oriented journalism. Although Scripps himself felt strongly about supporting the cause of the working man, the politics of the chain today has largely abandoned the philosophy of its founder.

While many of the Scripps-Howard newspapers are in large cities with competing dailies, papers in Birmingham, Albuquerque, Cincinnati, Columbus, Pittsburgh, Knoxville, and El Paso all operate under joint business, distribution, and mechanical agreements with competitors, as provided by the Newspaper Preservation Act.

Among the largest newspapers, only Denver saw an increase in circulation in the 1972 and 1978 period. There, the morning *Rocky Mountain News* jumped 22 percent while its slightly larger afternoon rival gained only 4.5 percent. In both Pittsburgh and Columbus, circulation losses were less than the competing paper. However, in Cleveland, the *Press* lost 18.1 percent, widening the gap between it and the larger *Plain Dealer,* which dropped 7.1 percent. In Cincinnati, the headquarters paper also lost a greater proportion of the readers than the *Enquirer,* although the *Post* continues its lead in circulation.

The Scripps-Howard chain has fared better over the years than its old rival Hearst. Like Hearst, however, it has properties in many of the older cities and faces many of the problems inherent in these situations. In Pittsburgh, for example, there have been several extended shutdowns of the papers due to continuing labor strife. In 1979, Scripps was successful in its bid to establish a joint operating agreement in Cincinnati and it may try the same strategy in Cleveland.

The Scripps group has not been particularly active in the acquisition binge of recent years. The parent E.W. Scripps Co. does have a separate broadcasting subsidiary. But even with relatively low profit margins, the newspaper group should be generating sufficient funds to permit future purchases for cash.

THOMSON NEWSPAPERS LTD.
Toronto, Canada

Properties

Newspapers

Alabama
 The Dothan Eagle
 The Opelika-Auburn News

Arizona
 Douglas, The Daily Dispatch

Arkansas
 Fayetteville Northwest
 Arkansas Times

California
 Barstow Desert Dispatch
 Eureka, The Times-Standard
 Oxnard, The Press-Courier
 San Gabriel Valley Tribune
 Lancaster Antelope Valley
 Daily Ledger-Gazette

Connecticut
 Ansonia, The Evening Sentinel

Florida
 Mariana, Jackson County
 Floridan
 Orange Park Daily Clay Today
 Punta Gorda Daily Herald-News
 The Key West Citizen

Georgia
 Dalton, The Daily Citizen-News
 The Cordele Dispatch
 The Valdosta Daily Times

Illinois
 Mount Vernon, The Register-News

Indiana
 New Albany, The Tribune

Iowa
 Council Bluffs Nonpareil
 The Oelwein Daily Register

Kansas
 The Leavenworth Times
 Atchison, The Globe

Louisiana
  Lafeyette, The Daily Advertiser
Maryland
  Salisbury, The Daily Times
Massachusetts
  Fitchburg, The Daily Sentinel and
    Leominster Enterprise
  Taunton Daily Gazette
Michigan
  Adrian Daily Telegram
Minnesota
  Albert Lea, The Evening Tribune
  Austin Daily Herald
Mississippi
  Laurel Leader-Call
Missouri
  The Carthage Press
  Cape Girardeau, The Southeast
    Missourian
New Hampshire
  The Portsmouth Herald
New York
  Oswego, The Palladium-Times
  Herkimer, The Evening Telegram
  Newburgh, The Evening News
North Carolina
  Rocky Mount, The Evening Telegram
Ohio
  Steubenville Herald-Star
  East Liverpool, The Evening Review
  The Salem News
  The Canton Repository
  The Coshocton Tribune

  Newark, The Advocate
  Zanesville, The Times Recorder
  Lancaster Eagle-Gazette
  The Portsmouth Times
  The Marion Star
  The Zenia Daily Gazette
  Middletown Journal
  Greenville Daily Advocate
  Piqua Daily Call
Oklahoma
  The Ada Evening News
Pennsylvania
  Lock Haven, The Express
  Hanover, The Evening Sun
  The Meadville Tribune
  Greenville, The Record-Argus
  Kittanning, The Leader-Times
  Monessen, The Valley Independent
  Connellsville, The Daily Courier
South Dakota
  Mitchell, The Daily Republic
Virginia
  Petersburg, The Progress-Index
West Virginia
  Fairmont, The Times-West
    Virginian
  The Weirton Daily Times
Wisconsin
  Fond du Lac Reporter
  Manitowoo Herald-Times
    Reporter

Average (U.S.) circulation, A.B.C., March 31, 1979:   1,089,899 daily
                                                               657,746 Sunday

British Columbia
  Nanaimo Daily Free Press
  Kamloops Daily Sentinel
  Vernon Daily News

  The Kelowna Daily Courier
  Penticton Herald
  The Vancouver Sun
  Victoria, The Colonist

Victoria, The Times
Saskatchewan
Prince Albert Daily Herald
Moose Jaw Times-Herald
Ontario
Thunder Bay, The Times-News
Thunder Bay, The Chronicle-Journal
Timmins, The Daily Press
Kirkland Lake Northern Daily News
Elliot Lake, The Standard
The Sudbury Star
The Sarnia Observer
The Chatham Daily News
Welland, The Evening Tribune
Niagara Falls Review
The Simcoe Reformer
St. Thomas Times-Journal
Woodstock, The Daily Sentinel-Review
The Cambridge Daily Reporter
Guelph, The Daily Mercury
Brampton, The Daily Times
Orillia Daily Packet & Times

The Barrie Examiner
The Oshawa Times
The Ottawa Journal
Peterborough Examiner
The Toronto Globe and Mail
Belleville, The Intelligencer
The Pembroke Observer
Cornwall Standard-Freeholder
Manitoba
The Winnipeg Free Press
Alberta
Calgary Albertan
Lethbridge Herald
Nova Scotia
Truro, The Daily News
New Glasgow, The Evening News
Sydney, Cape Breton Post

Prince Edward Island
Charlottetown, The Guardian
Charlottetown, The Evening Patriot
Newfoundland
Corner Brook, The Western Star
St. John's, The Evening Telegram

Average daily circulation in Canada, approx.:   1,420,000 daily

Thomson Newspapers owns more daily newspapers than any other group operating in the United States: 111 dailies, 67 in the U.S. and 44 in Canada, with total combined circulation of more than 2.5 million. Thomson also controls five weekly newspapers in the U.S. and 12 in Canada. The firm's revenue in 1978 was $306.5 million (Canadian), with its after tax profit of $56.6 million yielding the greatest profit margin (18%) of any major newspaper chain.

The company is part of a worldwide organization that also owns 16 daily newspapers and 31 weeklies in Great Britain, including *The Times* of London (which was closed for more than a year in 1978-79 by a labor dispute), plus book publishers, retail department stores and extensive oil rights in the North Sea.

With the exception of some large city newspapers in Canada acquired in early 1980 as part of FP Publications, Thomson's acquisitions have been almost exclusively in small to medium size cities with no direct competition. Often the acquired newspaper is in weak financial condition, but Thomson management has had a reputation for coming in, cutting costs, and bringing the property up to profit standards in 18 to 24 months. It has not been known for blazing trails in editorial distinction, but on the other hand there is little interference in editorial decision-making by the parent company.

The FP Publications purchase broke the mold for Thomson, in part because the availability of small town monopoly newspapers has grown scarce and the competition for acquisition fierce, hence their price is quite high. The cost of the FP Newspapers was relatively low ($186 per reader, compared to prices as high as the $450 reflected in the price Gannett paid when it purchased the two dailies in Wilmington, Del. in 1978). But newspapers in Toronto, Winnipeg and Ottawa face stiff competition and labor union problems, neither of which Thomson has had to deal with in the past. On the other hand, the eight FP newspapers (*Toronto Globe and Mail, Winnipeg Free Press, The Ottawa Journal, The Vancouver Sun, Calgary Albertan, Lethbridge Herald* and *The Columist* and *Times* in Victoria) added nearly 900,000 circulation in one swoop, almost twice that of the other 36 papers.

TIMES MIRROR COMPANY
Los Angeles, Calif.

Properties

Newspapers

> *The Los Angeles Times*
> *Newsday* (Long Island, N.Y.)
> *Dallas Times Herald*
> *Orange Coast Daily Pilot* (Costa Mesa, Calif.)
> *Greenwich* (Conn.) *Times*
> *Stamford* (Conn.) *Advocate*
> *Hartford* (Conn.) *Courant*

Average circulation, A.B.C., March 31, 1979:   2,100,016 daily
2,557,076 Sunday

Magazines

> *Golf*
> *Popular Science*
> *Outdoor Life*
> *Ski*
> *Sporting News*
> *How to*

Books

> C.V. Mosby Co.
> Matthew Bender & Co.
> Southwestern Co.
> New American Library
> New English Library
> Harry N. Abrams

Other

> Los Angeles Times-Washington Post News Service
> Newsprint and Forest Products Division
> KTBC-TV, Austin, Tex.
> KDFW, Dallas/Ft. Worth, Tex.
> Communications Properties, Inc. (cable operator)
> Printing, other publications
> Purchase of five television stations from Newhouse Broadcasting Co.
> pending FCC approval in 1980.

The Los Angeles Times, the second largest daily circulation newspaper in the United States, has seen its circulation flatten out and recede along with much of the industry. The 1,021,460 average daily sales reported in 1972 exceeds the 1978 level. But the *Times,* the world leader in advertising linage, ran 154 million lines in 1978, 28 percent more than in 1976.

In taking direct control of its distribution in 1976, the *Times* assumed responsibility for sales, service requests, billing, and collections of home-delivered copies. About $23 million of additional revenue was reported under this system in its first year since all circulation revenue is recorded at retail price, rather than at the wholesale price the independent contractors remitted for their newspapers under the old system (see Chapter 3). Nonetheless, the expense of the new delivery system exceeded the additional revenue by $3.7 million.

Newsday has continued its growth on Long Island, although it is experiencing renewed competition from the Tribune Co.'s *Daily News* and from *The New York Times.* On the other hand, *Newsday* had anticipated the demise of the **Long Island Press** and was already invading the Queen's Borough bailiwick of the *Press* before the end came in March 1977. *Newsday*'s 1978 circulation was up 16.2 percent from 1972 and linage had increased 14.6 percent to 59.2 million lines in that period.

Newsday has been one of the innovators in total market selling. As one part of this program, advertisements which appear in the regular paper may also be placed in a weekly supplement which is distributed to nonsubscribing households at no charge (to the reader). The newspaper moved into a $35 million offset printing plant in 1979. Across Long Island Sound, Times Mirror established itself in wealthy Fairfield, Conn. with the purchase of small dailies in Greenwich and Stamford. The Hartford paper was purchased in 1979 amidst some controversy.

The *Dallas Times Herald,* located firmly in Sunbelt country, pulled its 1978 circulation back to its 1972 level after having suffered several years of decline. Sunday circulation, however, climbed 14 percent, from 291,000 to over 332,000. Advertising linage, unlike daily circulation, has fared well. The 5.8 percent increase to 69.7 million lines in 1978 from 1972 established a record for total linage. (All figures for 8-column format.)

The newsprint and wood products division reflects the extreme boom and bust fortunes of that industry. Although a good hedge against continued escalation in newsprint costs and supply problems, cyclical demand and labor problems make this area one of continued suspense. Strong performances, such as in 1978, must be balanced with disasters, such as 1975, when an 11½ week strike at the newsprint mills and a depressed housing industry resulted in a 12 percent decrease in revenue and 57 percent in pre-tax profits.

Times Mirror's magazine operations were expanded in early 1977 with the purchase of *The Sporting News* and a trade magazine, *The Sporting Goods Dealer.* Although *The Sporting News* would seem to fit into the new magazine network of special interest magazines the company runs, it is actually quite different. Whereas *Golf, Ski, Outdoor Life,* and *Popular Science* are all oriented to those who are active participants in the subject matter of the magazine, the reader of *The Sporting News* is a passive observer. In terms of adding to the network, therefore, the *News* may add little, if any, synergy. *How-to* was added in 1979 as a bi-monthly.

The book publishing operations of Times Mirror have been aided by continued strength in law and medical school enrollments and continuing education by these professionals. The Southwestern Company sells its Bibles, dictionaries, and other products door-to-door. Harry N. Abrams specializes in coffee table art books at premium prices. New American Library is a mass market paperback publisher. Among its bestsellers are *Kramer vs. Kramer, The Omen* and *Fools Die.*

Times Mirror publishes quality products. All of its newspaper and magazine publications contend with direct competition and the success of the three major newspapers and several of the magazines is all the more impressive as a result.

In the adoption of technology, Times Mirror excells. Not only have its papers bought into the new technology, but in many cases they developed it to suit their own needs, such as the plastic plate injection molding process developed for the *Times.* The *Times* was the first to use EOCOM's laser plate-making device for positive to negative facsimile transmission from the main plant in Los Angeles to the Costa Mesa satellite facility. The *Times,* and to a lesser extent *Newsday,* have made extensive use of zoned editorial and advertising editions.

The firm picked up the pace of its media acquisitions in the late seventies, purchasing the three Connecticut newspapers and Communications Properties, Inc., which, combined with its existing cable franchises, made it one of the largest cable operators as measured by total subscribers.

Times Mirror did make a bid to take over Booth Newspapers in 1976 when some contolling stockholders of that group opposed the Newhouse bid and decided to seek out a more friendly acquirer. But Times Mirror management was not willing to go beyond $40 per share. A similarly conservative approach also cost Times Mirror the Kansas City Star Co., which Capital Cities Communications finally grabbed.

In August 1977, the *Los Angeles Times* became the target of a Federal Trade Commission complaint alleging that its advertising rate structure discriminated against smaller advertisers (see Chapter 4), an inquiry still open as 1980 began.

TRIBUNE CO.
Chicago, Ill.

Properties

Newspapers

>   *New York News*
>   *Chicago Tribune*
>   *Fort Lauderdale* (Fla.) *News* and *Sun-Sentinel*
>   *Orlando* (Fla.) *Sentinel-Star*
>   *Kissimmee* (Fla.) *Osceola Sun*
>   *Pompano Beach* (Fla.) *Sun-Sentinel*
>   *Van Nuys* (Calif.) *Valley News and Green Sheet* (4 times/week)
>   *Escondido* (Calif.) *Times-Advocate*
>   *Peninsula Times Tribune* (Palo Alto, Calif.)

Average circulation, A.B.C., March 31, 1979:   3,128,739 daily
                                                            4,168,766 Sunday

Broadcasting

>   KGNR-AM, Sacramento, Calif.
>   KCTC-FM, Sacramento, Calif.
>   WGN-TV-AM, Chicago
>   WPIX-TV, New York
>   WICC-AM, Bridgeport, Conn.
>   KWGN-TV, Denver, Colo.
>   KDAL-TV-AM, Duluth, Minn.
>   2 CATV Systems

Other

> 10 non-daily newspapers
> Newsprint and wood products manufacturing
> Insurance
> Hydro-electric generating plant
> Shipping
> Chicago Tribune-New York News Syndicate

The Tribune Co. was the first to blink in the highly competitive Chicago daily newspaper market when it suspended its afternoon entry, *Today,* in favor of an all-day *Tribune* in September 1974. Field Enterprises still could not make the *News* profitable and terminated publication in 1978, leaving Chicago a two newspaper city.

In the last full audited year in which all four papers were published, the *Tribune/Today* combination had a daily circulation of 1.1 million and 1.2 million Sunday. The *Sun-Times/News* combination was just behind at 1 million daily and 700,000 Sunday. The all-day *Tribune* failed to hold many of the former *Today* subscribers, but its daily circulation in 1978 was 111,603 above its 1973 level (out of 425,000 *Today* subscribers).

The *Tribune* remains the largest newspaper in Chicago, with a 110,000 edge over the *Sun Times* (794,000 vs. 684,000 daily) and 419,000 on Sunday (1,139,000 vs. 720,000). It has actually improved its market share of circulation from the four newspaper days, having 52 percent in 1973 and 54 percent in 1978.

Among major dailies the *Tribune* trails only the *Los Angeles Times* in total advertising linage, running 119 million in 1978.

In New York, the largest circulation daily in the United States is facing renewed competition not only from *The New York Times,* but from an energized *Post.* An afternoon paper (the *News* has a morning appearance), the *Post* is nonetheless trying to attract a similar audience. Long Island's *Newsday* has also made a bid for expanded readership in Queens Borough.

At 1.6 million daily circulation average in 1979, daily circulation has fallen 24 percent since 1973. It has been particularly slow to rebound from the 1978 strike, losing about 200,000 daily purchasers. But it continues to run more retail advertising than the other New York papers combined. It has used extensive zoned editions to good advantage, especially in classified advertising. Many individuals and businesses may not need the 1.6 million circulation which they must pay for at the full-run rate and now have the option of buying smaller, more local units.

The *News* has also installed what may be the largest electronic publishing system, a Mergenthaler mini-processor-oriented system which is supposed to include operational page make-up terminals, at a cost of $13.5 million. The *Tribune,* meanwhile, decided to equip itself with a slightly less ambitious Hendrix system, at a cost of $7.5 to $9.5 million.

The Tribune Co.'s three largest television markets are, curiously, all independent stations, unaffiliated with a network. All rely heavily on sports programming. WPIX-TV had its license renewal challenged by a group which subsequently lost its battle. Among the criticisms of the station were that its news operation was shoddy and it was known to run file film footage with the implication that it was current, without any notice to viewers.

None of the company's major markets is particularly growth-oriented, although there is still much room for profit improvement via technology savings in New York and Chicago. The company may also face cross-media ownership problems in these two cities. Losing television rights in two of the top markets would be a tough blow to the highly profitable division.

With a major commitment to Canadian newsprint and forest products, the company is tied in to a highly cyclical, low profit margin industry. Like the Times Mirror Co., it can look forward to continued boom and bust years, thus making the performance of the company as a whole difficult to predict.

The *New York Daily News* is in serious trouble, earning a scant 1.7% return on revenue of $325 million in 1979. There have been occasional rumors that the paper will be shut down or sold. Even the possibility of this is hard to imagine for the country's largest circulation general interest daily.

THE WASHINGTON POST CO.
Washington, D.C.

Properties

Newspapers

> *The Washington Post*
> *Trenton* (N.J.) *Times*
> *Everett* (Wash.) *Herald*

Average circulation, A.B.C., March 31, 1979:   728,521 daily
                                                            909,423 Sunday

Broadcasting

> WDIV-TV, Detroit, Mich.
> WJXT-TV, Jacksonville, Fla.
> WPLG-TV, Miami, Fla.
> WFSB-TV, Hartford, Conn.

Magazine Division

>*Newsweek* (Domestic)
>*Newsweek* (International)
>Newsweek Books
>Newsweek Broadcast Service
>*Inside Sports*

Other

>Los Angeles Times-Washington Post News Service
>Equity interest in newsprint mills

About 42 percent of The Washington Post Co.'s revenues come from *The Washington Post*. Its circulation increased to 530,000 in 1978, up 5.5 percent from 1976. In the same period, the daily circulation of the rival evening *Star* (owned by Time Inc.) fell 15 percent.

The *Post* changed to a company-controlled distribution system in late 1975. This means that most newspapers are delivered or sold by independent agents for a fee, with the papers themselves purchased at the retail, rather than the wholesale price. The *Post* reports that the increase in revenue of about $8.6 million in 1976 shown through this method was balanced out by the payment of agents' fees.

There has been repeated rumor to the effect that the *Post* was having second thoughts about its 1974 $16 million acquisition of the *Trenton Times*. Circulation at the *Times* had been declining steadily over the years, but the slide apparently was halted in 1976. The *Times*, an evening paper, still predominates over the competing morning *Advertiser*, which reported 64,000 daily circulation in 1978, up 7.5 percent from 1976, compared to 72,150 for the *Times*, virtually level with 1976.

A top executive at the *Post* acknowledged that the firm was approached by several prospective purchasers of the *Times*, but that the *Post* was not actively seeking a buyer. In the view of the *Post*, the Trenton situation has been turned around and the paper is making money with profit doubling from 1977 to 1978.

Although circulation still trails that of rival *Time*, *Newsweek* continues to lead in advertising pages. Among the three leading news weeklies (the third being *U.S. News & World Report*), *Newsweek* carries about 39 percent of advertising pages.

Meanwhile, Newsweek Books has reduced its scale of operations. As a result of the reduced expense, the division did yield a profit but it accounts for under 1 percent of total corporate revenue.

Newsweek is approximately 90 percent home delivered, which means that its fortunes are very much tied to postage rates. By 1980, second class rate increases added about $5.3 million annually to *Newsweek*'s 1976 postage costs. Further increases in first and third class rates, used for subscription solicitations, could add another $1 million to cash expenditures.

The Washington Post Co.'s broadcasting division is highly profitable. The smallest television licensee is in the 65th largest broadcasting market, Jacksonville, Fla. However, following the 1977 ruling by the U.S. Court of Appeals, the company terminated the cross-media relationship of its television, radio and newspaper operations in Washington (see Chapter 5), trading its Washington stations for the Detroit station plus $6.1 million.

The Washington Post has also benefited from the reduction in the number of union printers from 680 in 1974 to 517 in mid-1977 and the improved situation in the pressroom. The *Post* became 100 percent cold type in 1979—the news operation was still 60 percent hot metal in 1977. A new satellite printing plant, using offset presses, was scheduled for full production in 1980. Located in Fairfax County, Va., it should help improve distribution in the growing suburbs.

The *Times* had been burdened by the heavy cost of its plant, which has room for considerably greater capacity. With the installation of a front-end VDT system and a turnaround in circulation, the paper has seen significant sums falling to the bottom line. As the seat of New Jersey's state government, Trenton and surrounding Mercer County is virtually guaranteed a high level of employed state and supporting services workers.

Post management has been extremely firm in its attitude with organized labor and its ability to continue without the pressman's union has made its point with other locals. Nonetheless, management understands that further problems may still exist. Increased productivity is still being looked to from the mailing and composing room employees. The latter group has been particularly reluctant to accept the changes imposed by the new technology. In Trenton, only the pressmen are organized.

The firm is in an extremely favorable position for further growth through acquisition. Its interest in broadcasting may well lead it to acquire another television station. Management is also following closely developments in new media technology and can be expected to seek opportunities for profiting from these as they become feasible.

APPENDIX A

TECHNOLOGY UTILIZATION SURVEY

Instructions

For each of the following innovations in newspaper production, do *one* of the following:

1. If you judge that it was "widespread" by the end of 1976, place an "X" in Column I opposite that innovation.

2. If you felt it was not widespread by the end of 1976, in Column II write the year that you expect the innovation will have a 50% or better probability of being in "widespread" use; or

3. If you feel that you cannot make an educated judgment on the innovation, place an "X" in Column III.

Please make comments or explanations at the end.

	Column I Widespread use in 1976	Column II Year when 50% probability of widespread use	Column III Cannot answer
1. Reporter's portable keyboard for direct input to local new head-quarters with transmission via acoustic coupler or portable radio.	_____	_____	_____
2. Inside headquarters, keyboarding of all material into computer via paper tape.	_____	_____	_____
3. Inside headquarters, keyboarding of all material into computer directly in digital form.	_____	_____	_____
4. Inside headquarters, machine reading of typed hard copy for entry into computer.	_____	_____	_____
5. Storage in digital form of gross input for later callup and editing.	_____	_____	_____

	Column I Widespread use in 1976	Column II Year when 50% probability of widespread use	Column III Cannot answer
6. Editing and decisions on format by CRT and/or light pen with capacity for mutual interaction by two or more editors at their own consoles.	_____	_____	_____
7. Composing of whole page designs on a CRT and direct production from this of printing surface for some form of pressure printing.	_____	_____	_____
8. High speed electrostatic or ink jet printing with capacity for changing content electronically without interrupting production.	_____	_____	_____
9. No hard-copy production of final paper but large amount of text and graphic material stored in computer and available for selective retrieval by the computer.	_____	_____	_____
10. Facsimile capable of rapid reproduction of newspaper-like content to the home.	_____	_____	_____
11. High-resolution CRT for home video reading with capacity for making selected hard copy.	_____	_____	_____

If you wish to make comments or explanations for any statements, please use this space, and refer to the number of the statement.

Participants in the Survey:
   John E. Leard, Executive Editor, Richmond (Va.) Times-Dispatch and News Leader
   Uzal H. Martz, Jr., Publisher, Pottsville (Pa.) Republican
   George Milakovich, Production Director, Lee Enterprises, Inc.
   Kendrick Noble, Jr., Associate Director, Research, Paine, Webber, Jackson & Curtis, Inc.
   Peter P. Romano, Director, Production Department, ANPA Research Institute
   Jules Tewlow, Director, Special Projects, Lee Enterprises
   Joseph Ungaro, Vice President and Executive Editor, Westchester-Rockland Newspapers
   John R. Werner, Director, Pre-Press Operations, New York Times
   Ronald White, President, Graphic Systems Division, Rockwell International

SELECTED BIBLIOGRAPHY

Books and Directories

Bagdikian, Ben H. *The Information Machines.* New York: Harper & Row, Harper Torchbooks, 1971.

Bleyer, Willard G. *Main Currents in the History of American Journalism.* Boston: Houghton-Mifflin, 1927.

Bogart, Leo. *Strategy in Advertising.* New York: Harcourt, Brace & World, 1967.

Campbell, Angus, et al. *The American Voter.* New York: John Wiley & Sons, 1964.

Compaine, Benjamin. *Consumer Magazines in the 1980s.* White Plains, N. Y.: Knowledge Industry Publications, Inc., 1979.

Compaine, Benjamin, ed. *Who Owns the Media? Concentration of Ownership in the Mass Communications Industry.* White Plains, N. Y.: Knowledge Industry Publications, Inc., 1979.

Davison, W. Phillips, and Frederick T. C. Yu (eds.). *Mass Communication Research.* New York: Praeger Publishers, 1974.

De Fleur, Melvin L. and Sandra Ball-Rokeach. *Theories of Mass Communication.* 3d ed. New York: David McKay Co., 1975.

Editor and Publisher International Year Book. Annual. New York: Editor and Publisher, Inc.

Emery, Edwin. *The Press in America.* Englewood Cliffs, N. J.: Prentice-Hall, 1972.

Epstein, Edward Jay. *News From Nowhere.* New York: Random House, 1973.

Farrar, Ronald T. and John D. Stevens (eds.). *Mass Media and the National Experience.* New York: Harper & Row, 1971.

Gordon, George N. *Communications & Media.* New York: Hastings House Publishers, 1975.

Hynds, Ernest C. *American Newspapers in the 1970s.* New York: Hastings House Publishers, 1975.

Lane, Robert E. *Political Ideology.* New York: Free Press of Glencoe, 1962.

McLuhan, Marshall. *Understanding Media: The Extensions of Man.* New York: New American Library, A Signet Book, 1964.

Mott, Frank Luther. *American Journalism.* 3d ed. New York: Macmillan, 1962.

Owen, Bruce M. *Economics and Freedom of Expression.* Cambridge, Mass.: Ballinger Publishing Co., 1975.

Rivers, William L. and Wilbur Schramm. *Responsibility in Mass Communication.* rev. ed. New York: Harper & Row, 1969.

Schramm, Wilbur, ed. *The Process and Effects of Mass Communication.* Urbana, Ill.: University of Illinois Press, 1965.

Tebbel, John W. *The Compact History of the American Newspaper.* New York: Hawthorne Books, 1963.

Toffler, Alvin. *Future Shock.* New York: Random House, 1970.

Udell, Jon G. *Future Newsprint Demand, 1970-1980.* Washington, D. C.: American Newspaper Publishers Association, 1971.

————et al. *The Economics of the American Newspaper.* New York: Hastings House, 1978.

Journals, Monographs and Other Serials

"ANPA Newspaper Format Committee Simplified ADS Recommendations." *R.I. Bulletin,* No. 1224. Easton, Pa.: American Newspaper Publishers Association Research Institute, March 29, 1976.

Bagdikian, Ben H. "Report of an Exaggerated Death: Daily Newspapers that Failed, 1961-1970." *The Newspaper Survival Study,* No. 1. Oakland, Calif.: The Newspaper Survival Study (1976).

Bogart, Leo. "How the Challenge of Television News Affects the Prosperity of Daily Newspapers." *Journalism Quarterly,* 52 (Autumn, 1976), 403-410.

Borstell, Gerald H. "Ownership, Competition, and Comment in 20 Small Dailies." *Journalism Quarterly,* 33 (Spring, 1956), 220-222.

"CAMEX: Not Just Another CAM Contender." *The Seybold Report,* June 5, 1976.

"Computype's On-Line System for Smaller Newspapers." *R.I. Bulletin,* No. 1222. Easton, Pa.: American Newspaper Publishers Association Research Institute, March 22, 1976.

Denbow, Carl Jon. "A Test of Predictors of Newspaper Subscribing." *Journalism Quarterly*, 52 (Winter, 1975), 744-748.

"Detroit News Goes All the Way with Newsroom Electronics." *R.I. Bulletin*, No. 1151. Easton, Pa.: American Newspaper Publishers Association Research Institute, May 15, 1974.

"53 Dailies in 1978 Purchases; 46 of Them Go Into Group." *Editor & Publisher, January 6, 1979, p. 47.*

Guittar, Lee J. "Perspectives of a Changing Market: Focus on Sales and Marketing." *R.I. Bulletin*, No. 1235. Easton, Pa.: American Newspaper Publishers Association Research Institute, August 23, 1976.

Hicks, Ronald G. and James S. Featherstone. "Duplication of Newspaper Content in Contrasting Ownership Situations." *Journalism Quarterly*, 55 (Autumn, 1978), 549-554.

Howard, Herbert H. "Cross-Media Ownership of Newspapers and TV Stations." *Journalism Quarterly*, 51 (Winter, 1974), 715-718.

Jaffe, Erwin. "Experimental Dry Offset at the ANPA/RI." *R.I. Bulletin*, No. 1237. Easton Pa.: American Newspaper Publishers Association Research Institute, September 2, 1976.

"Laser Platemakers—Buck Rogers Tackles Plate Preparation." *The Seybold Report*, March 10, 1975.

McCombs, Maxwell E. *Mass Media in the Marketplace.* Journalism Monographs, No. 24. Lexington, Ky.: Association for Education in Journalism, 1972.

_____, L.E. Mullins, and David H. Weaver. "Why People Subscribe and Cancel: A Start-Stop Survey of Three Daily Newspapers." *News Research Bulletin*, No. 3. Washington, D. C.: American Newspaper Publishers Association, April 5, 1974.

McKinney, Frank S. "The Philosophy of Converting to the DiLitho® System." *R.I. Bulletin*, No. 1237. Easton, Pa.: American Newspaper Publishers Association Research Institute, September 2, 1976.

Meyer, Philip. "The Comic Strip Problem." *ANPA Research Report*, No. 24. Reston, Va.: American Newspaper Publishers Association, November 21, 1979.

Miller, Boyd L. "More Dailies Zoning for Suburban Readers." *Journalism Quarterly*, 42 (Summer, 1965), 460-462.

Mindak,William. "Do Newspaper Publishers Suffer from 'Marketing Myopia'?" *Journalism Quarterly*, 42 (Autumn, 1965), 433-442.

Nixon, Raymond B. "Changes in Reader Attitudes Toward Daily Newspapers." *Journalism Quarterly*, 31 (Fall, 1954), 421-433.

_____. "Trends in U.S. Newspaper Ownership: Concentration with Competition." *Gazette* 14 (1968), 181-193.

_____. "Who will Own the Press in 1975." *Journalism Quarterly*, 32 (Spring, 1955), 10-16.

_____, and Robert L. Jones. "The Content of Non-Competitive Vs. Competitive Newspaper." *Journalism Quarterly*, 33 (Summer, 1956), 299-314.

_____, and Tae-Youl Hahn. "Concentration of Press Ownership: Comparison of 32 Countries." *Journalism Quarterly*, 48 (Spring, 1971), 31 ff.

Penrose, Jeanne, et al. "The Newspaper Non-Reader 10 Years Later: A Partial Replication of Westley-Severin." *Journalism Quarterly*, 51 (Winter, 1974), 631-638.

Rarick, Galen. "Differences Between Daily Newspaper Subscribers and Non-subscribers." *Journalism Quarterly*, 50 (Summer, 1973), 265-270.

_____, and Barrie Hartman. "The Effects of Competition on One Daily Newspaper's Content." *Journalism Quarterly*, 43 (Fall, 1966), 459-463.

Ray, Royal H. "Competition in the Newspaper Industry." *Journal of Marketing*, 15 (April, 1951), 444-456.

Rinehart, William D. "Why the ADS (Advertising Dimension Standards) System?" *R.I. Bulletin*, No. 1236. Easton, Pa.: American Newspaper Publishers Association Research Institute, August 27, 1976.

Rosse, James N., Bruce M. Owen, and James Dertouzos. "Trends in the Daily Newspaper Industry 1923-1973." *Studies in Industry Economics*, No. 57. Stanford, Calif.: Department of Economics, Stanford University, 1975.

Schweitzer, John C. and Elaine Goldman. "Does newspaper Competition Make A Difference to Readers?" *Journalism Quarterly*, 52 (Winter, 1975), 706-710.

Sohn, Harold. "Regional Newspapers Face New Economic Pressures." *Journalism Quarterly*, 53 (Spring, 1976), 117-119.

"Some Experiences with the NAPP Plate." *R.I. Bulletin*, No. 1219. Easton, Pa.: American Newspaper Publishers Association Research Institute, February 23, 1976.

Stempel, Guido H., III. *Effects on Performance of a Cross-Media Monopoly.* Journalism Monographs, No. 29. Lexington, Ky.: Association for Education in Journalism, 1973.

Sterling, Christopher. "Trends in Daily Newspaper and Broadcasting Ownership, 1922-1970." *Journalism Quarterly*, 52 (Summer, 1975), 247-256, 320.

Stevens, John D. and Donald D. Shaw. "Research Needs in Communications History: A Survey of Teachers." *Journalism Quarterly*, 45 (Autumn, 1968), 547-549.

Trayes, Edward J. and Bruce L. Cook. "Black, White, and Overall Population Levels and Their Relation to Daily and Sunday Newspaper Circulation in the 20 Largest U.S. Cities, 1950-51 and 1970-71." *Communications Research Reports*, No. 3. Philadelphia: School of Communications and Theater, Temple University, 1973.

Udell, Jon G. *Economic Trends in the Daily Newspaper Business, 1946 to 1970.* Wisconsin Project Reports, Vol. IV, No. 6. Madison: University of Wisconsin, Bureau of Business Research and Service, 1970.

"U.S. Economic Growth and Newsprint Consumption." *Newsprint & Traffic Bulletin*, No. 1. Washington, D. C.: American Newspaper Publishers Association, January 5, 1977.

Wackman, Daniel, et al. "Chain Newspaper Autonomy as Reflected in Presidential Campaign Endorsements." *Journalism Quarterly*, 52 (Autumn, 1975), 417-420.

Weaver, David H. and L. E. Mullins. "Content and Format Characteristics of Competing Daily Newspapers." *Journalism Quarterly*, 52 (Spring, 1975), 257-264.

Westley, Bruce H. and Werner J. Severin. "A Profile of the Daily Newspaper Non-Reader." *Journalism Quarterly*, 41 (Winter, 1964), 45-50, 156.

Wood, Thomas H. "Depreciating the New Technology." *R.I. Bulletin*, No. 1236. Easton, Pa.: American Newspaper Publishers Association Research Institute, August 27, 1976.

Unpublished Dissertations, Speeches, etc.

Associated Press v. United States. 326 U.S. 1 (1945).

The Associated Press and the United Telegraph Workers, A.P. System, Division No. 14 of United Telegraph Workers, AFL-CIO. (William E. Simkin, chairman). Arbitration Award, March 29, 1971.

Citizen Publishing Co. v. United States. 394 U.S. 131 (1969).

Burns, Robert Kenneth Kavanaugh. "Collective Bargaining and Arbitration: The Case of the Daily Newspaper Industry." Unpublished Doctor's dissertation, University of Chicago, 1943.

"Dailies Build New Profit Structure on Newsprint," *Newsprint Facts.* [New York: Newsprint Information Committee], May-June, 1976, p. 1.

Fagan, Harrison Bernard. "Industrial Relations in the Chicago Newspaper Industry." Unpublished Doctor's dissertation, University of Chicago, 1930.

Grotta, Gerald L. "Changes in the Ownership of Daily Newspapers and Selected Performance Characteristics, 1950-1968: An Investigation of Some of the Economic Implications of Concentration of Ownership." Unpublished Doctor's dissertation, Southern Illinois University, 1970.

Hershfeld, David Charles. "Automation and Collective Bargaining in the New York Newspaper Industry." Unpublished Doctor's dissertation, Princeton University, 1970.

Langdon, John Henry. "An Intra Industry Approach to Measuring the Effects of Competition: The Newspaper Industry." Unpublished Doctor's dissertation, Cornell University, 1969.

Oakland Tribune Publishing Co. and Oakland Typographical Union No. 39. 60 L.A. 665.

Rosse, James. "Daily Newspapers, Monopolistic Competition and Economies of Scale." Unpublished Doctor's dissertation, University of Minnesota, 1966.

Tewlow, Jules S. "A Technical Director Looks at Communications Systems for Newspapers." Address at NEWSTEC '72 Conference, Brighton, England, November 22, 1976. (Photocopy).

Times-Picayune Publishing Co. v. United States. 345 U.S. 367 (1953).

Trends in Public Attitudes Toward Television and Other Mass Media. New York: Television Information Office, 1975.

United Press International, Inc. and United Press International System, Division No. 47 of United Telegraph Workers, AFL-CIO. (I. Robert Reinberg, chairman). Arbitration award, November 15, 1972.

Other

Various articles in *Advertising Age, Business Week, Columbia Journalism Review, Editor & Publisher, The New York Times, The Wall Street Journal.*

INDEX

About the Author

Benjamin M. Compaine is executive director of the media and allied arenas at Harvard University's Program on Information Resources Policy. Formerly director of books and studies for Knowledge Industry Publications, Inc., he is the editor and co-author of *Who Owns the Media? Concentration of Ownership in the Mass Communications Industry* and the author of *The Book Industry in Transition: An Economic Analysis of Book Distribution and Marketing, Consumer Magazines in the 1980s,* and other studies of mass communications. He is a graduate of Dickinson College and has an M.B.A. from Harvard Business School and a Ph.D. in mass communications from Temple University.

Other Titles in the Communications Library Series...

The Book Industry in Transition: An Economic Study of Book Distribution and
Marketing
by Benjamin M. Compaine
LC 78-7527   ISBN 0-914236-16-4   hardcover $24.95

Children's Books and Magazines: A Market Study
by Judith S. Duke
LC 78-24705   ISBN 0-914236-17-2   hardcover $24.95

Trends in Management Development and Education: An Economic Study
by Gilbert J.Black
LC 79-4435   ISBN 0-914236-24-5   hardcover $24.95

Videotext: The Coming Revolution in Home/Office Information Retrieval
edited by Efrem Sigel
LC 79-18935   ISBN 0-914236-41-5   hardcover $24.95

Who Owns the Media? Concentration of Ownership in the Mass
Communications Industry
edited by Benjamin M. Compaine
LC 79-15891   ISBN 0-914236-36-9   hardcover $24.95

U.S. Book Publishing Yearbook and Directory, 1979-80
edited by Terry Mollo
ISBN 0-914236-63-6   softcover $35.00

The Music Publishing Business
by Paula Dranov
ISBN 0-914236-40-7   hardcover $24.95

Religious Publishing and Communications
by Judith S. Duke
ISBN 0-914236-61-X   hardcover $24.95